DANILO DOLCI

Introduction by

Aldous Huxley

Translated from the Italian by

P. D. Cummins

Report
from
Palermo

The Orion Press

New York

American adaptation by John White

Designed by Wladislaw Finne
Manufactured in the United States of America

iv

contents

STATISTICAL-SOCIOLOGICAL SURVEY

introduction

BY ALDOUS HUXLEY

Without charity, knowledge is apt to be inhuman; without knowledge, charity is foredoomed, all too often, to impotence. In a society such as ours—a society of enormous numbers subordinated to an ever-expanding and almost omnipresent technology—a new Gandhi, a modern St. Francis needs to be equipped with much more than compassion and seraphic love. He needs a degree in one of the sciences and a nodding acquaintance with a dozen disciples beyond the pale of his own special field. It is only by making the best of both worlds —the world of the head no less than the world of the heart —that the twentieth-century saint can hope to be effective.

Danilo Dolci is one of these modern Franciscans-with-a-degree. In his case the degree is in architecture and engineering; but surrounding this central core of specialized knowledge, there is an aura of general scientific culture. He knows what specialists in other fields are talking about, respects their methods and is willing and eager to take advice from them. But what he knows and what he can learn from other specialists is always, for him, the instrument of charity. His science is applied within a frame of reference whose co-ordinates are an unshakable love for his fellows and a no less unshakable faith in and respect for the objects of that love. The love inspires him to use his knowledge for the benefit of the weak and unfortunate; the faith and respect keep him constantly trying to encourage the weak and the unfortunate to become self-reliant, to help them to help themselves.

When, seven years ago, Danilo Dolci came to Sicily from the North, it was on an aesthetic and scientific pilgrimage. He was interested in ancient Greek architecture and had decided to spend a week or two at Segesta, studying the ruins. But the man with the professional interest in Doric temples was also (and primarily) the man of conscience and loving-kindness. Dolci came to Sicily for the sake of its ancient beauty; but what kept him in Sicily—and Sicily is now his home—was the island's present wretchedness. What Keats called "the giant misery of the world" is more than averagely gigantic in Sicily—particularly at the western end of the island. On Dolci's mind that first glimpse of western Sicily's giant misery acted as a categorical imperative. Something simply had to be done about it. He settled down, some twenty miles from Palermo, in a rural slum called Trappeto, married one of his neighbors, a widow with five young children, moved into a small house with none of the usual conveniences, and from that base of operations launched his campaign against the misery that surrounded him. (I say "base" rather than "headquarters"; for "base" implies lowness and it is from the very bottom of society, on an economic and environmental level with those he is trying to help, that Dolci does his work. "Headquarters" implies elevation; but Dolci refuses to give orders or dispense largesse from some safe hierarchical perch above the common wretchedness; he prefers to live in the midst of it, to leaven the huge festering lump with love and knowledge, to stimulate it to rise of its own accord.)

At nearby Partinico and in the country surrounding it the problems facing the man of knowledge and good will are many and all are hard to solve. There is, first of all, the problem of chronic unemployment. For a large minority of able-bodied men there is simply nothing to do. No work, no way of earning a living, no reason, so far as society is concerned, for their existence. But work, Dolci insists, is not only men's right; it is also their duty. For their own sake, and for the good of others, they ought to work. Inspired by this idea, he organized a *sciopero a rovescio*, a reverse strike, in which the jobless protest against their condition by going to work. One fine morning Dolci and a group of Partinico's unemployed started to work—free, gratis and for nothing— on a local road that was badly in need of repair. Promptly the police swooped down on these unorthodox benefactors of society and began to make arrests. There was no violence;

for, with Dolci, non-violence is a matter of principle and of policy. In due course Dolci was tried and given two months in jail for trespassing on public property. The sentence was appealed, both by the defendant and by the prosecution. In the view of the local authorities, two months was too lenient a sentence. The case was reviewed by a higher court and Dolci has now (January 1959) the risk of being sent to prison to serve an additional term of eight months.

Hardly less grave than the problem of chronic unemployment is the problem of widespread illiteracy. Many of the people cannot read at all, and of those who are able to read very few can afford to buy even a newspaper. The three hundred and fifty outlaws who are responsible for most of the banditry, for which the district of Partinico has become notorious, have spent, collectively, seven hundred and fifty years in school and upwards of three thousand years in prison. With illiteracy there goes an enormous, primitive conservatism. Thus, the country people eat potatoes, when they can afford them—for potatoes have to be imported at considerable expense from Naples. But because their forefathers knew nothing of these new-fangled tubers, it never enters their minds that they themselves might cultivate potatoes. Similarly, there is no local tradition for carrots or lettuces; consequently carrots and lettuces are practically unknown in Partinico. Traditions in relation to "honor" are as rigid as traditions about vegetables. Any offence against an individual's "honor" demands the shedding of blood; and, of course, the shedding of blood has to be avenged by the shedding of more blood, which has to be avenged . . . and so on. To these murders for honor and revenge must be added the murders committed for money and power by members of the Mafia, that vast organized racket which for centuries has constituted a kind of secret state within the state.

We come now to the problem of land tenure. In this part of Sicily the land has been pulverized into holdings so small that their owners find it very hard to scratch up a living, and quite impossible to make the necessary investments for improving and conserving the soil.

And finally there is the heritage of millennia of improper land use—deforested and eroded hills, vanished or vanishing topsoils, rivers that either carry too little water or else, when a too rapid run-off turns them into torrents, too much.

To solve all these problems will take time, much time; but meanwhile Dolci has made a start. Children are being taught and parents are being persuaded to allow their children to go to school. (That they should need persuading is due to the fact that boys are paid four hundred lire a day, whereas a man must be paid a thousand. Not unnaturally employers prefer child labor to adult labor. And not unnaturally, too, the heads of a destitute family prefer four hundred lire a day to nothing at all.) Meanwhile from his base at the bottom, Dolci has reached up to his friends and sympathizers near the top of the social pyramid. The government has been persuaded to build a dam in the valley below Partinico. When it is completed, a good many thousands of now sterile acres will be watered and (at least until such time as the population outruns the new resources) there will be work and food enough for everyone in the district. The problem of what to do about the impossibly small holdings will have to be solved later on, when the irrigation system is ready. So will the problem of preventing the Mafia from getting hold of the water and levying a tribute on its users.

To do something about the wretchedness of Partinico is certainly difficult; but since the numbers involved are small and since the economic situation can be radically bettered by the simple expedient of building a dam, there is a good chance that the problems which beset this rural community will be effectively solved. Partinico, however, is not the only nor the most distressing scene of Sicilian misery. There is also Palermo.

Palermo is a city of more than half a million inhabitants, of whom well over a hundred thousand live in conditions of what can only be described as Asiatic poverty. In the very heart of the city, behind the handsome buildings that line the principal thoroughfares, lie acre upon acre of slums that rival in squalor the slums of Cairo or Calcutta. (One of the worst of these slum areas lies, ironically enough, between the Cathedral and the Palace of Justice.) In his *Report from Palermo* Dolci has set forth the statistics of this giant misery and has recorded, in their own words, how the inhabitants of the city's lower depths pass their distorted lives, what they do and think and feel. The book is absorbingly interesting and at the same time profoundly depressing—depressing, one might almost say, on a cosmic scale. For Palermo, of course, is in no way unique. All over the world there are hundreds of cities, thousands and tens of thousands of small towns and villages, where present conditions are at least as bad and where the future looks darker, the prospects of improvement seem incomparably worse. Sicily, after all, is a part of Italy; and Italy is a highly civilized country well stocked with men of good will and trained intelligence and already, in the North, thoroughly industrialized and therefore capable of providing not only the moral and cultural, but also the financial and technical resources that the rehabilitation of Palermo will require. Some day something will undoubtedly be done about those grisly slums and their chronically unemployed inhabitants. Meanwhile Dolci is doing what little a man of knowledge and good will, with a handful of like-minded helpers, can do to mitigate the present wretchedness and to find out, systematically and scientifically, what needs to be done in the future and how that which needs to be done can be accomplished. The task is far harder than that which confronted him at Partinico; for the physical conditions are worse, the numbers much greater, the unemployment just as chronic and much less easily curable. At Partinico the building of a dam will make all the difference. But the ills of a metropolis like Palermo can be cured only by mass industrialization. What kinds of industry should be introduced? Who is going to put up the necessary capital? And, when established, how are the new industries (manned, be it remembered, by highly unskilled and largely illiterate workers) to compete with the vast going concerns and well-trained labor forces of Milan and Turin? These are the questions which Dolci the engineer, Dolci the firm believer in scientific method, must somehow answer—first on paper and then, with the help of his friends at the top of the pyramid, in practice. Will he succeed? Can something be done in a reasonably short time to provide work for Palermo's unemployed, a decent life for the slum dwellers and a fair chance for their unfortunate children? Time will show. As I write these lines, Dolci is threatened with jail again; but his soul goes marching along and his good work is doubtless being carried on by the devoted men and women who are his helpers—the long-range scientific work of studying social and economic problems and finding technically feasible solutions, and the short-range work of love and compassion, the work of teaching, the work of curing and comforting, the work of bringing disinterested affection to the rejected, and to the despairing the glimmer, for the first time, of a new hope.

January 1959

Publisher's note: The appeals to a higher court referred to by Mr. Huxley were heard at a second trial which was held in March 1959. The result of this trial was a sentence of eight months' imprisonment. The sentence was suspended pending a review by the Supreme Court of Italy; this review has not yet taken place.

preface

This book is intended to be a small contribution to the initial stages of a study on the unemployed in the province of Palermo. Its object is to shed light on the conditions under which the totally unemployed, the partially unemployed and the self-employed (i.e., those who are carrying on some activity, legal or otherwise, which cannot be called work in the strict sense of the word) exist. The pages that follow, then, are an invitation to the reader to join in a discussion the aim of which is to arrive at the root causes of this unemployment; they pose a problem in order that it may be resolved.

If by work, we mean an activity which is of use, not only to the individual but to the whole community, then that of the executioner, the *feudataria*,[1] the prostitute, certainly cannot be said to come within this category. The prostitute, however, does at least offer her own body, whereas the landowner merely lives on the labor of others. As things are at present, even the judge whose rulings are based on a code which fails to guarantee full employment cannot accurately be regarded as a "worker." Nor can the banker whose dealings are confined to such members of the community as have means. This book is concerned solely with those who offer—or rather, try to offer—their useful labor.

The first two parts consist of the personal stories of the witnesses, told in their own words. None of them has been altered or touched up in any way. For the reader's sake, however, more familiar speech has been substituted for the dia-

[1] *Feudataria*—owner of an estate. The word *feudo* is anything but obsolete in Sicily, which is still largely feudal. *Translator's note.*

lects used by the *contadini*—a dialect incomprehensible to all but a few.

Certain aspects of unemployment have only been sketched in lightly in these accounts; others have been left out. The few facts and figures that are appended will not only help to fill in these gaps, but will still further emphasize the grim state of affairs that compels men either to live by their wits or to eke out a bare existence by the pitifully inadequate ways and means which are described in the pages that follow.

The last part is devoted to the answers given by a cross-section of the unemployed to five of the eleven questions that were put to them. This statistical-sociological survey was undertaken because it was felt that the best approach to those issues was made not by expressing personal views and opinions, but by eliciting those of the people themselves. In the eighty-one communes of the province of Palermo, more than five hundred agricultural laborers, mostly between the ages of eighteen and fifty, none of whom had any land of their own, were asked to reply to these questions. All these men were encountered by chance in the piazzas and streets of the various villages. There was no need to go in search of them; unfortunately, except for the brief spell when they are busy threshing, they are always to be found waiting about in the hope that some work may turn up. The same questions were put to another hundred people in the city of Palermo itself, picked at random from the many hundreds that stand outside the Labor Bureau day after day.

In order to discover exactly how the unemployed and semi-employed reacted to their circumstances, the following questions were put to each in turn in the simplest possible words:

1 Have you got a trade?
2 How many days do you work in a year?
3 How many years did you attend school?
4 When you are unemployed, how do you manage to live?
5 Why are you unemployed?
6 Do you think it is God's will that you are unemployed?
7 Whose fault is it that you are unemployed?

8 What do you think the various political parties in Italy ought to do?
9 Is the ballot secret?
10 When you apply for work are your political beliefs taken into consideration?
11 What do you think you and each of us should do to get rid of unemployment?

Particular importance was attached to the method of approach. Great care was taken to maintain the strictest impartiality, and never to question anyone in the presence of others since this might have led to replies that were purely rhetorical and demogogic. Again, equal care was taken to elicit the individual's true thoughts and feelings; obviously, instinctive and unconsidered answers were too superficial in character to be of much value. Finally, it should be stressed that the object of this survey was not to cross-examine and judge people, but to get them to participate, as it were, in a round table conference; it was by listening to what each had to say that, in the light of all the various views and opinions, a composite picture gradually emerged—very gradually, let it be said, for arithmetical formulae cannot be applied to men and women; ten plus ten equals twenty, but put twice ten human beings together and the sum total is far greater.

The problem of unemployment involving fishermen all along the southern coasts has yet to be examined in detail and does not come within the scope of the present book. With regard to statistics, exact figures were not always available, but by comparing such as were obtainable—and of these there was no dearth—and finding that they more or less tallied, a reasonably accurate approximation could be reached. The answers to the questionnaire, but for the omission of a small amount of irrelevant matter, are given exactly as they were received, since its purpose was not to criticize the ideas expressed but to gain as much insight as possible into the minds and lives of all those who were asked to reply to it.

That only one name should appear on the cover of a book in whose creation more than a thousand people—the people of the province of Palermo—played a part, directly or indirectly, and in many cases a long and exhausting part, is surely strange. Amongst those who provided me with statistical information, and afforded me such valuable help in carrying out the statistical-sociological survey, my special thanks are due to the following: Carola Gugino, Gino Orlando, Michele and Angelo Panteleone, Nino Sorgi, Adriano Alloisio, Enzo De Negri, Sandro Di Meo, Goffredo Fofi, Grazia Fresco, Emilio Honneger, Alberto L'Abate, Giovanni Mottura, Giorgio Mugnaini, Guido Neppi-Modena, Franco Parisi, Giovanni Piergallini, Carlo Ravasini, Lawrence and Maddelena Rayner,[2] Giuseppe Ricca, Vittorio Rieser, and Emilio Soave.

DANILO DOLCI

[2] I want to take this opportunity of expressing my own thanks to Lawrence and Maddelena Rayner who so generously helped me, not only with the dialect, which is incomprehensible to a northern Italian, but also with many of the obscure and difficult passages in this book. *Translator's note.*

some facts and figures

The following are the official figures given in the Vigorelli Report and the official statistical report of the Regional Administration of Sicily, dated September 1953, of completely destitute and semi-destitute persons in Sicily out of a total population of 4,462,000:

	Families	%	Persons	%
Completely destitute	284,400	25.2	1,200,000	26.9
Semi-destitute	243,800	21.2	900,000	20.2
Total of completely destitute and semi-destitute persons			2,100,000	47.1

Of the Sicilian "bread-winners" 47.7 percent are agricultural workers who are paid by the day and own no land of their own. In 1951 the population of the province of Palermo (about 1922 square miles) was 1,019,796—approximately 530 persons per square mile.

At the end of the first week in September 1951, the number of employed persons in Sicily, according to the Italian National Institute of Statistics, was 301,000. It is interesting to compare the figures of the "active" population with those of two cities, Milan and Naples: Milan 47.7 percent, Naples 32.5 percent, Palermo 30.9 percent (city of Palermo 27.6 percent, province of Palermo 33.7 percent).

A glance at the list of persons registered for work up to the end of September, 1952 is also informative. The figures, which are those given by the Central Institute of Statistics, take on a particular significance when they are coupled with the following words: "Sicily. There can be no incentive to seek what is manifestly impossible: what urge can there be to find work when the people are aware that industry is non-existent?"[1]

[1] Vianelli: *Unemployment in Italy,* Vol. III.

	Men	Women	Total
Totally unemployed	19,194	2,007	21,201
Young persons seeking first job	6,135	1,029	7,164
Persons living at home, pensions, etc.	614	2,627	3,241
TOTAL	25,943	5,663	31,606

Employment Analysis

	Men	Women	Total
Agriculture and Fishing	8,967	329	9,296
Industry, transport and communications	12,212	3,735	15,947
Commercial	598	285	883
Clerical	766	267	1,033
Unskilled labor	3,400	1,047	4,447
TOTAL	25,943	5,663	31,606

The total population of Palermo when the census was taken on November 4, 1951 was 488,079 (actual residents in the city: 482,960); at the end of 1955 the number of inhabitants had risen to 555,563 (actual residents: 541,896). In 1951, according to the census taken for that year, 111,131 families were living in 96,414 houses; a further 2,807 families were living in 2,367 grottoes[2] or shacks; in 1954, the "official" number of these grottoes and shacks had risen to 2,461; since then, no statistical reports have been published. In 1951, 3,551 marriages were registered, 101 of the brides were under the age of sixteen. Thirty children were born to mothers who had not yet attained their sixteenth birthday. 12,924 live births were recorded in 1951; against these, there were 2,812 reported miscarriages and 439 still births. In the same year, there were sixteen suicides and thirty-two murders.

Of particular value, since it is an official document, is the *Special Budget for the City of Palermo* drawn up under the auspices of, and unanimously approved by the Regional

[2] A grotto, a miserable hole in the earth, is some seven feet high and usually about nine feet long by six feet wide. The rent of a grotto varies from 500 lire to 300 lire a month, though occasionally it is higher. (At the time this book was written there were about 620 lire to the U.S. dollar.) The conditions of those living in the grottoes are indescribable. *Translator's note.*

Assembly of Sicily. The figures that appear in this budget are significant. In 1954, the Council's balance-sheet showed a deficit of 4,017,000,000 lire; in 1955, the deficit had rocketed to 5,703,160,000 lire. "The deficit shown in the balance sheet is organic in character; the moneys required for the maintenance of the city continue to increase annually, with the result that the balance sheet must become more and more unfavorable." In 1954, 13,111 persons were employed by the municipality, and in that year alone, the Council expended 1,316,060,250 lire on the sanitary services and the upkeep of the city police force.

"Fifty percent of the city water is wasted or contaminated owing to defective piping. One hundred and ten cases of typhoid were reported at Bocca di Falco, and a further seventy-six cases, resulting from water pollution, were reported in the Via Oreto zone.

"The Department of Public Works gives the number of families living in makeshift shacks and shanties as 15,000 (60,000 persons). And, according to the Regional Housing Department, as against 65,984 houses in good condition, 36,-131 houses (which provide accommodation for 200,000 persons) are in a dangerous state of disrepair.

"The living conditions of this part of the old city are similar to those that exist in the lowest slum quarters of Naples. Most families have only one small room, a few have a second room so small that there is not even space in it for a single bed; none have lavatories or proper kitchens. Hardly any of the rooms have running water or electric light. They are sunless, airless, filled with dust from the courtyard, and the stench that rises from the open drains below is unspeakable. These conditions, together with the appalling overcrowding and the consequent promiscuity, have led to a state of moral and physical degradation which can only be described as terrifying. . . .

"This section of Palermo covers approximately five hundred acres, including the districts of Tribunali, Palazzo Reale, Monte di Pietà, and Castellammare. The section is cut into four roughly equal quarters by Via Vittorio Emanuele and Via Maqueda. In addition to these four quarters, it also comprises several outlying zones—Danissini, Borgo Nuovo, etc.

	No. of occupied rooms	No. of empty rooms	Grottoes and shacks	No. of inhabitants
Tribunali	10,017	391	385	34,481
Castellammare	12,659	147	154	22,142
Monte di Pietà	13,842	275	164	30,941
Palazzo Reale	15,025	192	195	34,235
			TOTAL	121,799

"One third of these houses do not conform with the regulations of the sanitary authorities as fit for habitation; these should be condemned and pulled down. The demolition of such houses in Tribunali, Castellammare, Monte di Pietà and Palazzo Reale alone would lead to the disappearance of 20,000 rooms."

The average number of days worked in a year by each of the five hundred men interviewed in the province of Palermo amounted to 99.4. Of the hundred men interviewed in Palermo, the number of working days per man averaged out at 121.7.

report from Palermo

the witnesses in Palermo

Concetta, her two grandsons
their mother and a friend

CONCETTA: I'm sixty years old, and I've been working in the
fish cannery for twenty years.

We women clean all the fish except mackerel; the fishermen have to gut them as soon as they catch them; if they
didn't, they'd go bad. We fillet anchovies, cut their heads off,
and throw them in a pile on the ground. We clean sardines
and lay them in oil or salt. Tuna we put into oil, or brine. One
of us stands in the brine tub, and as fast as we throw the fish
in, she presses them down with her bare feet.

The stink is awful; there are plenty that can't stand it. It
sticks to us; we can't get rid of it. We smell so bad that when
we get on a bus people move away from us. A relative of my
sister-in-law, Angela was her name, got a job in the cannery;
her husband was in jail and she had to go out and work to
keep her kids. One day was enough for her; the stink got her
down, poor girl. If you're the kind that gets dizzy easy, or if
you got a weak stomach, you'd get sick just like Angela did.
Course you don't notice it so much when you're used to it.
All of us women have terrible rheumatism—not surprising,
seeing we're always soaked to the skin.

We boil the tuna and pack it into cans. We work eight
hours a day; we get sixty lire an hour—the rate's the same for
overtime. We knock off for half an hour in the morning and
half an hour in the late afternoon. I'm a widow; I've got a
pension of thirty-five hundred lire a month. My sons are
fishermen, but before I'd bother them I've gone hungry many

a time. I'd never go live on them—not me; I'd rather work for my living. I've got seven sons, six of 'em married, and one daughter that's single. These two youngsters here are my grandsons; they live with me now that their father's in jail. He got mixed up in a fight and they gave him seven years. I tell you it scares you to death to live in Palermo.

There's plenty of work in the summer when the fish come in from Tunis, but in the winter, for four or five months there's nothing doing. If a little frozen fish comes in from Norway, we get maybe a couple of days' work now and then. It's a hard job; the fish are frozen so stiff that the cold goes right through your bones; you can't even feel your hands. They take women in the canneries because they don't have to pay us as much as they would men, but we do a man's work, I can tell you that. We have to hoist iron baskets that weigh two hundred pounds apiece up on the ropes and stack heavy cases of fish, one on top of the other. Every case weighs twenty-two pounds.

About three hundred women get jobs in the canneries, but there aren't more than fifty of us regulars. In the season there might be as many as a hundred working regularly. They have all kinds of canneries at San Lorenzo, Acquasanta, Pallavicino, Castello, Sant'Erasmo, and fifty other places. Look at my hands; see what the brine does to them? It makes them so sore that they often bleed; it eats right into the flesh; our fingers are full of little holes, and they sting and burn like red-hot coals. When they get that inflamed, we can't use them. We put oil on them and lay off for four or five days. If you let them go too far, they get all covered with sores.

There are a lot of families that would starve if the women didn't work in the canneries. The men can't find jobs; they look after the kids. They don't keep a sharp enough eye on them, though; one kid fell down some steps, and when her mother went home at the end of the day she found her lying there dead. Another time a child was left alone while her mother was putting the fish in the brine, and she fell in the sea and drowned. God knows how many accidents there've been; they're always happening. There're worse things than accidents, though. Take my daughter-in-law's brother. He wanted to join the police, but he was too short, so they wouldn't take him. He worked a little while in the curing sheds, but then they laid him off and he couldn't find another job. In the end he killed himself—jumped off the balcony. Poor fellow; he'd gone out of his mind.

All kids have to go to school—that's the law—but plenty don't go; their families can't send them; they don't have the cash for clothes and books. I share my room with three families. Have we got a toilet? Sure—the courtyard!

We start work in the sheds when we're twelve and go on till we're sixty or more. Some of the young married women, so they can make a few extra soldi, take care of the boss . . .

When the *Camera di Lavoro* sends anybody around to see what kind of conditions we're working under, we all sneak away and hide; we would never say anything against the boss. If we did we'd be out of a job for good; none of the canneries would take us.

Do we go to Mass? Certainly we do; we're all Catholics, every one of us. Religion is going to Mass on Sundays and the big feast days. Before we begin to clean the fish, we always cross ourselves. It comes natural to us to cross ourselves after we finish work too. Maybe there's a few that don't, but only a very few. We've got our religion, and we stick by it.

Most people vote C.D. because if they vote C.D., they're voting for Our Lord . . .

FIRST GRANDSON: Once upon a time the *parrini* came on shanks' mare to beg for charity; nowadays they do their collecting on Lambrettas or in the latest model Fiats.

HIS MOTHER, WHO HAS JUST COME IN, REPROVINGLY: Tut, tut!

FIRST GRANDSON: Some of us young guys vote Communist. For four pounds of pasta, though, Mamma and Papa vote Monarchist!

HIS MOTHER: Sure I vote for the King. Poor man, he lost his throne and everything. If they got up a petition for him, I'd put my name on it a hundred times, a thousand times, as much as they wanted me to . . . Why am I sorry for him? I just told you why—because they made him give up everything he had. What did they want to do that for? Why couldn't they let him go on being king?

FIRST GRANDSON: Poor people scrape together a living in all kinds of ways in Palermo. There are some guys that go around selling sandstone to clean copper.

SECOND GRANDSON: Other guys sell zucchini squash—they carry them in covered baskets around the streets.

FIRST GRANDSON: There're some that sell *stigghiole*—that's cow or horse or sheep lungs stuck on a skewer and roasted over charcoal. There are hundreds of them.

SECOND GRANDSON: And some that sell *frittola*—pig's liver cut up small and boiled. And all the ones that peddle salt, charcoal, liver sausage, sawdust, boiled beans and boiled chickpeas—there's too many of them to count. Then for a month in the winter there's the ones that sell blueberries.

FIRST GRANDSON: Don't forget the ones that sell fig marzipan—they boil the figs down to a paste, roll it in flour and bake it in the oven. They always stand around near schools because kids love it. When they're going in and coming out, they shout to them: "Hey! try your luck with *strumbula*—five lira a throw! The *strumbula*'s a kind of dice, and the kid that rolls the highest number gets a big hunk of the candy.

SECOND GRANDSON: Other guys entertain people in the public gardens of the Villa Bonanno by telling stories about the adventures of the Paladins. Some people give them five lire; they don't make much. Then there are the characters that sell all kinds of things in the piazzas: bottles of brilliantine, pills to loosen your bowels, all different kinds of medicine, little cakes made out of rice, with an orange flavor, pens, penknives, and souvenirs of Sicily: toy bagpipes and little models of Sicilian carts.

FIRST GRANDSON: And what about the moneychangers that cheat the people that come here from Catania by giving them phony bills? These crooks are getting scarce, though; even the foreigners are beginning to know good money from bad.

SECOND GRANDSON: And the shoeshine boys that hang around hoping for customers.

FIRST GRANDSON: And the ones that'll make you an offer for whatever you want to hock and save you the trouble of standing in line outside the pawnshops—right under the noses of the *carabinieri* that are there to keep order. They're mostly women. They can look the stuff over, figure what it'll bring, and ask you if you'll take so much. They pawn whatever they buy and make a little on the deal.

SECOND GRANDSON: There's the *panerara*—maybe fifty of them. They keep an eye on the houses of rich people and get to know their schedules. When a signora comes out to do her shopping, one of them'll be waiting outside the door with a basket. "Carry your parcels for you, *Baruneddu?*" They call her a baroness to flatter her; if they offer to run an errand for a gentleman, they always begin: "God bless you, noble *Cavaliere . . .*"

FIRST GRANDSON: What about all the kids in the cafés that give the owners so much to fill up thermos bottles for them, and then go in the banks and the offices selling cups of hot coffee? They have to make the coffee go as far as possible, otherwise they wouldn't make a soldo.

SECOND GRANDSON: Then there's the *munnezzara,* guys that go out at night with wheelbarrows and shovel up manure—manure's city property, so they're really stealing it. They sell it to the market gardeners for five hundred lire a load.

FIRST GRANDSON: And the old-fashioned barbers that bleed sick people and put leeches on them to bring their fever down.

SECOND GRANDSON: And the sword swallowers, the magicians, and the characters that twist their bodies inside out and make all the kids think their heads are cut off.

FIRST GRANDSON: There are the guys that sell mulberries. They're mostly skilled workers, like carpenters, that only do it to make ends meet; half the time they're out of work. Oh, yes, and the ones that sell little bottles of jasmine perfume.

SECOND GRANDSON: There're some that make a few soldi drawing pictures on the pavement and making designs. And I don't know how many fortunetellers and magicians there are going around.

FIRST GRANDSON: All the beachcombers, too. The customs police keep a sharp lookout for them though; anything that gets washed up on shore belongs to the government.

SECOND GRANDSON: There're cooked-snail sellers and water sellers with big jars made out of clay.

FIRST GRANDSON: And guys that push boiled cuttlefish, *frutti di mare*, sea urchins, and bait: little shrimp and worms.

SECOND GRANDSON: There are maybe fifty hucksters that go around every day on Lambrettas or in cars with oil, wine, eggs, hens, whey, and *mozzarella* for sale.

FIRST GRANDSON: Early in the morning and all day long people come into Palermo from the country with stuff to sell: kegs of wine and marsala at forty or fifty lire a keg, twenty-quart cans of oil, sacks full of live chickens, sacks of cheeses, sacks of horsemeat, not from animals that are properly slaughtered, but from any old nag or mare that's dead (we buy this horseflesh around here), and goats, dead or alive. As soon as the train hits the outskirts of the city, they give the engineer a bottle of wine so he'll slow down, and then, so they won't have to pay the tax on their stuff, they toss everything out; sometimes they have just time enough to get off the train themselves; sometimes they don't get the chance. Many times an engineer that wants to arrive on time will pick up his speed, and then the stuff gets thrown all over the tracks. There are people that wait beside the tracks for the train to pass; they get fifty lire for every sack or bundle they pick up. A customs guy gets on the train just before it gets to Palermo. The tax on the country produce is very heavy.

One time, when the stuff was thrown out on the tracks at Cortile Cascino, there was a guy in the bunch that picked it up that went and sold it on his own. A fight broke out. The ones that were regulars at watching the tracks, about twenty or so of them, started accusing one another of doing the same thing; they began swinging right and left; they bit each other and scratched, and the women pulled each other's hair and rolled on the ground and wouldn't let go till they'd ripped out a fistful. It was a real mess; they used to trust each other before it happened, but they don't any more . . .

A FRIEND: Now it's my turn. What's the Mafia got to do with coffins? I'll tell you. Coffin making's one of the very few industries in Palermo; it may not be big, but it's very profitable, so the competition's fierce. This year four or five coffin makers were murdered. The coffin-making industry's controlled by the Mafia of the wholesale markets. Everybody in Italy's heard about these *mafiosi* who make a regular practice of bumping each other off. The coffin makers' places are surrounded by flower shops where you can buy wreaths and crosses; as for the coffin makers, they're so anxious to get all the stiffs for themselves they wipe each other out! The guy who was killed in Via dei Giudici the other day was a coffin maker. He was also a big shot in the cigarette black market. The cigarettes are often stashed in coffins, you know, and as coffins have to be taken here, there, and everywhere, it's a pretty safe way of delivering the goods.

The credit for spiriting away live people in coffins doesn't belong to the Mafia though; it belongs to the government. When the prefect Mori was sent to Sicily in 1922 to put down the Mafia, he insisted on having a free hand. He started off by arresting everybody, no matter whether they were right, left or center, which was a mistake because quite a number of them turned out to be high-ups of the Fascists. Mori was warned from Rome that he better be more careful, so he changed his tactics and only rounded up the small fry, and told the big shots they'd have to emigrate—a certain Rocco C., he said, would arrange everything for them. Well, Rocco C. hid them in coffins in which he bored airholes; then the coffins were stowed away on a ship bound for the States, and Rocco made the trip with them to deliver the remains to the heartbroken relatives. A good thing he made out of it too; he was paid twice: first by the guys he smuggled aboard, then by their enemies for making corpses out of them for real! As soon as they were a good distance out at sea, Rocco used to dump four or five coffins complete with "bodies" into the drink! In fact, the minute the "corpses" left Palermo they were written off; none of them ever arrived in America, and that was that!

Today you'll find the center of the coffin-making industry in the Via dei Giudici, Via dei Calderai, Rua Formaggi, and Via del Ponticello. As I said, it's controlled by the Mafia. That coffin maker I was telling you about that was murdered in the Via dei Giudici was mowed down by machine guns outside his own shop . . .

Up until a short time ago the leftist parties used to tell the people: "Take the pasta the Rights offer you, but don't vote for them." Nowadays, though, men are beginning to realize that this pasta is an insult to human beings and instead of taking it they ought to throw it in the faces of the C.D.'s.

Yeah, times are changing. Many of the old customs are dying out: *giacchiotto,* for instance. It used to be quite the thing for a rich, aristocratic family to adopt some poor little kid, bring him up, and make a servant out of him. They put him in a uniform, a striped coat, when he answered the door —that's how it came to be known as *giacchiotto.* The kid grew up to be a servant his whole life for no pay; he was just part of the furniture, and he was passed on with the rest of the property from father to son. Rich people that "adopted" children for their own use would make a big show of how they did it out of charity, out of the kindness of their hearts. Sometimes a kid would be turned into a pervert by his "generous" master.

Giacchiotto hasn't quite gone out, though. If the "adopted" child's a girl, it often happens that, as soon as she's developed, the master takes advantage of her. If she gets pregnant he makes her have an abortion, or if she has the baby he won't let her keep it, it's turned over to the authorities. He gives her a dowry of a little land or a cow, and he marries her off to one of his tenants. It's considered very kind of the master, but the girl's husband takes to drink or goes wrong— he's ashamed of his wife; he thinks of her as being no better than a whore and himself as nothing but a jerk. The master's a wonderful man, but him, poor bastard, everybody knows he has horns . . .

Some people leave their cars in the street and pay men to sleep in them. It's cheaper than a garage . . .

Go inside the vestibule of the courthouse. You can be sure some guy that knows you're there for legal advice will stop you and ask you if you've seen X. "X is one of the most brilliant lawyers in Palermo," he'll say, and build him up for all he's worth—of course, X has paid him to do it. But suppose you ask him where you can find Y, who doesn't go in for greasing palms. He'll give you a black look. "Y? Y?" he'll say. "Never heard of him. Funny, I've been in and out of this place for thirty years. You sure he's fully qualified?" Of course, you don't like the sound of this at all, so you decide to see X!

There's another racket that goes on at the courthouse. Some poor dame that's had a fight with her husband or some trouble with a neighbor in the courtyard'll rush in there, thinking, simple soul that she is, that she'll get justice. But does she? An usher (or maybe some minor official) very kindly takes down the charge or the complaint for her and sends her to see the lawyer that he works for. The lawyer asks her for a fee; when she's gone, the lawyer splits it with the tout . . .

The *mafiosi* that emigrated to America had hardly organized the Black Hand there when the federal authorities cracked down. The famous detective Petrosino was sent at once on a secret mission to Sicily—it was so secret, in fact, that even the Italian police didn't know a thing about it. But Petrosino had hardly landed when a man in the Piazza Marina pulled out a revolver and shot him point-blank; he fell dead right opposite the Palazzo di Giustizia, in front of which heretics and witches used to be burned at the stake in the days of the Inquisition. Witches weren't always burned, though; sometimes they were flung out of the windows. The ignorant, narrow-minded crowd would hoot and howl while they hurtled through the air and then crashed to death on the stones below.

Don Totò

I used to buy and sell old iron and junk; I had a license and a regular spot. I wasn't like the guys from Cortile Cascino that push their stuff in the streets. They came to me and offered me whatever they had, and I'd buy anything I could use: old hammers, pincers, crowbars, those watchacallums you life up a car on when you're changing a tire—oh yeah, jacks—suppressors, lamp bases, razors, phonographs, books in all kinds of condition, used bicycle tires, saucepan lids, and so forth and so on.

Towards the end of the war, I got sick. When I was discharged the Council gave me back my old job as a streetcleaner, but I had to keep running to the doctor, and it ended up with my getting canned. I had no pension, nothing, so in order to get something to eat I took up selling junk. Sometimes, though I didn't know it, I bought stuff—bicycles, for instance—that was stolen. I used to write down most of the names of the people who sold me things in a little book, but when I felt sure they were aboveboard I didn't bother—I never would have believed they were crooks. But the stuff I bought from them was hot, and the result was I got sent to prison.

Sometimes people would come to me who didn't have the money to pay for whatever they wanted. It seemed lousy not to trust them, to say "no," so I'd let them have it, and that was the last I ever saw of them. Then too, there were the spongers. "Don Totò, lend me enough for a meal," they'd beg, and I'd do it. In the end I got wise, though. I realized I was being robbed left and right and stopped giving money to anybody.

When it was raining I hardly sold a thing, but everybody was after me to buy something. The rain put the hawkers out of business, so the peddlers that sold roasted nuts, cooked vegetables, fish and so forth brought me all their household possessions looking to raise some cash.

I had a licensed spot by the wall of the old fort before it was torn down to make room for the court buildings—a good deal it was, too. Well, a few days before His Excellency Mussolini was due to come to Palermo to lay the cornerstone of the new building, the police took my license away. After the state visit, what do you think? The bastards gave another guy a license for the same spot that was mine— they did me in, me, a municipal streetcleaner for twenty-four years. And as if that wasn't enough, the Council gave me a spot where there was absolutely nothing doing.

As I told you, I've got no pension—it's a dirty swindle. I was in the army during the war, I obeyed orders, and when I was in the Twenty-third Como Brigade, our outfit was in the trenches. What happened? The guns were too much for me and I went off my rocker. My commanding officer, acting on the medic's orders, sent me to the loony bin. "He must go to the asylum at once," the medic said after he took a look at me. There was nothing wrong with my head before the war; I can prove it, because if I hadn't been in perfect shape I'd never have been in the First Engineers, a crack outfit that some guys even paid to join. I was sent from asylum to asylum: Cittadella, Mantua, Reggio Emilia, Central Emilia—I don't remember whether I was in Aversa or not. But no pension.

DON TOTÒ'S WIFE: It took four medical orderlies to get him to the asylum. You'd think that was proof enough that he was raving mad. But when he was discharged (the war was almost over), they just let him out—they never gave him a medical discharge or anything, so he doesn't get a pension.

DON TOTÒ: Since my health's gone to pieces, I've tried to make a living in all kinds of ways. I even went in for clock repairing, but I smashed a lot more than I fixed, which didn't please the customers. People were always in and out of the room where I worked; I'd be bending over my job, and when I looked up I'd find some of the clocks and watches gone. The guys who go around from street to street yelling, "Any old clocks or watches to sell?" used to bring them to me to repair, but I made a real mess of them—they never ran again. Nowadays, although we've got no license, my wife and I sell a few odds and ends at home, like needles, or thread, or candles.

I've done everything I can to cure myself; I've got asthma, a bad heart, my blood doesn't circulate right, I'm a mass of nerves, I've got aches and pains all over. I've taken medicine by the bottleful—I don't know how many lire my wife's spent on doctors and pills. Nothing's done me any good. We've been to the wise woman, too—she's not a witch but a real saint. She consecrated herself to God and she knows through prayers whether somebody's request will be granted or not. She doesn't use incense or herbs or anything like that, she just prays. She told us to go to church, but even though we went I wasn't cured.

I honor St. Rosalia with a Triumph in the hopes that she'll make me better. We're going to have another Triumph for her soon. This is what you do. You get everything in the room in order, then you hang a silk bedspread on the wall, and right in the middle, over the door, you put the picture of St. Rosalia. Underneath the picture you fix up a little table like an altar—you set two vases of flowers on it, two big candles and four little ones. You take a tray, the kind waiters use for coffee cups, you stand a statue of St. Rosalia on it, and you ask the people passing for contributions—they give what they can afford, ten or twenty lire. You can have a Triumph that costs four or five or six thousand lire—you can spend less if you like, or more. My wife and I pay for our Triumph out of our own pockets and so do a few others, but most people still stick to the old custom and hold the tray out.

When the money's collected, part of it's spent on hiring musicians, the rest goes on wine and food for the guests. We buy rabbit, *fave* beans, garlic and oregano, and oil and pepper for a great stew. When we're all together for the Triumph, the musicians strike up a song, then we start eating and drinking.

We have three musicians; one plays the cello, one the mandolin and one the guitar. They take turns singing a verse of the Song of St. Rosalia. It begins like this:

At St. Rosalia's birth,
All men did rejoice on earth,
She had such beauty and such worth,

and it goes on:

One day within her glass she spied
Jesus, our Savior, crucified.

There are dozens of verses, and each one tells of some miracle that St. Rosalia performed. She did a lot of miracles at sea, and so, when a boat's in danger of shipwreck, the sailors pray to her and promise to offer her a Triumph if she'll bring them safe to shore. Sick people pray to St. Rosalia and promise her a wax arm or leg or heart—it all depends on what part of the body they beg her to heal.

After the Song of St. Rosalia, the musicians sing and play the Dance of the Virgins and Saints. It's a tarantella:

Cicca, Veronica,
    Victoria and all
The virgins and saints
    Take part in the ball.

Pretty? Listen:

Concetta dance, Paola dances,
    Concetta turns with Marianna,
Marianna with Concetta,
    And Concetta with Vincenza.

DON TOTÒ'S WIFE, BREAKING IN: It begins like this:

The fair young virgins
    With steps light and airy,
Dance around the altar
    To thank God and Mary.
Who are the happiest?
    Maria, Constanza and Beatrice—
Who are the most joyful?
    All, all the fair young virgins.

Then we all start dancing the tarantella:

See Concettina,
   With Peppina,
Gesualda
   With Giovanna,
Giovannina
   With Rachela . . .

The tarantella lasts for half an hour. We twirl around until all the saints and virgins have been called into the dance, and when we've named every one of them, we wind up with:

Saints and young virgins,
   Dance round about,
Link hands together,
   Not one is left out.

DON TOTÒ TAKES UP THE STORY: We have a great celebration on St. Rosalia's Feast Day. "Long live St. Rosalia!" everybody shouts. We give the musicians a special meal: codfish with tomato sauce, pasta with anchovy sauce, fruit, lemonade and wine. When C., a friend of ours, came here for St. Rosalia's Feast, we ate twelve pounds of pasta, four pounds of bread, and two pounds of beans, and we drank quarts and quarts of wine. Now, thanks to her, he can't eat more than a tenth of a pound of pasta! When we're celebrating St. Rosalia's Feast, one of the guests'll call out: "Those who believe in St. Rosalia and love her, join with me and shout: 'Long live St. Rosalia!'" and we all shout: "Long live St. Rosalia."

AS DON TOTÒ SPEAKS, HE BEGINS TO WEEP. THEN HE CONTINUES: When we reach the top of Monte Pellegrino, before we climb the steps to St. Rosalia's shrine, we recite the Rosary, and before and after every decade, we say:

A hundred thousand times
   St. Rosalia we praise,
Who keeps us safe from harm
   And from all evil ways.

We recite this verse ten times, then we say:

St. Rosalia of Palermo, descend, then climb once more,
Deliver us from famine, plague, earthquakes and war,
Deliver us . . .

This is the story of how St. Rosalia delivered the city of Palermo from plague. One day, a hunter who had climbed to the top of Monte Pellegrino saw St. Rosalia appear at one of the windows. She spoke to him. She said:

"Where are you going, good man?"

"I'm going hunting."

"Where have you come from?" asked St. Rosalia.

"From Palermo."

"And what do you do in Palermo?"

"Ah, don't ask me what I do there," said the huntsman. "The people are falling in Palermo like ripe pears."

"What is causing them to drop?" she asked, and when the huntsman told her the plague was raging in the city, St. Rosalia said:

"Return to Palermo, tell the Cardinal to have a special chariot made, and to have my image carried on it through the streets. As soon as this has been done, the plague will pass. But three days after you have given the Cardinal my message, you will die."

Well, everything happened exactly the way she said it would. The hunter died and Palermo was miraculously saved from the plague. The body of St. Rosalia was found, and the key to the coffin (the coffin which is carried through Palermo in the procession of July 15, her Feast Day) was thrown into the ocean to make sure it would never be unlocked.

No medicine does me any good. I'm worn out from suffering. I'm exhausted from sickness and I pray and pray to St. Rosalia to take pity on me. Every year for the last five years I've given her a Triumph.

Look, we keep those lamps burning before her day and night. I talk to her, and once—once she looked down at me, she bent her head head towards me and she said, "Yes . . ." I pray to her, I talk to her almost every night—(*sobbing*) but, but it was only that one time when she bent her head towards me that she said, "Yes . . ."

Giuseppe F.

Every time a new invention comes along, another poor guy goes under. We barkers used to make quite a good living in the old days. Whenever a new shop was opened—a bakery, a butcher's, a grocery, a wine shop, any kind of store—the owner would send for us. If he was opening up in a big way, he'd hire four or five of us. We were well paid because we knew how to advertise a store. Nowadays all the advertising's done on the radio. When there's a *festa*, though, we earn a little—there's still some work for the barker.

My outfit has a clarinet, cymbals, a big drum, and two trumpets. We dress ourselves up in tails and top hats or else chefs' hats to make the crowd laugh. We rent the clothes from the Massimo Theatre and have to pay a deposit on them.

Sometimes we march through the streets, sometimes we ride in a carriage. Every few yards or so we stop and advertise the new shop at the top of our voices. Suppose it's a shop that sells wine. "Oi, oi, oi!" we shout, "go to number so-and-so, such-and-such street. For only a hundred and forty lire you can buy the very same wine that'll cost you two hundred anywhere else! Only a hundred and forty lire for this superb wine! The proprietor was born and bred in the wine-growing country—he's rich, he doesn't need to make money, so he's lowering his prices! What a stock he has! If his casks accidentally broke open, the city'd be flooded with wine!"

This patter, of course, is just to make people think the proprietor's filthy with money, even though he may be as poor as a church mouse.

We do everything we can to draw a crowd and amuse them. We begin with a lot of cross-talk. One of us sets the ball rolling like this:

"Our sponsor's got a real fistful of cards!" (By cards he means money.)

"Oh, he has, has he? Name a couple of them—"

"The Seven of Swords and the Ace of Wands!"[1] (The crowd roars.)

"You son of a so-and-so! You don't call those cards, do you?"

"What do *you* call 'em, Mister Shit-eggs?" (He turns around three times.)

"I'll tell you what, I'll take you home with me and you can shit a hundred eggs a day. At thirty lire apiece, that'll come to three thousand lire. But if you cackle like a hen, I'll kick you out!"

Say a baker's hired us to advertise his bread. "Oi! Oi! Oi!" we yell, "go to So-and-so if you want the very best bread that money can buy! Baked to a turn, crisp and crunchy, just asking to be crunched, whiter than white! Made of the very finest flour! He won't have anything but the very finest flour—any inferior flour he dumps in the ocean!" Sometimes we butter up the guy who's hiring us by shouting: "Jesus! Our patron's hammered in a nail, hammered it home for good!" which means: "Our patron's opened a shop and he'll never go broke!" We make a lot of use of the kids in the crowd: "Come on, now, boys and girls, let's have three big cheers for the new owner: Long live So-and-so, hip-hip-hurray! Clap your hands, all of you—any kid that doesn't clap will die at midnight for sure—he's chicken, he wets the bed! Altogether now —clap!" So they all clap like mad, and we blow a loud flourish on the trumpets.

See those certificates on the wall? They're certificates of merit for the poems I've written. That's right, I'm a poet, though I'm not lucky. Sometimes, if a shopkeeper opens his wallet wide enough, I make up a poem in his honor. Sometimes I compose songs for the mandolin and guitar.

We have all sorts of ways of drawing a crowd. The shopkeeper who's hired us'll give us a bag of candy for instance, and we'll throw handfuls to the kids, who scramble like mad after them, fight for them and fall on top of each other in the road. People rush up to find out what's happening, what all the screaming and yelling's about. Sometimes we strike up a

---

[1] These cards refer to a man's sexual prowess. *Translator's note.*

lively bersagliere's march, and off we go with a chain of kids behind us, each one holding on to the one in front. Everybody flocks to their windows and onto the balconies to watch.

Of course, the sort of show we put on depends on what we're paid. The less we get, the less we do, but when the money's really good, we go to no end of trouble.

Once when we were out in our tails and top hats we played a practical joke that gave us a really good laugh. It was during the Fascist regime, when everybody had to give the Fascist salute. When we were close to the Pioppo, we hid all our musical instruments except the trumpets, which we used to blow a warning blast. Naturally, everybody thought that the entire Municipal Council of Palermo was coming! But a minute later, when we sat down at a table outside a café and ordered drinks, the people realized quickly that we had taken them in! "The sons of bitches! They're bastards from the Capo, that's what they are!"

One way we had of advertising was to praise the goods of the shopkeeper who hired us and run down the goods of his competition.

"Buy your pasta from Y," we'd shout. "Beware of X's pasta, it's garbage!"

"You guys have got two voices—you keep changing them!" somebody in the crowd would call out. "Can't help it in our business," we'd say. "We *do* change our tune, that's true, but we guarantee you we're speaking the truth today! Buy Z's pasta . . ." and so forth.

Whenever a shopkeeper hired the rival outfit, we did our best to make a fool of him. I'd drape myself in a white sheet, for instance, and hold a lighted candle in each hand; the band would strike up the funeral march, and we'd march off real solemn, with a crowd of kids alongside us, boo-hooing their eyes out—we paid them a few soldi to make with the tears. As soon as we reached the shop, I'd kneel down outside it and act like I was as dead as a corpse. "Aren't they a riot?" the crowd we'd drawn would say. "Where in the devil do they find such funny characters?" A little later I'd get up, and we'd march to our sponsor's shop. "Long live Italy, long live our generous sponsor, and long live all of us," we'd yell. Then our musicians would say, "Where's the wine?" and everybody would laugh again, and our sponsor would run to get the wine.

We'd pay the kids to bother our competitors any way they could—fart at them loud, boo them, and so forth. There are six of us in our outfit, and we're all masters at our trade—the flower of Palermo, eh? The other bunch are amateurs, they don't even count.

Suppose we've been hired by a fellow who's opened a wine shop, we've got a special trick for amusing the crowd. I ask the shopkeeper to pour me a glass of wine, then I go into the street and hold it up. "See this?" I say to the kids. "It's a prize for the first one that gets his big behind on the ground. Ready, get set—GO." As fast as that, they all flop down on their backsides. "A tie," I say, and we start again. As soon as I see they're busy getting up and sitting down, and always tying with each other, I wind up by pouring the wine over their heads. If our sponsor's a baker, we throw bread to them, and there's such a scramble and hassle to get hold of it that quite often there's a good deal of blood from noses getting punched and so forth.

Nowadays I don't make enough money to live on as a barker, so I write poetry and compose songs. My brain's made of gold when I'm writing poetry, but I don't seem able to make any money at it. I make up all sorts of poems: love poems, poems of hate and revenge, poems in praise of somebody's products or goods. Some people I write them for give me a present, some don't. Things are better for us barkers in the summer, when there are more feast days, but in the winter when it's icy—well, as the old saying goes: "Your back's at ease, but not your empty belly."

The way things are, we're actually worse off than beggars. If a man wants to live honestly he just has to chew his nails. The lucky ones are the ones who know how to steal a wallet— they can eat to their hearts' content. But you have to be cut out for that sort of thing.

During the war I made up a poem to the tune of a popular song, and sent it in to a paper. The editor printed it and paid me twenty-four lire. I'll say it for you:

England, go back, you've lost the game,
You rule the seas, you've often said,
To rule *our* sea, you cannot claim,
You cannot fill *our* hearts with dread.

Your troops are not a match for ours,
Your bombs fall wide both day and night,
See how your puppet army cowers,
Grovels and cringes to our might.

Our hour of victory draws nigh,
Triumphant, glorious, complete,
England, each second that goes by,
Makes still more certain your defeat.

England, in my own native tongue,
I warn you of your coming fate,
For you the bell of doom has rung,
Withdraw before it is too late.
All, all your puny efforts fail—
The glorious Axis will prevail!

Even now, I still can't believe we lost the war. If we ever
took the world seriously here in Palermo, instead of kidding
it, we couldn't go on living.

There are one or two barkers in the city who may have a
stronger voice than mine, that's true, but they can't pronounce
the names of the streets and the shopkeepers as clearly as I
do. I don't want to brag, but as far as pronunciation goes,
they're nowhere near me.

the Capo

The Capo is the section southeast of the Massimo Theatre and some thirty yards behind it, in the very heart of Palermo. The hundred families under consideration were picked at random; thirty-one in Cortile Scalilla, nineteen in Vicolo Catara, twenty-nine in Cartile degli Orfani, thirteen in Cortile Capellaio and eight in Cortile Maestro Carlo.

The Streets are narrow; in some places they are less than three feet wide. In one alley, close to a second-hand-clothes stand, we saw a naked child squat down to do his business and pass a tapeworm twenty-five inches long. The houses are high; some have as many as four stories.

At night the floors of most of the rooms are strewn with mattresses, rags and blankets. If a child gets up to do his business, he has to fumble and grope every inch of the way in the dark to avoid walking on the body of a sleeper. Families sleep on the table, as well as under it; one old woman managed to bed down her ten grandchildren, for whom there was no accommodation in their own home, in this way. Another tiny room was shared by three young married couples.

The hundred families number five hundred and seventy-six persons, all of whom live in eighty homes, or ninety-one rooms. The average number of persons to a room, then, is 6.33.

Only one family has a proper toilet; the other families do their business in an open drain which is frequently situated just below the kitchen. Fourteen families have water taps, but in summer the water is cut off as it is needed for the plants in the public gardens. The "Christians" can do without it!

Forty-nine families have electric light. Two rooms have floors of packed dirt; seventy-nine, of broken tile; and one, of coarse cement. The floors of the remaining rooms are fairly good.

There are two hundred and twenty-three places large enough for one person to sleep. This means that the average number of persons to one such place is 2.58.

Among the children three through six years old, four go to kindergarten and fifty-three do not. Among those six through thirteen, forty-nine go to school, fifty-eight do not. On the average, the four hundred and forty-four persons over six years old have finished only a third of the second grade.

As for the occupations of the heads-of-family, twenty-eight are hawkers; nine are laborers; eight, shoemakers; four, bricklayers and carpenters; three, candy sellers; three streetcleaners; one is a stevedore; one, a tailor; one, a plasterer; one, a painter; one, a craftsman who decorates carts; one, a chauffeur; one, a doorkeeper; one, a wood inlayer; one, a cooked-meat vendor; one, a lathe operator; one, a poolroom attendant; one, a barber's assistant; one, a mailman; one, a sawdust merchant; one, a moneychanger; one, a grocery assistant; and one, a cigarette seller. Four of the men are disabled, and ten have no trade or calling. Thirteen of the families are on relief.

As for the women, ten are chambermaids, two are dressmakers, one is a hawker, one is a beggar, one is a laundress. The other women do not go out to work, but help out by doing various jobs at home for the stores; for example, stringing string beans.

With few exceptions, the children follow the family calling.

Twenty persons have had typhus, from which there have been several deaths. Forty-one children have suffered from various chest diseases, nearly all of which were diagnosed as tubercular. Infant mortality is due largely to some form of blood poisoning.

The authorities frequently refuse to issue licenses to peddlers, hence they are forced into far less harmless "work." It is difficult to say how often these unfortunate have been fined. They can not remember how many fines they have incurred, but can only give a rough monthly estimate. The twenty-eight hawkers interviewed in Capo have been fined approximately eight thousand times in the last ten years.

The Capo has its own underworld argot, largely thieves' slang. The argot is constantly changing. A word may be used for only a few months, or it may survive for a year or for years. For obvious reasons, the substitution of one code word for another regularly occurs; squealers who give away the meaning of such a word to the police double-cross them by warning the underworld not to use it in the future. An instance of this substitution is the number of words that have been employed in thieves' slang to denote "wallet." *Lascagno* was dropped for *quaglio*, *quaglio* for *curamo*, *curamo* for *surci* and *u porto*. Certain words picked up in other cities have found their way into this argot; for instance, *addumannusa* (stranger, foreigner) has given way to *farlocca*, which comes from Rome.

The argot of the Capo and other disreputable sections, which does not form part of the true Sicilian dialect, has gradually become familiar; hence, in the last twelve years, more and more use has been made of back-slang—i.e., *"nepa"* for *pane* (bread). The speed at which back-slang is now spoken is astonishing.

Gino O.

What's my background? I'll tell you. My mother was a *spiccia-faccende*—you know, a person who makes a living getting legal papers for other people. She was a widow—her husband had been a shoemaker by trade. She had to keep going to the Town Hall, and among the people she met there was the man who was to become my father. She was a real good-looker, and he was crazy about her; by promising to marry her, he got her to do what he wanted. He didn't bother to tell her he was married already.

I was born in 1912, a bastard. My mother couldn't bring herself to part with me, and since I had no name, she gave me hers. I remember very little about those early days; I have a dim recollection of playing in the street and of being left in charge of a neighbor while my mother was at work, but that's all.

When the Spanish flu epidemic hit Sicily, my mother caught it and died. Her family had written her off because she'd gone wrong, and because I was a child of sin none of them would give me a home.

I had a grown-up half-brother who was engaged, and he got his girl's family to take me in. There was a young pickpocket living in the house, and after a while he started to teach me the tricks of the trade. He began by showing me how to lift the stuff out of a woman's handbag (a *magghia appendente*, a trawling net, it's called in thieves' slang) in the *il frontino* way—that is, from the front. What I had to do was this. I had to pass the victim, walk on five or six steps, then turn around sharply so that I was face to face with her; as soon as I came level with her handbag, I had to unfasten it in a flash. I had to be able to handle every kind of fastener: buttons (some handbags fastened with buttons in those days), snaps, clasps and zippers. The minute I had the bag open, I had to slip my hand inside and grab the wallet or whatever else I could.

When a kid mastered his trade, his problem was to convince people he could be trusted and get somebody to take him on. After a while, some guy that'd been a pickpocket himself in his young days would get to hear about him. "There's a kid that knows his job and one that won't crack," he'd say to himself, and he'd hire him. The two of them would travel all over the place, and work every city in Italy. My first master was a certain B. I'll never forget the first day I went out with him. I was in such a panic I wet my pants: I was scared stiff that the woman we'd picked out would get wise to what I was doing, grab me and scream for the police. If I hadn't been still more scared that B. would call me yellow and drop me, I never would have gone through with it. Lots of kids used to get their courage up and steady their nerves with booze or drugs; after that first time, though, I was all right. B. gave half the money from the hauls we made to his family; he didn't give me any, but he paid for my room and board. He never told how much was in the wallets, which he always opened himself. I usually nabbed two or three a day, and while I was at it, B. made sure that none of the passers-by would spot my game.

Almost every family in the street I lived in had a kid like me who was learning to be a pickpocket. In Via Sant'Agostino, Cortile Catarro, Cortile Salara (Scalilla) and in practically all the streets around, there was either a master thief or a school for thieves. Here in Ballarò you'll find hundreds of young pickpockets; there are mobs of them, too, in Via Montalbo, Via Castro, Rione Borgo—half of Palermo's alive with them. Some of the expert thieves emigrate to America; others go to the big Italian cities—Milan, Turin, Genoa— where they aren't known and where they find things much easier than they do here, because the people aren't wise to their tricks; stealing their wallets is child's play. In Rome a prostitute will often lend pickpockets a hand; she'll rub herself up against a guy while they're frisking him, so he doesn't notice what's going on. Well, I don't want to give away too much; I wouldn't want to see all the thieves rounded up and hauled off to stir. The authorities wouldn't dream of helping them live any different by finding them honest work, so once they come out of the jug, they're far worse than when they went in. Things haven't changed since the days when the Saracens landed; men thought then, as they do now, that prison was the only cure for all the wickedness in the world, and what happened? They clapped not only sinners, but saints, too, behind bars.

Nowadays squads of so-called special police patrol the city on the lookout for thieves and pickpockets, but the fact is, there's nothing very special about them. In my time, though, there were some famous squads—Sciabbica's, for instance. He was a holy terror, Sciabbica was; he's on the retired list now, but the work is in his blood, you might say, he can't live without it, and he still does a little on his own account. Sciabbica could run like a rabbit. Then there were the squads under the orders of a character we nicknamed the Little Gentleman because he slicked his hair down with brilliantine.

One day—I'll never forget it—I was going to work with my gang when all of a sudden, at the corner of the Via Sant'Agostino and the Via Maquedo, where windowshoppers are easy marks, I caught sight of one of Sciabbica's squads. I managed to say, "Sciabbica! Beat it!" and we instantly scattered and ran like hell up the side alleys. I never stopped running till I got home; my side ached, I was panting, but I didn't dare slow down—I knew if they caught me I'd get at least three days in stir. Even when I did get back I couldn't calm down— the thought that the cops might have spotted me was enough to make me shake all over. The guys in the house all gathered around me the way they always did when one of us rushed home unexpectedly; they stood there waiting for me to get my breath and tell them whether the police were after me or whether I'd made a bolt for it after nabbing a wallet. Alarms, escape, pursuit, panic, thrills and triumphs—that's the life of a pickpocket. When a gang sets out in the morning, so do the police squads.

So far, I've only told you about the pickpockets that lift from *minule,* women; now I'll tell you about the ones that specialize in robbing *u vascu,* a man. These gangs work with a *sciammaru,* a kid of twelve to fourteen, who has to be the right height—that's to say, he has to come up to the victim's elbow. It's the *sciammaru's* job to move the man's arm, without his noticing it, to the right or left, depending on which side he keeps his wallet—*u surci,* the mouse, as it's called in thieves' slang. The *sciammaru* brushes against the man, gives his coat a jerk and makes sure that the mouse is there; then he touches one of the gang who's directly behind him, either on the right shoulder or the left to show him where the mouse is, and gives the coat a second jerk to turn it around a little more, then his accomplice passes his hand under the guy's armpit and grabs the mouse.

When the street's crowded, and the man the gang has spotted is trying to pass people or is waiting to cross the street, the whole thing's fairly easy. There are usually four or five in a gang, and sometimes they work with stooges whose job is to create a diversion so the victim doesn't notice what's going on. The stooges are old ex-cons who've had more than enough of prison and prefer to do the less risky part of the business. They act as lookouts too—they're through with the active side of the game, but they haven't given it up. A stooge is like an old whore who's been working a street in a neighborhood twenty years, and who goes on making a living there, not by selling herself but by washing down the door-steps. The stooge either bumps into the victim or takes him by the shoulders as if he were in a hurry to pass him. When the gang has nabbed a wallet, the money inside it is split up; one half is split between the *sciammaru* and the guy who actually lifted the mouse; the rest is divided among the others. The stooge gets whatever the gang wants to give him. He's not one of them, strictly speaking; he has no standing.

Most of the victims are *contadini*[1] who've come to Palermo to visit the hospital, look for work or do some shopping; they always bring all their savings with them. Pickpockets also keep a sharp lookout for *fardailoi,* emigrants who've been in North or South America for years, and have just returned

[1] Farmers, or farm workers. *Translator's note.*

to Sicily; they're almost certain to have in their pockets *u surcu abbuzzatu*—a wallet stuffed with bills. Besides thieves, there are confidence men who have their own particular ways of making *u coppo*, a bundle—*a bidone*, they call it in Rome. There's the lone wolf, for instance, who rigs himself out in a blue jersey and a peaked cap with an anchor on it, and makes like he's a Yank that's just landed. "Hey, can you direct me to the Amurrican Consulate?" he'll say to some sucker, and then he'll mutter: "I've got some real good English[2] stuff in my suitcase—you can have it cheap." It ends up, of course, with his unloading a lot of rubbish on the dope. Then there are pickpockets who frisk passengers on the buses, but they don't always carry it off—in winter, for instance, it's not so easy to get into the pants pockets of a guy wearing an overcoat.

Well, now you know the sort of life I led as a very young pickpocket—the life I went on leading until I was twelve. Sometimes, to encourage his "apprentices," a master would promise to take them to a house. One time four of us were taken into the room of a prostitute who catered specially to kids like ourselves. She threw herself flat on the bed and— But let's leave it there; talking about it makes me feel sick. There's one thing I have to tell you, though, dirty as it is: if we found out that one of the gang had turned squealer, the rest of us got hold of him and screwed him to show him what a rat we thought he was, and to teach him a lesson he'd never forget.

By the time I was twelve I'd made quite a name for myself. There was a kind of thieves' hiring market, and one day a big shot—let's call him X—came to see the family I was living with, told them he'd like to take me on, and agreed to give them so much for me. So I left home and began traveling around with him; I was on my way now—he even took me abroad. To do what? The very same thing, of course. It makes me feel bad when I think of it. One gimmick we worked between us was a regular tear-jerker. X would stride along the street with a leather belt in his hand. "Have you seen a kid of twelve anywhere?" he'd ask the passers-by. "My kid's run

<hr />

[2] The term "English" is used indiscriminately in Sicily and other parts of Italy to mean superior. *Translator's note.*

away from home, been missing for three days—wait till I get him! I'll tan his hide!" The next minute, he'd let out a shout. "There he is!" he'd yell, pointing at me, and away I'd run with him at my heels. As soon as I spotted a guy that was sure to have a nice fat "mouse" in his pocket, I'd clutch at his legs and howl: "Save me! Save me! Don't let my father beat me!" I clung to him for dear life while my "father" raised the belt and began to slash at me; I lay on the ground and writhed, and while the kind gentleman was doing his best to shield me from the blows, X would neatly lift his wallet. Then he would clear his throat, the signal that he'd got the mouse, and I'd let go, get up, and go off with him sobbing and sniffling.

We often hired a carriage whose driver was in the know to follow us in case we had to make a quick getaway. Once when we were in Palermo, on the Corso dei Mille, near the Mulino Pecararo, a man came along carrying about ten empty bottles. X was in the act of frisking him when he suddenly got wise to it and asked a guy who was passing to hold his bottles for a minute. "My pants are coming down," he said. No sooner were his hands free than he whipped out a pistol and began to fire at us; scared out of our wits, we made for the carriage, jumped in, and off we went. The crowd that heard the shots thought it was the usual story, that a girl had been kidnaped and somebody was firing at her abductors.

We stayed for a while in Naples, where we had a room in a hotel; we wore decent suits and looked really respectable— X made out he was a traveling salesman. We went to Turin, Milan—all over the place. One time X managed to get himself a press card and posed as a journalist. Every so often we'd return to Palermo, our base.

When I was fourteen I hooked up for a while with two other pickpockets, both in their twenties. One night, when we were working a certain city, we picked up a woman and took her back to the place where we were staying. When they'd had her it was my turn; afterwards, while I was lying in bed with her, she began to ask me a lot of questions, and before I knew what was happening I'd told her all about myself and what the three of us were doing. When I woke up in the morning she wasn't there—she'd skipped while I was asleep. The next thing that happened was the police came, and when they started to question me I soon realized it was the whore that'd given us away. The cops kept asking me about a certain corporal in the *carabinieri*, a Sicilian from Palermo—he's a sergeant now—who'd helped us by pushing people around; if I hadn't told the woman about him, they could never have known that he had any connection with us.

A year later the authorities decided to send me to the Santa Maria Capua Vetere Institute, in the province of Naples. I was put on the boat in the custody of a policeman who had no idea that a pal of mine who was determined that I shouldn't be put away was among the passengers. When we landed, and the cop had me safely on the train, my pal gave me some stuff to rub into my eyes that would make them red and inflamed. "They'll think you've got some infectious disease and won't admit you," he said. I told myself that anything was better than losing my freedom, so I rubbed the stuff in. It made my eyes so bad that the doctor who examined me when I arrived told the superintendent he couldn't let me pass the physical. The trouble cleared up in a week, but to this day I still suffer from conjunctivitis.

I went home for a while, then I started roaming all over the place again. Twice I was arrested and hauled into court; the first time I got twenty days, the second, thirty, but although both sentences were entered on my record, I didn't actually serve them as I was under age. Then, when I was in Rome, the cops got hold of me once more; I was finally sent to the Emmanuel III Institute, in the province of Mantua.

It was the time I spent in this institute that made me a rebel. They beat us, and the superintendent did things that I won't repeat. If we so much as dared to play a little ball while he was having his siesta, he gave us two or three days in solitary. We were always starving. We used to creep down at night, force the lock of the kitchen cupboard and steal a piece of bread, or else we'd tiptoe out into the garden and grab some tomatoes and a melon or two. The day came when we were so sick of being constantly beaten and kept on short rations that we decided to complain to the mayor. The letter was signed by all the older boys, and I was chosen to deliver it. When I got back I found the superintendent waiting for me: he raved and swore and threatened me with his pistol.

But the mayor investigated our complaints, and in the end the superintendent was dismissed.

I spent three years in that place—three years of hell. We were always dying for a smoke, and we used to save a slice for two of our bread ration to swap with the *contadini* for one of their homemade cigarettes. We had a long walk to school; people used to look at us as we marched along and say, "Poor kids—come on, let's give them some bread and a drop of wine." Since I could read a little, I was put in the third grade; I had already started to shave, and I looked like the father of all the little country kids that were mixed up in the classroom with us. I still remember my first day at school. The teacher drew a triangle on the blackboard and said: "To find the area of a triangle, multiply the base by the height and divide the answer by two." He fixed his eyes on me and asked: "You, boy—do you understand?" "Yes, sir," I said, though I didn't have the faintest idea what he was talking about. After geometry, we had language. He dictated: "Oh pony trot—comma" —"comma," I wrote—and, "You were good but you don't know how to speak—period," and I wrote "period."

By the time I got in the sixth grade, I was eighteen. I'd been put to work in the garden; one day I was caught kissing the mayor's niece in the bushes, and I was expelled on the spot. So there I was, left to face the world without a trade. What sense was there in teaching me, a city kid, country stuff, I ask you—did they expect me to grow cucumbers in St. Peter's Square?

The tribunal found a foster home for me in Rome; I lived there for three years, and during that time I learned the barber's trade. I hadn't forgotten my old friends, but I wanted to make a new life for myself. Then, although I begged them to let me stay with my foster mother, the Rome police transferred me to Palermo. The Palermo police didn't know what to do with me. They finally solved the problem by exiling me for two years to the island of Pantelleria.[3]

I won't dwell on the horrible corruption I found on the

---

[3] Exile—i.e., *confino*, a means of getting rid of unwanted persons— originated by the Fascists. The exiles were free to go where they liked within certain limits, but had to report to the police morning and evening. *Translator's note.*

island. Was that the way to make a decent human being of a guy—was that the way? Let me give you just a faint idea of what went on there. It was a common thing for the village kids to walk by and offer their services for a lira. Even telling you about it makes me feel ashamed. The whorehouse was out of bounds, and we were so sex-starved that one guy who had a female dog for a pet nearly went crazy with jealousy if anybody touched it. If I hadn't been through it, I'd never have believed such things were possible. And it was this sewer that the authorities proudly called a center for moral rehabilitation!

When I left Pantelleria, I was twenty-two. I was called up for military service, but was rejected because of my conjunctivitis. I went straight back to Rome and started to work as a barber. I got customers, cut their hair at their houses, made new friends and lived a normal life. I'd reached a point when I knew I had to break with my past once and for all; I wanted a family of my own, I wanted not only love, but responsibility. If a man doesn't feel the need for responsibility, what's to become of him?

Gradually I grew more and more homesick for the city where I'd spent my childhood, and so I went back to Palermo. But how different things were for me now that I'd become a respectable citizen and earned an honest living as a barber; now I could enjoy a drink in the Caffè delle Rose and wander about at ease under the clock of the Massimo Theatre, the favorite rendezvous of the upper classes. When I walked through the Capo, the miserable slum where I was born, I felt like a stranger. Sometimes I'd meet one of my old buddies. "Listen," I'd say, "you'll pay plenty in the end for the easy money you make. I used to lie awake shaking all over at the thought of Sciabbica, but that's over and done with—I'm going straight now, and when I go to bed at night, I sleep sound till morning." I still hadn't solved the problem of my future, though; I was still too exhausted with all I'd been through to see things clearly, to make any kind of constructive plans.

I met a girl, fell in love with her and got engaged; I was desperate to get married, but I was making barely enough to live on—I couldn't put anything away. Finally I asked a friend of mine if he knew of any job that would bring me in a little more; he said there might be one in a cement factory and promised to put in a word for me in the right place. The "right place" was a paralyzed old bastard, an ex-*pezzo di novanta*,[4] who had the last word on who was hired and fired. I got a job, but the work was too heavy for me; I worked like an ox, stoking the furnace and carrying loads of baked bricks around on a great big iron shovel. I just didn't have the strength for it, and three, four or five times a day I'd pretend I had to go to the toilet so I could get a breather. It got back to the *pezzo di novanta*, of course: "We've got no use for lazy bastards like you," I was told, and was fired just like that.

I did everything I could think of to earn the money I had to have before we could get married. I worked on commission, trying to get orders for wax figurines, materials, watches, etc., I made a few lire as a *spiccia*, and did some ladies' hairdressing, which I'd learned a little about. But as hard as I tried, I still couldn't make enough to save anything—there didn't seem to be any way out. "Never mind the money, Gino, let's get married," my girl urged me. "Two can live as cheaply as one, and we'll be free to love each other." I wouldn't hear of it, though. "It's no use going on, then," she said at last, "we'd better break it off." But I couldn't bear to think that all the sacrifices I'd made were in vain, so I asked her if she'd leave Palermo with me. "Yes, Gino," she said. People who knew us both thought she was crazy. "Poor girl, she must be out of her mind," they said. "Imagine running away with a guy who's got no work and can't possibly keep her."

We went to Rome, and my foster mother, who had showed me the only kindness I ever knew, took us both in; what little she had she shared with us. So my girl and I got married; there was no show, no nothing—just the usual wedding of poor lovers. Not long afterwards my wife got sick and had to go to the hospital. I couldn't find a job, and things went

[4] *Pezzo di novanta*—a heavy cannon—thieves' slang for master thief. These criminal types are the paid bullies of the Mafia, which controls most labor in Sicily, both industrial and agricultural. They see to it that the protection money extorted from the employers is paid over to the *mafiosi*, and collect from the wretched workers, who grease their palms in the hope of getting hired or in their anxiety not to lose the jobs they are holding. *Translator's note.*

from bad to worse; I went to bed hungry very often. But what I hated most was having to go empty-handed to the hospital to visit my wife. It made me terribly ashamed of myself—I felt I wasn't a real man, a good husband. What a red-letter day it was for me when I was able to take her an orange. An orange—what's an orange, you'll say. To me it was everything.

I felt desperately alone. I went from barber shop to barber shop in the hope of a job, but I had no luck. I reached a point where I was tempted to look up my former pals and go back to work with them; it was the fear of losing my wife if I returned to that sort of life that held me back. One day I ran into one of my old pickpocket friends accidentally. He gave me five lire. I bought a present for my wife and some food for myself—I made it last two days. I tramped the streets looking for work in vain, and at last, in despair, I told myself I had no choice—there was only one way out and I'd have to take it. I *would* have taken it if my foster mother hadn't guessed my thoughts. "Gino," she said, while I sat brooding over the bowl of *minestra* she had put before me, "don't do anything stupid. Remember you've got a wife now—she's only a girl, you've got to look after her. I know what's in your mind, I know it seems the only thing you can do—but you mustn't do it." Her words comforted me and calmed me down; maybe they brought me luck, too, for a few days later I was taken on by a Neapolitan barber. He paid me twenty-five lire a week and allowed me to keep whatever tips the customers gave me; if he hadn't he'd have had to pay me thirty-five. Work! I'd found work at last, and I was happy.

When my wife left the hospital we went to live with a cousin of mine in the Marinella district. I paid regular visits to my foster mother, and now that I was earning something I did what I could to help her. Her husband had been a railroad porter and some of his buddies who were still working chipped in and gave him a percentage of what they made. But it didn't amount to much, and he couldn't afford to buy himself a glass of wine or a cigar. I knew how much he craved them, and I was always glad when I had enough to treat him to these small pleasures. Sometimes his wife would go at him tooth and nail because he'd keep a few soldi for himself, and then I'd step in and do my best to restore the peace. He was seventy, the poor old guy, and if he did tell a few lies about the money—well, you couldn't blame him. He could only buy himself one pipeful of tobacco a week; when he'd smoked it he used to scrape out what was left in the bowl and chew it just to get a taste of the real thing. On Saturday nights he'd come home a little tight and rub his damp mustache against my cheek. "Poor boy," he'd say, "poor boy . . ."

We had an argument with my cousin and decided we'd leave Rome. So we packed up and came back to Palermo.

I knew my father by sight because people had pointed him out to me, but I'd never exchanged a word with him. I was on speaking terms with my grandfather, though, and when I met him in the street I used to beg a few soldi from him. I'd saved a little money in Rome, but not much, and since I had no job, and all my wife and I possessed in the world was some household linen, I finally forced myself to go to my father. As we were strangers to one another, I had no natural affection for him; I couldn't even feel that he *was* my father. He said we could come and live with him, but when we arrived we didn't get what you could call a warm welcome from his wife. It was plain that she didn't want us, but she had to put up with us just the same—she couldn't go against her husband's orders.

My father had come by very hard times. He had been fired from the Council because he was a Constitutional Socialist; he hadn't been able to find another job and he was flat broke. When we moved in, I became the provider. I bought food for the whole household out of my savings. My father had been driven into becoming a *spiccia*—it was lucky for him he had friends at the Town Hall.

There's one particular evening that stands out in my memory. I'd been out, and the moment I got back my stepsisters came to me crying with hunger; there wasn't a bite to eat in the place. "Papa's got some money, Gino," one of them said, "but he won't buy us any food." "We'll see about that," I said, so I went off in search of him. Well, I found him, and asked him straight out if it was true. "I've got a few lire in my pocket, Gino," he said, "but they don't belong to me—a client gave them to me to get him some papers he needs." I was amazed at his honesty, because I was well aware that most of the *spiccia-faccende* in Palermo are crooks. They'll double-cross anybody; not only that, they're in with certain officials, and are always prepared, if need be, to supply customers with false papers, documents, etc.

We only stayed for a very short time with my father. His wife was determined to get rid of us by hook or by crook, and what do you think she did? At night, while we were lying on our mattresses on the floor, she used to throw pebbles at us to make us think the house was haunted! One night my wife got up to go to the toilet. "G-gino, are there gh-ghosts in this place?" she asked. Her teeth were chattering with fright. The "ghosts" had just pelted her with stones. But two could play at that game. Close to the bed where my father and stepmother slept there was a tiny altar with a lighted candle on it; the next time the pebbles came flying, I picked up a shoe, threw it straight at the candle and put it out. "The ghosts! The ghosts!" I shrieked, then, wrapping myself in a sheet, I rushed over to the bed and gave my dear stepmother a good clout! In the morning I listened with a completely straight face while she told me of the awful goings-on. "I saw it as plainly as I see you, Gino," she said. "A ghost—all in white, it was, and—" "A ghost!" I burst out. "I won't spend another night in a haunted house! Thanks very much—I'm going!"

So we moved out and I rented a barber shop. You've got no idea how careful a barber has to be not to give his customers the slightest cause for offense—for the least little thing, they'll walk out on him and never come back. Many a time I lost a customer just because I hadn't helped him into his overcoat or straightened his jacket the way he liked it. Believe me, if you leave a single hair on a man's chin or don't bow to him as low as the barber next door, that's the last you'll ever see of him. Flattery's the barber's stock-in-trade. When a new customer came in you should have heard me! "What is your name, sir?" or, "Would you be kind enough to give me your name, sir?" I'd say, as if he were my boss, poising my pencil over my book. If you're a barber's assistant you work very long hours; one barber I worked for in Rome at least stuck to a timetable, but another one, the Neapolitan, wouldn't put up his shutters until his rival across the street had closed his; many a time I didn't get home till ten o'clock at night.

In my father's house I'd noticed the photograph of a well-dressed girl, and one day I asked him who she was. "Your sister," he said, "your real sister—your mother's daughter and mine. She's seven years older than you." You can imagine my surprise. He told me she was living with an uncle, and I thought I'd like to get acquainted with her, so I wrote her a letter and said I had a message for her from another uncle who lived in Rome. This was just a story I'd cooked up, of course, as I couldn't be sure she'd be willing to see me; people are so anxious to keep up appearances, to be thought "respectable," that they'll hide their natural feelings, and deny their own flesh and blood, as well I knew. If only my father had had the guts to say "That's my son," as my mother did when I was born, mine would have been a very different story. But to go back, an answer came from my sister to say she couldn't very well invite me to her uncle's house, but that she'd arranged for us to meet at a cousin's. Well, I went, the cousin introduced us to each other and left us alone. We sat down on the sofa in dead silence. After a minute or two I began to fidget impatiently: was she waiting for me to speak, or did I have to wait till she opened her mouth? At last I got up courage and broke the ice. "Why do you live with our uncle and not with our father?" I asked. "My uncle doesn't have any children of his own," she said. "I've become a daughter to him—he loves me dearly, sends me to school, does everything for me. But tell me, where have you been all this time? Papa told me I had a brother—why haven't you been to see me before?"

"I didn't even know I had a sister till the other day," I said.

Then she began to ask me all sorts of questions: what school had I been to, was I a Catholic, was I a Fascist? (This was during the Fascist regime.) I told her I hadn't got past the sixth grade, and that I never bothered my head about religion or politics. "What! You're *not* a Catholic, *not* a Fascist!" she said in a shocked voice, and right away gave me a lecture on both subjects. She had specialized in literature, and she was still more taken aback when I said: "My dear sister, if I had had the same education as you, no doubt, with a little luck, I would have graduated too, and become both a Catholic and a Fascist in the bargain!"

I couldn't get up an ounce of brotherly affection for her. They talk about the call of the blood, but hers certainly didn't call to mine. Before I left we agreed to see more of each other, but I really didn't care whether we did or not.

However, we did meet again. One evening she asked me to go with her to the Fascist H.Q. in the Piazza Bologna so she could renew her party card. While we were on the way she said, "If you see a short young man coming towards me, would you mind leaving me? He's my fiancé, and—well—he might be jealous . . ." Although she didn't come straight out with it, it was plain what she meant: she didn't want anyone to know we were brother and sister.

That was the end of it as far as I was concerned. I left her abruptly, and it wasn't till years later, after the war, that I saw her again. We met at my father's funeral; she was married, by this time, and I had become a Communist. For a while we were quite friendly, and I often went to her house. Then one Christmas Day when I showed up for dinner there was a ring at the door. "It must be some of my in-laws—hide, Gino, don't let them see you," she said. I cleared out without a word, and never set foot in her place again.

It was mainly on account of all the misery and hardship I'd been through that I became a Communist. To me communism meant a new life for people, it meant work for everybody, salvation for everybody; it meant a world where there wouldn't be any need for a Sciabbica since no one would be driven to steal any more—there'd be no more light-fingered characters left, except kleptos. A world where men could live like men—that's what communism stood for to me. Let me tell you how I became a member of the Party.

After the American forces had occupied Sicily we all existed by dealing in the black market. I sold contraband cigarettes in my shop—I got them direct from a customs guard— and as every barber in Palermo was doing exactly the same thing, I had no scruples about it. With the money I made in this way I was able to buy food for my family, but all over the city people were starving. The sight of so much misery, the awful injustice of it, stirred me up to such anger that at last I resolved I had to try to do something about it. So I shut myself up in the room at the back of the shop, and after a lot of thought, wrote a manifesto that ended with the words: "Long live Stalin! Long live Roosevelt! Long live Italian communism!" I scraped up enough money to have a number of copies printed, got some friends together and formed the Antifascist Action Party. We plastered the walls with this manifesto of mine, and handed it to passers-by in the crowded streets in the center of the city.

One day while I was busy in my shop a shiny American car drove up outside. "An important customer," I thought, and I asked my wife to get me a clean towel. The next minute, in walked a bunch of U.S. officers who told me they'd come to arrest me for disobeying General Alexander's directive. "Haven't you read it?" they demanded. "Don't tell us you didn't know what his orders were." But I didn't know what they were; all I knew was that people were dying of hunger. I was tried by the military tribunal and sentenced to one year, but the sentence was commuted.

Soon after this I received a visit from a schoolteacher who had heard about my manifesto; he invited me to attend a Socialist meeting with him. As all political meetings were strictly banned, it was held in secret. I went to a few more meetings with him, and at one of them a certain resolution was put to a vote. I was against it, and I was so outspoken that I was severely reprimanded. I had applied for membership, but I had grown very sick of the Socialist Party's jabber-jabber-jabber—it was actions, not words, that I wanted.

When the ban on political meetings was lifted I started to attend them. I became active on my own account, and organized a mass demonstration of barbers. The day it was held a Communist came up to me and said, "Why don't you join the Party?" This was in 1943, when anybody who wanted to join the Party was free to do it. As soon as I got my Party card, I was made responsible for a cell in my street, and a little while later I was promoted to leader of a section. I read all the literature eagerly, not only because it helped me understand the doctrine of the Party but because I always had a thirst for knowledge. I got up a workers' study group, and we started with Marx. I sweated over his dialectical materialism for months before I could get the full meaning of it into my head. We followed Marx with Gramsci's *La Città del*

Socialismo, from which I learned an enormous amount. It taught me, for instance, that society is like a train made up of old, dilapidated coaches pulled by a streamlined, up-to-date engine. Each coach stands for a system of government that's been tried in the past, and each one has its own characteristics, its own weaknesses. The trip is very difficult and slow because first a door'll come unhinged, then a screw'll work loose in one of the coaches; the driver has to stop, and the passengers have to join in to fix things. Then, thanks to their united effort, the damage is repaired, the train starts off again, and so, little by little, it pulls nearer to its destination, the city where all men are equal . . .

Well, I picked up a Marxist culture, and at the same time went on working in my shop. But a barber can't make much in Palermo, and as I now had four children, I was in bad need of some other job that would help me make ends meet. One day a comrade who'd had a decent education said to me, "Why don't you join the Agricultural Workers' Federation and take the study course?" I took his advice and enrolled for the political correspondence course that the Party had just started.

I took tremendous pains to learn and I worked hard at my books; I realized that the more I knew, the more use I would be to the Party. "Learn all you can; the revolution is a revolution of men. The revolutionary movement needs new and responsible leaders." These words of Gramsci's had become my inspiration. I sat up till all hours, and to save electricity I studied by candlelight. But in my eagerness to go ahead I drove myself much too hard; though I didn't realize it, I was close to a breakdown. I grew more and more depressed, I told myself it was hopeless, that I was no good, that I'd never get anywhere. Finally I wrote to the heads of the correspondence school in Rome to ask them whether they thought there was any use in my going on with the course; I was beginning to doubt, I said, that the Revolution would ever take place in my lifetime. Nothing could have encouraged me more than the reply I got. "To continue studying in such difficult conditions as yours is a positive gain in itself," it said. "As for the Revolution, bear in mind that history can't be measured by the span of a man's life." I pulled myself together, persevered, took the examination, and when the results came out, I was congratulated on doing remarkably well—I passed sixteenth out of four thousand. From this time on I worked on the Party's local committee, and became responsible with the other members for all the problems concerning agricultural workers.

The first time I was sent to address a meeting of peasants, there were looks of disappointment when I came into the brightly decorated hall. "We were expecting Comrade P., not you," they said. Comrade P. was the Party leader. They had evidently made a hero out of him, and this was all wrong, so I did my best to impress them that in the class struggle all men are equal, that it's the masses that count, not the individual. The individual must be subordinated to the masses, I said, especially when the individual doesn't understand and further their interests. When I sat down, the applause more than made up for the cold reception; I went home happy, knowing that, even though I still couldn't express myself in technical terms, I had succeeded in speaking straight from the heart to people who were struggling for the right to live. I had succeeded because I had made their struggle my own struggle. In the past I had fought for only one person: myself; now I'd learned to identify myself with the cause of others, and so I'd made the first move to redeem myself.

In 1949 I was sent to Mantua to the congress of the Agricultural Workers' Federation. It was then that I realized with a great thrill that the Sicilian peasants who were getting ready to take possession of the land, far from being alone in their struggle, had the full support of all the workers in Italy. I'll never forget the countrywoman from Lecce who jumped up onto the platform, excused herself for not being able to speak good Italian, and exclaimed in her dialect: "As long as they won't give us land, as long as my children have to go barefoot, I'll fight side by side with my comrades. Let them send for the police; to hell with the police—that's what I say!" I was so moved by her sincerity that tears came to my eyes.

Right after I got back from Mantua I was sent to Marineo, where the struggle for the occupation of the land was in full swing; I was picked to replace a comrade who had turned out to be incompetent to handle the situation. The morning after my arrival I led the peasants to an estate; it was then that I learned a hard lesson, that theory and practice are by no means the same thing. The night before, I had talked to the *contadini* about the *kolkhozes* and they had listened attentively when I said that, following the Russian example, we would cultivate the estate collectively. The second they set foot on the land, however, they forgot every single word I said, and they ran around as if they were crazy, marking off plots for themselves by pegging out mule reins or piling up stones. They were just like passengers rushing into a train and reserving seats for themselves by dumping down newspapers and suitcases. I was completely taken aback. "This is all wrong, you know," I said to one man. "Excuse me, Comrade Gino," he said, "but I look at it like this. I've got a mule, my neighbor doesn't, so it stands to reason my crop'll be twice as heavy as his. It's only right, then, that I should have the plot of land I need."

But I've gone ahead too fast, I have to go back to the night I arrived in Marineo. It had been agreed that the estate should be occupied in the morning, and we leaders had taken great pains to make the *contadini* feel they were organizing the whole thing, that we were only there to help them in any way we could and to make sure their plan succeeded. As soon as we had decided on the meeting place where we were all to come at daybreak, the meeting broke up. Morning came, and we leaders were the first ones to arrive, but in a few minutes there was a crowd of *contadini*, some of them carrying hoes, some of them leading mules. It was still dark when we started out for the estate; men, women and children marched along, chattering happily about the coming harvest as if the land was already theirs. It was really something to see these peasants who had already played their part in the war of liberation starting out to fight another war that they had planned by themselves. They crowded around me, their faces full of hope, but for all our excitement we didn't forget to keep a sharp lookout for the *carabinieri*.

At last we came in sight of the estate. It stretched out in front of us like a big sea—I don't know how many acres there were. Wherever we looked, there was only earth and sky. The few miles that separated us from it seemed endless, we felt as though we'd never get there. Just before we reached our goal, we came to a little rise and called a halt. It was quite possible that one or two *mafiosi* might be lurking about on the lookout for us, and we wondered which would be the wisest course: to occupy the land all together or to break up into groups of four. But while we were discussing it, the local Party leader made up his mind and marched onto the estate. Concerned about his safety, we all followed.

Well, as I've told you already, the peasants instantly started to mark off their plots. The land was unused, but in order to prevent it from being expropriated, the owner, who knew what was in the air, had had it plowed up in the last few days. Without any delay the *contadini* began to break up the clods and till the furrows.

After a while we stopped for a much-needed rest. Families got together and sat down to eat the bread they'd brought with them—a few had a little wine.

Earlier we had caught sight of a man in the distance, dressed in the Mafia style: riding breeches, jacket, boots and felt hat.

Silk hat, felt hat, you asked me here to meet you,
I got your invitation and here I am to greet you!

says the song, and I'd gone to meet *him*. He had a rifle on his shoulder. "What did you come here for? What are you up to?" he asked. "We're taking possession of the land under the Segni-Gullo law,"[5] I told him. I was careful to speak politely, because I knew it was dangerous to cross him—get this type of guy sore, and he'll snipe at you under the cover of the nearest fig tree: bang! and you're done for! After I talked to him awhile, he disappeared.

Towards evening there was a heavy downpour of rain. I found shelter in a nearby cottage and waited there until my clothes had dried off well in the oven. The peasants called it a day and started to walk back to the village, all but two of

[5] Under this law, all uncultivated land was to be given to the peasants or the peasants' co-operatives. Signor Gullo, a Communist, and Signor Segni, a Christian Democrat, each served a term as Minister of Agriculture during the period 1946-50. *Translator's note.*

them who couldn't tear themselves away from the land. As soon as the rest had gone, the *carabinieri,* who'd been lying low while the whole crowd was there, came up and arrested the two unlucky ones.

I can't tell you what happened after that in Marineo, because that same evening I was ordered to go to Montelepre, and as I was arrested and sent to prison because of what happened there, I never learned the rest of this particular story. The *contadini* of Montelepre, Cinisi, Carini, Partinico and Terrasini were agitating for the expropriation of the Piano degli Aranci estate, and my job was to find out exactly what the situation was in these villages. I was supposed to address an open-air meeting in the piazza at Carini, but since it was the local saint's day, and the celebrations were being put on there, it had to be held in the *Camera di Lavoro,*[6] which was packed. Squads of *carabinieri* had been stationed outside the building and in all the nearby alleys; among them were soldiers of the C.F.R.B.[7] It was obvious that the authorities were determined to do everything they could to stop us from occupying the estate. When the meeting was over, I left Carini, spent a short time in Terrasini and Partinico, and then went on to Montelepre. I had never seen so many radiant faces; the peasants were fired up with the thought that their great dream was finally about to come true—the dream of paradise on earth, a little land all their own. I can't describe my own feelings at the sight of so many happy faces—I can't put them into words.

At this particular time the exploits of Giuliano[8] had made the little village of Montelepre world-famous; here I was, in the heart of the bandit country. The bandits didn't terrify me, but I must admit that I couldn't help thinking from time to time about the thirty-six leaders of the peasants' union who had been murdered in different parts of Sicily, shot down by hidden assassins, actually riddled with lead. In spite of this, however, I took some awful chances. Once, for instance, when I had to go to Carini, a peasant from Montelepre came with

[6] House of Labor—any local hall of the Communist union.

[7] *Comande Forze Repressione Banditismo,* the special militia drafted to deal with bandits. *Translator's note.*

[8] See *Bandit,* by Gavin Maxwell, New York (Harper), 1956.

me, and instead of sticking to the road we took short cuts through the fields. I didn't follow the beaten track, either, the time I walked to Partinico and back—I went across the fields, and ran the same kind of risks. You know what risks I mean, I take it. I don't mind telling you that I was far more scared during those short walks than I had ever been during the war. It's not so bad when you know where the enemy is, but the thought that a sniper may be hiding behind a fig tree ready to pick you off is what you might call unpleasant.

One evening I was addressing a meeting in the *Camera di Lavoro* in Montelepre when a *carabiniere* came in, said the sergeant wanted to speak to me, and asked me to go to the barracks. "Tell your sergeant I'll be there as soon as the meeting's over," I said. When we broke up, twenty peasants insisted on coming with me. The sergeant who was expecting me didn't seem at all upset. "I'm sorry to have to put you to this trouble," he said, "but this is a danger zone on account of the bandits, and we have to have particulars on any strangers who come here; we want to know who they are and what they're doing in Montelepre. You, for instance—what brings you to these parts? I've nothing against the *Camera di Lavoro*, I may say—I'm a workingman myself. What's more, when I was in Turin I made the acquaintance of Togliatti's wife— what do you think of that, eh?"

He kept me for some time, but when I left the barracks all twenty of the peasants were still there, patiently waiting for me outside.

It was while I was in Montelepre that I realized that very few of the *contadini* had any idea of the real purpose of their union. They just thought of it as an organization they could turn to for help; hardly any of them grasped the fact that our struggle was not only economic but political—that it had to be both if we were going to achieve what we were after, which was an entirely new form of government in Italy.

I went to Carini to make arrangements for the occupation of the estate. The entire district was swarming with *carabinieri*, and we had to try to think of how we could reach it without getting arrested. Obviously we couldn't all go in one bunch, it would bring them down on us right away. For two hours we leaders discussed ways and means in the *Camera di*

Lavoro; I didn't know the locality, but those who did suggested different side roads and footpaths we might take in order to avoid being spotted immediately. Finally we decided to set out in groups of four or five, carrying hoes to make it look as if we were going out to do a day's work in the fields. We were all to assemble at the Case Nuove; from there, with our banners flying, we would make the steep climb up to Sagana, and from Sagana we'd descend in a body to Piano degli Aranci and take possession of it.

Some of the leaders went off to the other villages to tell the *contadini* what we had arranged. The rest of us spent the night in Carini, and as soon as it was beginning to get light, we got dressed and went from house to house, knocking on every door. "Wake up! We're going to start for the estate!" we called out. "Land, land—who wants land?" In a very few minutes everybody was awake, and soon the first groups were on their way. We met a small detachment of *carabinieri*, but as we'd hoped, they took us for laborers out to do a day's hoeing. I suffered something awful climbing up the rough paths— I was wounded in the leg during the war of liberation, and it gave me hell. Sometimes I kept going by hanging on to the tail of a mule; once I just slid to the ground and had to rest there for a while before I could take another step.

It was seven o'clock when those of us who'd started out first reached the Case Nuove. One by one the other groups arrived, and as soon as we were all there, we raised our flags and began to ascend to Sagana. We had just reached the outskirts of the village when we saw another band of peasants coming towards us with their flags flying—it was the contingent from Partinico.

We joined forces, hugged one another, and marched on. But when we reached the tiny piazza we saw that it was crawling with squads of *carabinieri* and C.F.R.B. An officer stepped forward and asked us why we had come. "We're going to occupy the estate," we said straight out, and he immediately began to threaten us in hopes we'd turn back. "It's against the law—do you want to put yourselves in prison?" Meanwhile the sergeant had gone up to a group of flag bearers, one of them carrying the Red flag. "Down with it! We're not Communists here!" he roared. It was a bad moment; in

Bisacquino, a refusal to lower the Red flag had ended up in shooting, and a number of villagers and *carabinieri* had been wounded.

We were told to pile our flags against the wall; however, we were allowed to leave them unfurled. If they thought the sight of their machine guns would scare us, they were wrong. The officer went on talking to us—although we didn't know it, he was playing for time. He told us that at that very minute the prefect was in Montelepre assuring the peasants that there wasn't any need for them to occupy the estate because it was going to be expropriated right away.

While we were waiting for our comrades from Montelepre to arrive, we played cards to pass the time. But after we'd waited for I don't know how long, somebody—I don't know who—said, "Come on, let's not hang around here any longer —let's go and occupy the estate." We decided the best thing to do was to send a messenger to Montelepre to find out what was happening there; he'd been gone quite a while when we caught sight of figures in the distance coming towards us. There were shouts of "The comrades! Here they come!" But as they drew closer we could see the glitter of gold braid and the glint of steel. Comrades! The figures that were advancing were *carabinieri*, armed to the teeth!

Bandits—that's what we were to them and the C.F.R.B. The real bandits were probably watching the scene through field glasses from their mountaintop hideout, and splitting their sides at the joke!

The *carabinieri* rounded us up and made us all march into the big courtyard where the prison used to stand in the time of the Bourbons. The sergeant sat down at a table and ordered us to line up so he could see which men came from which village. I stood apart from the rest. "You, there, what village do you come from?" he said. "I'm one of the union leaders," I said, "I don't belong to any village—I belong to them all." The sergeant then took down our surnames, our Christian names, our parents' names, and called us to attention. "Now, all of you, we know who you are. I warn you, we'll keep an eye on you in the future, so I advise you to watch your step—if we catch you again it'll be too bad for you." After this we were marched out of the courtyard and into the piazza, where we were ordered to halt outside the police station; it was the turn of the officer-in-charge to have his say: "You'd better be careful," he said. "If you break the law—" but we cut him short. "It's not your business to hold a meeting—stick to your job as a cop!" we yelled. The peasants had been told to disperse, but since the *carabinieri* were still holding us, their leaders, and were not making any move to let us go, they stayed right where they were. The *carabinieri* trained their machine guns on the crowd. "Break it up!" they shouted. "Get moving—go home!" We wanted to avoid bloodshed at any price, so we told them to obey. We leaders were hustled out of the piazza to the road, where a couple of trucks drove up. Just as we got to them a car came along and one of the *carabinieri* officers saluted—the passenger inside it must have been the prefect. They made us get in the trucks, and they drove us off to the barracks.

In the meantime, however, the messenger we'd sent to Montelepre had got back to Sagana. He'd found the village surrounded by *carabinieri*—that was why our comrades hadn't been able to join us. He was a North Italian, a rough type, who didn't give a damn about the police. "Come on, all of you," he shouted. "Follow me. We'll occupy the estate, and to hell with the cops!"

When we got to the barracks and the officer in charge learned that, leaders or no leaders, the *contadini* had marched off to seize the land, we were driven to Palermo and consigned to the Ucciardone, the prison where the bandit Pisciotta[9] was handed a cup of poisoned coffee to drink and died in agony. Here we were formally charged with inciting the peasants to take unlawful possession of the estate.

Four of us were jammed into a cell barely big enough for two; there was hardly room enough for us to turn around. What with the rancid soup they gave us to eat, and the pot we had to do all our business in—well, you can imagine the stink. I made as much as I could out of this "holiday," though, and spent the time teaching myself more about social problems. At the end of six months I was released. I went back to

[9] Giuliano's cousin. He was poisoned with strychnine. Eight more of Giuliano's company of bandits were poisoned in the Ucciardone; one died and the rest recovered. *Translator's note.*

Sagana, where I helped some comrades found a Communist cell, and we succeeded in getting a few more men to join the Party. Then I went back to Palermo and picked up my activities with the Agricultural Workers' Federation again.

When Eisenhower came to inspect the Allied troops in Italy, the Sicilians organized a "Stop the War" demonstration. I was in the crowd in the Piazza Massimo when an incident occurred; I saw a woman struggling with the police who were hauling her into the wagon over the protests of Deputy Colajanni, the representative of the Regional Assembly of Sicily. Those who couldn't see what was happening thought it was Colajanni being arrested. Shouts went up: "Long live Sicily! Long live the Sicilian Assembly!" and in a second all hell broke loose. The *Celere*[10] went into action instantly, and one of them grabbed hold of me by the collar. "Let me go—can't you see I'm a disabled soldier?" I said, and tapped my badge. Actually, because I've been in prison I'm not allowed to wear it, but I have a right to it, so I pin it on just for the hell of it. I get a war pension from the state, but because I've done time, the Disabled Soldiers' Association won't give me a membership card. They'll most likely have the gall to get my pension stopped because I told you this—we'll see. But to go back. I struggled to get free but the *Celere* cracked me over the head with their rifle butts, dragged me into the wagon and drove me to the Faletta prison, where they had already taken a lot of men and women they had arrested in the Piano dei Greci—which, incidentally, commemorates the name of Damiano Lo Greco, a peasant who was shot and killed while he too was demonstrating for peace. I spent eleven days in a cell in the Faletta before I was brought before the commission that deals with political first offenders. That was when I realized the value of *Unità*; even though I was shut off, it kept me in touch with everything that was happening outside. In one issue there was an article in the form of an open letter signed by the leaders of the various Party organizations and by several deputies. To my great surprise, it was all about me. "Who is

[10] No English equivalent. The *Cerele* are similar to the *Garde Mobile* —they are armed squads who are rushed up in jeeps to disperse crowds. The occasion when the Communists hold their annual rally is a field day for the *Celere*. *Translator's note.*

Gino O.?" the letter began, then after that the story of my life, my efforts to lift myself up out of the gutter, the success of them, the way I'd redeemed myself by becoming one of the leaders in the struggle for freedom and peace—it was all there. If my comrades hadn't taken up my cause, and helped me and supported me, I'd undoubtedly have served a sentence of five years.

When I was brought before the commission, the chairman asked me what I was doing in the middle of the crowd and deliberately flung at me: "A good many wallets were stolen, you know." I felt ashamed and humiliated. The room I was in was furnished expensively—there was a couch covered in heavy velvet where the coats were thrown, and the air was heavy with the odor of expensive cigarettes. The chairman made a lot of noise about the overcoat I had on. "Very handsome, I must say—it must have set you back quite a bit," he said sarcastically. It was American, of course.[11]

I was put on probation for two years, which meant I had to report to the police regularly and keep within a certain area so that I couldn't carry on my political activity. How could I go to a police sergeant and say, "Look, I'm on probation, I'm not allowed to go beyond such-and-such a street, but I'm going out to the village of X to hold a political meeting"?

Although I was pretty useless for these two years, the Party allowed me to keep my membership card. I'm sure this was a gesture of comradeship and support so that I wouldn't lose heart and go bad. But the police—I had struggled with all my might to escape from my past, and now they were doing their best to push me downhill. They were trying to make me a rat, as they tried to do to everybody who had to report to them regularly.

All the time they found some excuse for calling me to the station. One time the inspector, saying *"tu"* to me as if I were a kid, and here I was already the father of five children, asked me:

"Have you ever been to prison?"

"No," I said.

[11] Bales of second-hand clothes are sent from the U.S.A. to Sicily, where they are sold by weight. See the following story, "Peppino." *Translator's note.*

"In that case we'll tear up the probation order," he said, but a day or two later he sent for me again. He had my record open on his desk.

"So you've never been to prison, eh?" he said.

"But I thought you were asking me if I'd ever been in prison for a political offense, sir," I answered.

His manner changed; he became fatherly.

"Listen to me, boy, keep your nose out of politics," he said. "Politics aren't your business. Stick to your own line—find yourself a job."

"What sort of job, sir?"

"Take out a peddler's license, or—"

"But I can't take out a license—you won't let me take one out. I've got a record."

"Oh, you make me tired! Do you wonder that we have to keep people like you under special surveillance? Now if you'd only try to live a decent life, and come in if you hear of anything interesting—come to me personally, mind you, not a word to anyone else . . ." and he looked at me meaningfully.

I understood, of course, but I would have rather died than become a *cioccolattaro*, which is what we call a squealer in Palermo.

The *cioccolattari* work in gangs of four or five; all of them have police records. They run a lottery which is a real swindle. First they buy about four hundred chocolates, then they make holes in some of them and insert tiny slips of paper with numbers on them, the lowest being ten, the highest five thousand.

Then the chocolates are wrapped up, and the foil on the ones containing the high numbers is marked with very tiny dots so the *cioccolattari* know them. The numbers represent lire—that is, if you buy a chocolate which happens to have a slip with the figure ten, then they pay you ten lire. They don't mind paying out small amounts, but they make sure that the chocolates with the slips from a thousand up go to their own gang.

To draw a crowd, the *cioccolattari* do a lot of clowning, and perform magic tricks: they bring an egg out of a hat, etc. Then the member of the gang who gets the most applause starts selling the chocolates. If business is slow, he's quickly replaced by the expert among them, whose patter soon warms up the onlookers. Once in a long while he makes a mistake, and the five-thousand-lire chocolate goes to one of the crowd. The winner passes up his slip in great excitement, but do you think he gets his prize? He does not. The *cioccolattari* drops it into his hat, which has a false bottom. "Five thousand—did I hear somebody say he handed me a slip for five thousand?" he shouts, "I'm afraid he's made a mistake. If you don't believe me, ladies and gentlemen, see for yourselves—there's nothing inside my hat!" And of course, there isn't !

There are about two hundred *cioccolattari* in Palermo. If they weren't rats they wouldn't be allowed to run this lottery, which is nothing but an American-style swindle. All lotteries, even if they're straight—all games of chance—are strictly illegal. The *cioccolattari* also work the three-card trick: "Spot the lady! Now you win and now you lose!"

It's sheer necessity that governs the relationship between the poor and the rich—between the poor bastards that eat one day and starve the next and the rich ones they depend on, the rich ones who'll look after them provided they toe the line. Take, for instance, the hawkers that sell tripe and lungs; tripe and lungs are hard to get, so they treat the merchant they get their supplies from like God Almighty. If he shuts them off, they've had it. He's a little Caesar whose word is law as far as they're concerned, who forces them to vote for certain candidates; generally speaking, they don't give a damn for politics, all they're voting for is their livelihood. The tinhorns who make them sell themselves—that's what it amounts to— are *mafiosi* acting on orders from higher up. Talking of the Mafia, let me tell you about one of its favorite rackets. The shop of a guy who's paid his protection money is broken into and looted; his "protectors" promise him they'll search every neighborhood and get his stuff for him. Well, in a little while the goods are found and returned to him. Then he has to show his gratitude by putting up the ante for a blowout—some ante, too, because the "thieves" that ransacked his place have to get their cut!

Although I'm still working as a barber, I no longer have a shop. I have six children to keep, and as the Party's short of funds, it can't afford to pay me. I attend to my regular customers at their own houses, but the trouble is there aren't enough of them. However, I'm well known by sight, especially in the Capo, and when they see me coming along with my bag, a lot of the guys bring out their chairs and a bowl of hot water, and I shave them on their own doorsteps. In that way I manage to make ends meet.

But what makes life such a terrible strain on me is that every morning when I start out I know I've got to make so much. While I'm at X's house busy shaving him, I'm already thinking of the fifty lire I'm going to get when I've finished, and which, half the time, I don't get. "I'll pay you tomorrow," he'll say, and that's it for me—it happens time and time again. If a customer gets sick, the chances I have of getting the money he owes me are just about dead. I've been married sixteen years, and we still haven't been able to buy half the household stuff we need. We used to live on the third floor of a broken-down house in a room that was about thirteen feet long by six feet wide, all eight of us jammed into it—you can imagine what it was like. A few days ago the house really began to fall to pieces, and my family and seventeen others were moved out. They put us into this classroom, but when the school opens, in five days' time, we'll have to move. What'll become of us then I have no idea.

I get my unemployment card renewed every month. For nine years my name's been down at the unemployment office, and I've never had the offer of a single day's work. What makes it worse is the fact that I'm an ex-serviceman on a government pension, and there's a law that makes it mandatory that all men in this category be given employment. I went yesterday to get my card renewed—for the umpteenth time I had to go through the same old routine. I handed my card to a clerk who has to do the work of five or six men—he doesn't know whether he's coming or going, poor bastard, no wonder he yells at you for the least little thing—all you have to do is look at him to see he's a bundle of nerves. He has my sympathy—even the cops have my sympathy nowadays. When I was a kid they treated me like a menace, they chased me and persecuted me without any mercy, all because they didn't know what to look for. I've gradually come to see that they're not to blame for the things they do, they're just another bunch of workers exploited by the government. When I was a kid the very sight of one of them heading my way was enough to scare the hell out of me; I reacted just the way a rabbit does when he's caught in the headlights of a car. But now when I meet them I feel sorry for them. Their mentality hasn't changed a bit, they haven't taken a single step forward. They still don't know.

Where was I? Oh yeah, the unemployment office. As usual, the confusion there was awful. Everybody shoved and pushed everybody else—you felt as if any minute you'd be trampled down. Let me try and picture the scene for you. A voice suddenly makes itself heard above the racket.

"Quiet, please!" There is silence, and the official begins to reel off a list of names. "Mazzola—Ganci—Di Maggio—"

"Present!"

"Present!"

"Di Maggio—where's Di Maggio?"

"Di Maggio's not here."

A VOICE: "Get out of the way, you!"

ANOTHER VOICE: "Who're you shoving? I was here first!"

Then everybody starts complaining in a loud voice: "It's a disgrace, that's what it is! Is this what they call keeping order?"

A VOICE: "There's only one way to clean up this place—that's throw a bomb in it!"

ANOTHER VOICE (warningly): "Shut up, or you'll get yourself arrested like you did yesterday."

There are women in the crowd as well as men. A young fellow takes advantage of the confusion to put his hand up several skirts. He keeps one hand in his pocket and enjoys a free feel with the other.

It begins to rain; the crowd that's waiting outside pushes in trying to get under cover, and as fast as anybody forces his way in, the ones inside toss him right out again. "Keep back—keep back, can't you?" yells the cop who's on duty at the door.

But they won't keep back. A disabled man tries to elbow his way through.

"Your papers!" the cop shouts. "Where do you think you're going?"

An official appears. "Minasola! Minasola!"

He disappears, and the door closes. Inside, an uproar breaks out. "Has my name been called yet?" "Please—my card—" "Come back tomorrow—" "But I'm not well—" "Well, what do you expect me to do about it?"

It isn't an employment office, it's a Tower of Babel . . .

Sometimes I think: "Here I am, forty-two, and what have I got to show for all those years? Nothing." But then I tell myself I've at least spent some of them trying to help others so they wouldn't have to go through all that I did. I carry on because I have to—for the sake of my family, for the sake of the Party that made a new man out of me. Before I leave home in the morning, I nearly always stop by the little bed where two of my children are lying asleep, and I bend down and kiss the baby. I've given him the love that I never had. "Even a guy like me isn't altogether useless," I think. But if I were to let myself slip back . . .

All the kicks and knocks I've taken have left me unsure of myself; they've given me what's called an inferiority complex and I've never got rid of it. Although I've learned to look at life in a different way, it's still there, deep down inside me, and when I've had to stand up for a democratic principle in the Party, it's come to the surface more than once. I'll give you an example. It happened pretty soon after the election before last, when I was responsible for organizing the provincial *Amici dell'Unità.* One day I went into my office and I was surprised to find that my table with all my papers on it was no longer there; it had been moved out into the hall, near the toilet. I couldn't think why it should have been moved there, and when I discovered it had been done at the orders of one of the heads, I was very depressed. I couldn't get out of the rut I was in, I was tormented with doubt, and I kept on asking myself: "Am I a worthwhile human being or am I just a nothing?" A little later I was transferred to another section, but my mood kept up and my work went from bad to worse. Finally I was called before Comrade B. Instead of finding fault with me, he talked to me in such a friendly and understanding way that I got my confidence back. The knowledge that he—my leader—still believed in me and still valued my work gave me the feeling that I'd been reborn.

If I had to keep fighting on and on, measuring my own strength against the men around me, hemmed in by what I see happening on every side, I'd lose heart often, but there's one thought that keeps me going. If you shake a bottle of vinegar and oil, the vinegar and oil will mix, but let it stand a minute, and the oil floats to the top. To me, the oil stands for the truth, and the truth, by the nature of things, can't be kept down forever—sooner or later it's bound to come up to the surface.

It's because I'm so certain of this that while I'm struggling to support my family I can continue fighting alongside my comrades for the good of the community. If any problem that involves the interests of a particular area or even a particular family happens to come up, I'm always ready to be called on, I'm always ready to fight. Here, read this letter I've just received from a comrade:

"I'm writing to thank you and all the other comrades for your kindness to me during the months when I was doing my military service in Palermo. I can't tell you how much it meant to me. Thank you, too, for helping me understand a bit more about politics—I'll put my new knowledge to good use, I promise you—and still more thanks for the marvelous farewell dinner—I'll never forget it. Thanks a million for all your friendliness and hospitality to me and my army pals. I'll always remember you, and when I'm old and I take my grandchildren on my knee, instead of telling them fairy stories, I'll tell them about my heroic friends in Palermo who fought to make a better, more progressive Sicily, a Sicily freed from the exploiters and oppressors who sucked at her very life blood. Be sure, too, that I'll tell them of the brotherly hand you held out, not only to me, but to all the comrades of faraway Emilia. . . ."

I'm a shoemaker, one of the fifteen thousand shoemakers in Palermo. You won't find many of us who've managed to put away any thousand-lire notes; except for a few odd days, we only work for four months in the year. In September and October we're kept busy making children's shoes for All Souls' Day. November, December, January, February—nothing. Then for eight weeks before Easter we're at it hard—everyone buys new shoes for the holiday. During the rest of the year we do a few repairs and that's all.

When there's no work to be had, our wives go out every day and do housework; any number of family men like myself sell American clothes. Sometimes, if the wholesalers want to get rid of their stock, they let us have them on credit; nearly a third of the people in Palermo dress in American clothes, you know. How many of us sellers are there? I ask you: can you count them in the Via Oreto? In Ballarò, Piazza Carmine, Via dei Cipressi, Borgo, Buon Riposo? Then there are the wholesale stores—every store employs from five to twenty street vendors. There are thousands of us.

The bales of second-hand clothes are sent from America to be resold and are unloaded at Resina, near Naples. There they're sorted out: coats are put in one pile, trousers in another, and so on. Then the stuff's bundled up again, and the men who've come from Palermo to buy a few lots take pot-luck. They have no idea what they'll find inside—it's a kind of lottery. Some bundles are a dead loss, but some are winners. This isn't the only business we out-of-work shoemakers go in for; many of us go through the streets selling bread and rolls, or vegetables bought wholesale in the market.

Whenever I have to peddle stuff, hardly a day passes without my being gypped. As soon as I start talking the customers beat me down—they haven't any cash, they're out of work. "Will you let me take this?" a woman'll say. "I'll get some money from my husband on Saturday night—I'll pay you Sunday for sure." Well, I let her have the goods, and on Sunday, what happens? She tells me to come again next Sunday. Some of the customers I help never show up again.

Palermo rigs out the whole province, the big villages and the little villages, with American clothes. Sometimes the police come along and confiscate our stuff—we have no license, you see. The authorities won't give us a license. They won't give licenses to the fig sellers, the vegetable hawkers and the rest of the men in that line either; maybe they think too many stalls would spoil the look of the city for the tourists. When our goods are confiscated, we're finished—bang! goes the capital that we scraped together by borrowing a bit here, a bit there, and by buying small gold articles at a thousand lire a gram and selling them at a small profit.

About a third of those in the shoemaking trade are women; they do the stitching. We're a poor, weak-brained lot, we shoemakers, and we've never managed to make our employers treat us fairly. Even the *Camera di Lavoro* hasn't been able to improve things for us. I'm completely at the mercy of my boss. If he wanted to, he could keep five of us in steady work, but no, he takes on ten men. An order comes in for two hundred pairs of shoes, let's say, to be ready in two weeks' time; in three or four days we've done the job, and there's nothing more for us to do till another order comes along—if it ever does. I have to sweat eighteen hours a day to make ten pairs of shoes in a week. For eight hours' work, I'm paid five hundred lire. How can a man like myself with six kids live on such a wage? We can't possibly send the children to school every day—either we can't buy them the books, or they're barefoot and too ragged to go.

Here's the sort of thing that happens when I go to ask my boss if there's any work for me.

Likely as not he'll say: "Come back later—I haven't bought the soles yet."

Back I come.

"I haven't bought the soles yet—come back this evening."

In the evening it's the same old story.

After I've been to see him another three or four times, the soles are there.

"All right, you can start work now," says the boss.

"What about the vamps?" I ask.

"The vamps? They're with the stitcher."

So I hurry off to the stitcher.

"Can't let you have them," she says. "They never sent me the lining."

It's *her* turn to go to the boss, and nine times out of ten he'll tell her: "Come again tomorrow."

I leave the stitcher, and pay another visit to the boss to ask him when I can have the vamps. We fifteen hundred shoemakers live in a kind of delirium. We do our work at home, and this is the sort of thing we have to put up with.

But that isn't all. Say I'm in a spot, my children are ill and I have no cash. Although I've worked for the same boss for two years, I have no insurance card and no employment card. "Will you see about my cards?" I ask. "All right—you'll have them tomorrow." Tomorrow comes—no cards. "You'll have them when the accountant comes," he promises. After two or three days, I show up again. "You must have patience," he says. "There's nothing for you right now, my salesman didn't bring back any orders." What can I do? If I complained in the right places, word would be passed around to the other bosses, "So-and-so's a trouble-maker," and none of them would give me any work. Even the shoemakers who are Communists don't dare to speak up, they're scared of being unemployed. Some bosses, if they suspect that a man is a Communist or sharp enough to stick up for his rights, won't have anything to do with him.

HERE PEPPINO'S BROTHER, WHO WORKS AS A CLERK, CHIPS IN: What else can you possibly expect in a city like Palermo, where Pisciotta dropped dead in his cell after drinking that famous cup of coffee? How did the poison get into it? They all make out they don't know, they keep their mouths shut tight. There isn't anybody with guts enough to try and get to the bottom of the business. It's the ones on top that hold the strings; you can't get anywhere without a friend at court. *O l'amicizia o la soru bedda,*[1] as the saying goes.

In Palermo there are bunches of hoods, gangs, each one the

---

[1] "You must have either an influential friend or a pretty sister."

boss in its own territory. If anybody dares to cross one of these gangs, all the worse for him—he'll get paid all right, he may even get knocked off.

Take Galioto, the bandit, for instance; they say he got his because he tried to lay down the law to the *mafiosi* of the wholesale vegetable market. Then there was that guy who was shot to death American-gangster-style yesterday—fifty bullets in the back. Only this evening one of Lucio Tasca's mob was rubbed out. And what about Baron Francesco Agnello, who was kidnaped over a week ago and who's still missing?

Like I said, what sort of justice can you expect in a city like Palermo? Look at the officials of the Agrarian Reform Board: according to what I've been told, there were 1900 vacancies, but instead of advertising them and conducting a competition the way they do in other parts of Italy, they just took on men who had friends among the big shots. We all know that with the money they're pouring out in wages, they could, if they wanted to, have made a present of the land to the peasants. Let's figure out how much they spend on salaries. Say each employee gets two thousand lire a day, the total layout for a day—one day only, mind you—is nearly four million lire—one billion, two hundred million lire a year. In eight years, just eight miserable years, the cost of wages comes to nine and a half billion lire. Rather than give the land to the peasants. . . .

Peppino: And think of the crowds that take their cans every day for "soup" to the Engineers' Barracks in the Borrazzi, the Territorial Headquarters, the Distretto, all the barracks in the city. Morning after morning they line up outside; they're a familiar sight to the guards, who let them fill up their empty cans with stuff from the garbage cans. These poor beggars fasten their cans to their belts and sling them behind them— that's why we call them tin bums in Palermo. There are hundreds and hundreds of them. . . .

The cooks on American ships collect whatever the passengers leave on their plates—they save everything. They save up scraps of ham, chicken wings picked clean, slivers of pork skin, cheese rinds, the heel of a salami, and so on, hide the stuff under their jackets, and when the ship nears the dock, there are men who row out in a rented boat to buy it from them. The Yanks take the cash, and the men row back and sell all these messed-up scraps in the poor sections of the city.

a jeweler and moneylender

I used to be in business, then I worked for a while in the post office. Now I sell small gold articles and lend money. I walk about all over the city. Roughly speaking, a quarter of the people who live in Palermo couldn't make ends meet if they didn't go in for some kind of racket. A hundred thousand Palermans are well-to-do, two hundred thousand earn a decent living, but there are another two hundred thousand inhabitants, and of these, half get only occasional work, maybe one week in a month, while the rest, who are totally unemployed, exist by selling contraband cigarettes, pimping, prostitution, and so on.

I sell small gold articles by weekly installments to hawkers who peddle them in the streets. Naturally I have to make sure that I'll get my money. One of my customers was a thoroughly reliable person; one day I met a nephew of his who invited me into his room. I had a good look around, saw that he had some nice furniture and said to myself, "He's safe," so when he asked me if I'd let him have some stuff if he put down a deposit, I made no objection. A few days later his wife came to see—she wanted a few articles, too. She put down a small amount, and I let her take them.

Next, her sister-in-law came along. She told me she worked in the bank as a cleaner, and as the money seemed safe enough, I obliged her, too. Shortly, after that she brought her husband to me. "All right," I said, when he'd paid the deposit. Each of them in turn said to me: "Keep my account separate —I'll pay you myself for what I've had." Four separate debts, four separate promises to pay. It didn't stop at four, though. Their friends, their relatives came to me, paid their deposits and took away the stuff. To start with, all of them paid up like clockwork every week, so, as I didn't see any reason not to trust them, I supplied the whole tribe with earrings, necklaces, watches, and rings to the tune of three hundred thousand lire. Well, once they'd got their hands on all these articles, they sold them for half what they were worth, and never paid me another lira. They'd gained my confidence by paying me every week for the first few weeks; they'd played me for a sucker, in fact, and left me to whistle for the rest of the money. There are swindlers, too, of a different kind, who pawn whatever you let them have on deposit, and then sell the pawn tickets.

You can get taken in all kinds of different ways. I'd go to a certain courtyard, for instance, to see a man who'd missed several installments, but when I came he was never there. "Where's So-and-so?" I'd ask his neighbors after I'd been there several times, "I haven't seen him around these last few days." "Didn't you know? He's been taken to the hospital," I'd be told. They were covering up for him, of course—he wasn't in the hospital, not on your life, he was hiding from me! When somebody won't pay up, we "bloodsuckers"—that's what they call us in Palermo—take out a warrant to attach his goods. (*The speaker laughs.*) Well, when the "bloodsucker" comes along, the man who owes him money won't let him in, and puts up such a fight that he runs off to get the police. While he's gone, the man moves every stick he has into a neighbor's room, and when the "bloodsucker" and the cop force an entry, they find the place as bare as the back of your hand! More than likely, too, the things he's moved out don't even belong to him—it's all stuff that he's bought on credit!

Would-be customers ask me into their rooms so that I can admire their brand-new furniture and satisfy myself that they're in a position to pay me; believe me, in a month's time it's disappeared completely! The price of gold in the piazza is eight hundred lire a gram, but to safeguard myself I charge a thousand lire. When you're new to this line of business you let anybody take what he wants if he pays the deposit, but after a while you get to know who are the regular payers and who aren't, who are the ones you can trust, and who are the crooks.

I always pay the wholesaler right on the dot, so he lets me have whatever I want—he knows I won't let him down. At one time I had a woman working for me, and she let people have far too much credit—she nearly ruined me. There are about a hundred of us in this line of business in Palermo. In addition to us, there are at least a thousand moneylenders; some won't lend more than five thousand lire, others'll make unlimited loans. About 40 percent of the borrowers always fall behind with their payments; 10 percent are crooks who deliberately default.

Sometimes I make loans to civil servants who bring me notes from their superiors as security. Say one of them wants to buy goods worth fifty thousand lire; he gets his superior to make out a note for fifty thousand lire; I lend him twenty-five thousand lire on it, buy the goods, which I let him have on credit, and the loan, plus the interest, is repaid by installments which are deducted from his salary by the cashier and paid direct to me.[1] When I was working in the post office my superiors would come to me for loans, and I used to oblige them. I had a fistful of promissory notes, but that didn't stop them from ordering me around: "Go here—go there!" And I had to go here, I had to go there. I was the underdog, the two of clubs, you might say—I couldn't take the trick!

If you have to go to the Council for anything you want done, you won't get anywhere unless you grease countless palms—you'll be blocked all the way unless you shell out. Last year, for instance, I wanted to add on some rooms to my place, so I applied to the sanitation authorities for the necessary permit. My application never got as far as the official who issued such permits, so I got no answer. At last I went to inquire about it, and was told: "Go see So-and-so." So I went to see So-and-so, who said, "I'm afraid these plans won't do" —I had had them drawn up by a qualified architect—"we shall have to have them altered. Of course you understand that a

[1] This is a fairly common arrangement in Italy, and a great convenience to an employee who wants a sum of ready money. Certain banks will accept these notes, but both banks and moneylenders are wary of advancing more than half of their value, since there is always a risk that the borrower may lose his job. *Translator's note.*

good deal of time will have to be spent on them." "Of course; if you'll do what's necessary, I'll see that no one loses by it," I said. So I did what was expected of me, gave him a little present, and nothing more was said about any alterations of the plans. Next, I went to see the official who issued the permits, and he told me that everything would go through, so I parted with some more lire, hoping that now my business would move ahead. But no such thing—it simply folded up. Back I went to the Council, where I was told that the matter now rested with the head of the department. Accordingly, I went to his house and gave him a nice little present; once more the wheels were set in motion, he gave his approval to my plans, which were then passed on to another department. And there they stuck. So I bribed the doorkeeper to put my application on the chief's desk ready for his signature, and I went to see X, who sent me to Y, who sent me to Z, and after I'd greased I don't know how many palms, I got the letter of authorization. I never would have got it otherwise.

I needn't tell you that we don't lend money without some kind of security. That's understandable, isn't it? We're forced to protect ourselves. We only make loans to those who are in a position to repay them. But careful as we are, we still make mistakes. I don't charge a high rate of interest myself, but some moneylenders ask as much as 10 percent per day on a loan. Last week the police commissioner, who's a friend of mine, came to see me to tell me about a certain woman, a widow who, after her husband's death, had gone in for the same line as myself, selling small gold articles which purchasers could take away after putting down a deposit and agreeing to pay so many weekly installments. The difference between her way of doing business and mine, though, was that I made my customers sign promissory notes and she didn't, so naturally people flocked to her from near and far— some of them even came from the waterfront, nearly a mile away. When they'd stripped the poor woman completely bare, it was good-by—that was the last she saw of them. I don't know how she got to know about me, but when she went to the police to tell her story she brought my name up and said that some of the crooks who had robbed her had taken me, too. The inspector sent for me and told me to bring a charge against them on my own account, which I did. He said that in the future, should anyone default, I was to prosecute under Article 641 of the Penal Code, which states: "Any person failing to discharge a debt in respect of which he has put his signature to a promissory note will be prosecuted and will be liable to a sentence of two years' imprisonment. Should he, however, discharge his liabilities prior to the date when he is due to appear in court, no further proceedings will be taken against him." (*The speaker laughs.*) I know Article 641 by heart, it comes in very handy. Mind you, I don't say it's correct word for word—if you like, I'll get the Penal Code and we can check it!

Zi X

I'm seventy-four, and I've lived all my life in Palermo. It's poverty that forces hundreds of girls into prostitution. During the war it was carried on openly in the parks and public gardens. The gardeners put mattresses in their sheds and rented them to the whores who charged a dollar a lay. Business boomed when the Yanks—the whites and the blacks—were here. You should have seen the streams of women. The American troops set up their camps in the parks. Husbands brought their wives to them, and took the money. I wouldn't have any dealings with married women, though—that's one thing I never did.

A woman could earn hundreds of dollars a day. As soon as one man came out, another went in; they waited in line. *Ol rait. God foc. Uon dollar.* The park keepers provided the mattresses so that the Yanks would be comfortable. The man who'd brought the girl kept the first dollar for himself; the rest of her take he split up into three equal shares: one for her, one for himself and one for the park keeper. The men who came with the girls had learned a little English—"dames," "broads," they didn't need any more.

There were hundreds and hundreds of private pimps—some of them were old, but most of them weren't over eighteen or nineteen, young fellows who'd picked up a little American and were out of work. If the vice squad spotted them they were arrested and imprisoned. The women who were hauled in were given a medical examination; the ones that had V.D. were kept in the hospital for three days, or maybe a month, two months. Then they were discharged. Work? No, they never found work for them—they were whores, let them sell themselves—see?

Sometimes a woman would talk another woman into going with her and taking the money, but mostly it was men that took the girls along and saw to that side of the business. Plenty of trade was done in the courtyards, too. A procurer would bring the G.I.'s and Tommies who wanted to get laid, and a man who lived there, and who acted as lookout, would ask: "Which women are you taking them to?" "Giovanna, Maria . . ." the procurer would say, and very often one of them would be the man's wife. The lookout sold tickets for the women, kept their accounts, and pocketed a percentage of what they earned.

While a woman was on the job with a customer, quite likely her lover'd be hiding under the bed, and he'd pinch the Joe's wallet or watch or whatever else he could lay his hands on. Some of the women were so filthy that they stank, but the G.I.'s weren't particular—a piece of ass was a piece of ass. There were married women, girls of twenty-one, twenty-two, twenty-three, twenty-four. Very young girls were few and far between, but swarms of old pros went back to the game and did a roaring business—ass, it was all ass to the Yanks. The blacks were crazy for it.

The streets used to be full of small boys hustling for customers like real gypsies. It's no different today. Whenever a ship puts in, trade booms. Every *carrozza* driver knows what American sailors want. "Broads!" they say, and the driver, who's not only a driver but a procurer as well, takes them to the dames. He gets paid by the girls as well as the Yanks. Some drivers are also "pimps."

After weeks at sea, all the sailors want girls. "Broads—where are the broads?" So do the officers—it's human nature, isn't it? Most of them go to the private brothels and licensed houses.

There are hundreds of private brothels in Palermo, and some sections are swarming with girls and their pimps. Then there are the streetwalkers who charge five hundred lire plus another five hundred for the room. A thousand lire for the works, that's the tariff. You can't go to a private brothel for less than a thousand, but the licensed houses are cheaper.

Licensed House	Price	Number of Women
La Palermo	310	18
La Messinesa	210	3 or 4
Inta le Vecchie	210	3 or 4
Pensione Igea	310	10
Di Via Gaggini	310	20
Pensione delle Rose	800 or so	?
Pensione Aurora	420	10 or so
Pensione Bucaneve	310	10 or so
Taibbi	420	10 or so

In most of the licensed houses the charge is two to three hundred lire, and the Joe's expected to leave a ten-lira tip for the service. Sometimes, if a woman takes a liking to a man or feels sorry for him, she'll only ask for a hundred—she may even give herself to him for nothing. When a *carrozza* driver takes a customer to a girl she has to pay him according to the tariff: if she gets two thousand lire for a quickie, she gives him six hundred, and if the man wants to spend the whole night with her and she asks ten thousand lire, the driver's cut is three thousand.

Fresh young girls, newcomers to the game, fall into two classes, and the price is all according to how attractive they are. The girls in the first class are cheaply dressed, and the lowest charge is from five hundred to a thousand lire. The girls in the second class are much better dressed and more refined, and you can't have one for less than two thousand lire. There are lots of married women who sell themselves to provide for their husbands and kids; some husbands have no idea where the money comes from, but those that do know pretend they don't. These married women may take their Joes home with them or else to a room in a café or hotel. They spot a likely-looking prospect on a bus, rub themselves up against him, and touch him you know where. "Could you tell me the time?" they'll ask, or "Have you got a match?" When they get off the bus with their pickups, they take them to a house or to their own place.

Then there are the call girls who oblige men with a night of love in the hotels where they're staying.

The private pimps protect their women. "She's mine—she's my whore," they will say of their particular girl. Very often it's the pimp who fixes the price and makes sure of the money for fear of the *brucia-paglione*, fellows who have their fun and won't pay up. Some pimps are stool pigeons: they keep their eyes open at night and pass on anything they see to the police. A whore is madly jealous of her pimp, and you won't often find one who'll go with a pimp who's protecting another woman—most of them wouldn't do such a thing for all the money on earth. It's the rottenest trick one girl can play on another, a real insult, and she risks being slashed in the face or knifed if she does do it. If a pimp finds out that his girl's gone with another pimp he gives it to her in the ass to make her feel how low she is, and to rub her nose in it. He tells everybody what he's done to her. It's the most terrible, most shameful thing that can happen to a whore in Sicily. A pimp, though, is only jealous of another pimp, never of a Joe.

If a fellow wants to be a pimp, he has to be quick-witted, he has to have an eye for business, and he must be able to read and write a little. He doesn't take a percentage of his woman's earnings, he lives on her. He wears good clothes, has a gold ring on one finger, a diamond ring on another and a gold chain around his neck. You don't see many pimps around in the daytime—they sleep most of the morning. In the evening they walk around looking for customers, and see to it that their women don't lower their prices. Nearly all of them have records, and have to report regularly to the police; that's how they become informers—respected partners of the cops, no? There are hundreds of them in Palermo. They play billiards and cards, gambling games like poker. They can well afford it—a good-looking girl can earn at least four thousand lire a day. When an American ship puts in the prices soar; the Yankee sailors don't care how much they throw away.

Pimps are very religious, it makes them feel they're protected. They all wear a gold chain with a gold medal of the Madonna around their necks (from time to time they pawn their chains and medals and then redeem them again), and pray to her to guard them from diseases. They're nearly all Fascists or Monarchists or Christian Democrats. I'm not allowed to vote because I've served a few terms in prison, but I'd vote for the Communists if I could. Not that it would do any good—we haven't got a chance in hell of getting rid of this gang of chiselers.

When a woman's at her wit's end for cash, she comes to me. "Zi, find me a foreigner," she says, "a man who doesn't live in Palermo—someone from the country." (A Yank is no good because he'd be spotted by the neighbors and they'd know what she was up to.) Sometimes it isn't the woman who comes to see me, but her brother or her mother or her father. Often it's her husband. He sits and rocks the baby, while the mother ... When a girl who's been on the streets gets married, do you know what she does? She stuffs the insides of a pigeon up her, tightens her vagina by douching it with alum, and the moment her husband pokes her, the blood gushes out. "O-o-oh! You hurt me," she moans, "you've taken my virginity ..."

It's not only women and their relatives who come to me when they're in need. Men from the outlying districts who know where I live and don't want to be seen going into a brothel, young fellows, students, daddy's own dear little boys, ask me to oblige them. "Zi," one of them will say, "got a nice girl for me? How much?" "What do you like?" I ask. "A clean, healthy girl who won't give me syph." "No fear of that where I'll take you," I say, and off I go to the place where the girl lives, with him following behind me. Maybe a neighbor spots him going in and asks me who he is. "Oh, a cousin, an uncle up from the country," I say ...

Cortile Cascino

The section known as Cortile Cascino is barely two hundred yards from the Cathedral; it extends from Via D'Ossuna to Cortile Grotta and is bisected by the railroad tracks. In 1945, forty cases of typhus were confirmed by the health authorities; since then, however, not a single step has been taken to improve conditions. No matter how often one has seen it before, the sight of swarms of naked children playing in the mud and filth, or scrambling about on the tracks, comes as a fresh shock. There are five sordid two- and three-story houses in the last stages of dilapidation, and in the southern part of the section, a few squalid huts and shacks. The walls sweat with damp and the rooms are alive with scorpions, fleas and cockroaches.

Here, the hundred and thirty families, numbering four hundred and ninety-eight persons, live in a hundred and eighteen rooms (plus five cubbyholes). The average number of persons to a room, then, is 4.22. In one room measuring nine by twenty feet, eleven people sleep. In another, measuring sixteen by seventeen feet, ten. Some fifteen families live in dark, windowless cellars. About half of the remaining families have no light except what filters in from other rooms.

Four rooms have floors of packed dirt; seven have floors of packed dirt and broken tile; thirty-seven, of broken tile and cracked cement; fifty-one, of broken tile; and four, of coarse cement. The remaining fifteen rooms have floors of sound tile that are fairly good.

There are no water taps. Only one family has a toilet. The other families work, eat, sleep and do their business in their own room. ("Decent men relieve themselves on the railroad tracks.")

Among the children from three through six years old, two go to kindergarten, forty-three do not. Among those from six through thirteen, thirty-three go to school; but forty-five do not go and have never gone, although school is compulsory. On the average, the three hundred and eighty-six persons over six years old have finished only four-fifths of the first grade. Only three families can boast of a mother and father who are able to read and write; in the previous generation of these families, two couples alone were literate. Keeping this in mind and allowing twenty years to a generation, we can estimate that twenty-five hundred years will pass before the couples in this section will be literate.

As for the occupations of the heads-of-family, thirty-nine are junkmen; eighteen are ragpickers; four, laborers; two, stevedores; two, street cleaners; two, shoemakers; one is a draftee; one, a hawker of vegetables; one, a blacksmith's apprentice; one, a doorkeeper; one, a housepainter; one, a stonemason; and one, a parsley seller. Fourteen of the families are on relief.

As for the women, eleven are laundresses, eleven are chambermaids, and two are wigmakers (they buy the hair at forty lire for two hundred grams); a few women earn a little washing down steps; the rest stay at home.

The boys usually take up their fathers' callings and become junkmen, ragpickers, etc. Thirty-one of these youngsters have been to prison, most of them for "nothing much."

Since 1945 there have been nineteen cases of typhus, two of them fatal, in Cortile Cascino.

There are sixty-seven babies under the age of three, many of them suffer from malnutrition and are frequently ailing; the commonest illnesses are digestive complaints, chest diseases and various forms of blood poisoning. These illnesses are aggravated by the inability of a large number of mothers to breast-feed their babies. Eighty babies have died here within the last ten years.

Ignazio P.

We older men who live in Cortile Cascino—Via D'Ossuna, Cortile Grotta—never get taken on in the building trades. Most of us are ragpickers and junkmen; the women earn a little by doing washing. Some of the young men get a few odd days as laborers, but when they're fired they come back to the rag-and-bone trade—there's one thing to be said for it, it never stops.

About seven years ago, typhus broke out here and ten people died. They sent the *carabinieri;* we weren't allowed to leave the district for fear we'd spread the infection. The whole place stinks; the courtyard is one mass of mud and filthy puddles. Every morning the women empty the toilet pots over the railroad tracks; some of them are sluts, though, and they just dump the stuff in the space by the water tanks. The slush and slop piles up higher and higher in the winter; the firemen come along, pump off a little water, syphon some of it from the cellars, and leave it at that.

"That's the best we can do," they say, and they go. The lousy typhus is always breaking out here, you know what I mean. Once, two people died, and a number of kids went down with it—it's generally kids who die from typhus.

That time I was telling you about, when the *carabinieri* were sent to see that we kept within limits, our food was cooked for us in great big pots. As soon as it was ready the *carabinieri* blew a blast on their trumpets, and hundreds of us came with our cans, bottles, empty jam jars and so on, and waited in a long line like soldiers. When we had to relieve ourselves, we had to do it in the courtyard; sometimes the *carabinieri* were decent and let us go as far as the railroad tracks. The food they dished out to us had medicine in it to kill the germs; it must have been a laxative because all fifteen hundred of us—men, women and kids—had terrible runs.

It's no wonder we get typhus. Look at the filth, look at the way the houses are all crowded together on top of each other. There's no running water, and eight, ten, twelve people live in a room where there isn't space to swing a cat. Most of the rooms have dirt floors, several are nothing but cellars. We hardly have any furniture; some families haven't even got chairs and have to sit down on empty cans or on broken stones. Fleas and bugs? There are tons of them—when you lay out the dead, you find their bodies are covered with them. The sanitary units come by and sprinkle powder in the streets and houses. Men and women loosen their clothes so the D.D.T. can be sprinkled on their skin.

This winter the rain was so heavy that some of the houses were flooded. The inspectors came, had a look around and went away. Families with rooms under water piled their mattresses and cushions and what little rags they had on pushcarts, and with other people from the different areas that had also been flooded out, they tried to find other rooms. At last the Council had to take action. The whole lot of them were rounded up and taken to the empty sheds in the market; the men were put in one part, the women in another. There were hundreds of them herded together, stuck like horses in stalls. They slept on the ground with just a few rags for covers. After they'd squatted there for four or five days, they demanded to be rehoused. What happened was that each family was given fifteen hundred or two thousand lire and sent back to where they came from—there was nowhere else for them to go.

Every morning we men do our business on the railroad tracks. (It's been the custom as long as I can remember, my father did it, and his father did, too.) Sometimes, if we're caught doing it, we're fined twenty-five hundred lire for disorderly conduct. It costs us one hell of a lot. The women do theirs indoors. The kids pee and squat down in the street or on the tracks; six months ago a five-year-old kid who was doing it on the tracks was killed by a train. Another kid fell asleep in the tunnel and was also run over and killed.

When you think that all this goes on two hundred yards from the Cathedral, in the heart of Palermo . . .

There's any number of people in the neighborhood who don't do a stroke of work. Some earn a few lire by making little flags with pictures of St. Rosalia on them; many of the women earn a little on the streets. They work some other parts of the city, though; the houses are so close together here that the neighbors would soon spot what they were up to, and they don't want anyone to know what they're doing.

Hardly any of the kids go to school. They play all day long in the filth in the alleys. As soon as they're twelve or thirteen the girls start looking for husbands, boys their own age. The little washerwomen in the courtyard marry the little rag-pickers.

I was taken prisoner in the war, and after a trip that lasted a month I arrived here on October 8, 1944. I was single then, and I found my mother and father and the rest of the family half-dead from hunger. I met a couple of friends in the city who asked me if I had any work, and I said no. I went with them to bombed-out buildings, and we collected as much wood as we could find. But a lady spotted me and asked me what I was doing. She called the *carabinieri* and accused me of stealing stuff from the ruins of her house. They searched my home, but of course they didn't find a thing. The sergeant asked for my papers, but I didn't have any because I'd just got back. Well, they shoved me in prison—me who'd never once been in any trouble with the police. After I'd been in for five months, I was taken to court and charged with attempted theft. I got twelve months.

I had no one to defend me—how could I pay for anyone to defend me when I didn't even have the price of a bite to eat and my family was starving? I appealed my sentence, and it was reduced to six months. But I've got a black mark against me; I've done time, and according to the law I'm a criminal.

That was the first and last time I was in prison—I've had the good luck not to get pinched again. But though I've kept clear of jail, I have a hard life and I've been through the mill, let me tell you. I can't make enough in the junk business to support my family, and my wife has to go out as a cleaning woman.

Once I was sick for eighteen months with undulant fever . . . I can't read or write—you don't find many around here who can . . . I get up at seven, summer and winter, and trudge along the streets with my pushcart, shouting: "Any old rags, bottles or bones?" I buy old iron, any kind of junk. You don't get much for old iron—six lire a pound. It's not worth selling at the price. I work for a man who gives me the cash to buy with; the cart's his, and I rent it from him for fifty lire a day. Some days I may make three hundred lire, but there are whole weeks when I don't earn a soldo. Of course, you may just strike it lucky and make a thousand lire or even more in one day, but I don't have to tell you it hardly ever happens. At noon we pack up, business is over. There are about two hundred of us junkmen; this section's the center of the junk trade.

Besides scrap, we also buy orange, tangerine and lemon peels at five lire a pound, and sell them to the wholesalers who supply the soft-drink manufacturers; they charge them eight-nine lire for a pound of peels. Plenty of kids in this section collect cigarette butts from off the streets—they sell the tobacco that's left in them. They don't spend the money on themselves, though; they give what few lire they get to their families—it all helps out.

Some of the poor bastards who work in the building trades can't afford to smoke real cigarettes, so they buy ten or twenty lire worth of this loose tobacco, and roll their own. The kids go into the center of Palermo, Via Libertà, Piazza Massimo, to look for butts; if they get caught by the police, they're sent to the house of correction at Malespina. It's against the law to collect cigarette butts, it's a horrible offense, a real disgrace; I'll say it's a disgrace—to the rich, and how well they know it.

In wet weather there's nothing doing for us junkmen. During the winter we only put in a few odd days. We buy pasta and bread on credit; no storekeeper will let us charge more than a thousand or fifteen hundred lire, so we're forced to run up bills at different stores.

As you know, business is over for us at noon, but in the afternoon you'll find us hanging around at the end of the alley that runs into the street where the junk shops are, in the hope of picking up a lira or two; there's always a chance that someone might come along with some old iron, a few rags—you never know. We play cards to pass the time, or go to the *cantina;* the ones who have no money just stand around in the sun. In the *cantina* we talk about the price of old iron or copper, about what we've made or haven't made, and do our best to cheer each other up. "How much did you take in today?" I'll ask one of the others. "Five hundred lire," he may say, or "damn little" or "not a soldo." "Hard luck," all of us say, and we do what we can to pick his spirits up.

My family's been in the junk trade in this neighborhood for a hundred and ten years. That's the truth—I haven't told you a single thing that's not true.

When a man goes home with his pockets empty, there's a scene. "What have you been doing in the streets all morning? Didn't anyone call you?" his wife shouts.

"I didn't get a break—it's not my fault," says the husband, hoping he'll be able to make something the next day. If he doesn't, there's a worse scene that ends up with them coming to blows.

Our section's what you might call a dead end; we never get to know anything outside the junk trade. We're not even interested in anything that happens in the rest of Palermo unless it's a murder.

Religion? There's no such thing here. I registered Christian Democrat, not because I wanted to vote C.D., but so I'd be allowed to carry on my trade. At election time a few priests and some men and women come along and hand us packages of pasta to get us to vote for them. We get more Monarchists than C.D.'s, though; they give us tickets with addresses on them where we can go for free pasta. Most people vote the way they're told to; they're scared stiff at the thought of what would happen to them if it got out that they voted against the party. Hardly any of us go to church; there aren't any Sundays or feast days for people like us. On Sundays we're too busy wondering what we can find to put on the table.

This is a tough neighborhood. Once two strangers came

through to take pictures, and a man who was rolling drunk, though it was only half past ten in the morning, lurched over and before they had the slightest idea what he meant to do, he got ahold of the camera and yelled that he'd stop them from taking the pictures. A real mess they were in—it was touch and go whether he smashed up their camera, which was worth eighty thousand lire.

Most of us married men have six or eight or ten kids—making them's our one pleasure—it's the only pleasure the poor can afford . . .

Just before the elections some priests came around to teach the kids their catechism. We cleaned up the courtyard as much as we could, cleared away the slop and stamped the earth down flat. After they gave the children two or three lessons, they brought a projector along and started showing a movie all about the Madonna and the saints. But in spite of what we'd done the priests couldn't stand the filth, and the kids were too much for them—they wouldn't sit still and pay attention—so they packed up the film in the middle, and off they went with the kids shouting dirty words at them: "You give us a pain in the ass, you shits! You only come here when there's an election! Screw you!"

Well, they went, and that was the last we saw of the priests, the catechism books and the movie.

Uncle Andrea

Here in Palermo, you've got to distinguish between the methods of the *affaristi* and the shady dealings which became such a public scandal that, owing to the ignorance of the authorities, *affarismo* was confused with *zuinismo*, tarred with the same brush. *Affarismo*'s legitimate business, *zuinismo*'s not, and quite right too.

Affarismo's been a respectable profession, just like any other, right from the start. It's the unemployment of all the poor people who've been driven into taking it up that has given it a thoroughly bad name. They say there are at least a thousand *spiccia-faccende* in Palermo, but I believe five hundred's nearer the mark. Men and women who have no jobs wait around outside government departments and administrative offices hoping to make a few lire by coping with official forms for people who can't make head or tail of them. They stand around the federal courts, the civil courts, the records office, all day long, ready to obtain whatever papers or forms a customer may need—birth certificates, death certificates, marriage certificates, legal documents, pension books, etc., etc.

The *affarista,* who's looked on as a bloodsucker by the clients for whom he's done his best, hardly makes anything at all out of the hard, exhausting work he has to do—he doesn't make more than enough, in fact, to buy himself a crust of bread. Suppose, for instance, I charged a customer a hundred lire for getting him a copy of a birth certificate. Well, first of all I'd have to go and apply for it, then I'd have to pick it up the next day, pay the fee—fifty-five lire—and take it to my customer's house. For all my time and trouble, I'd make the great sum of forty-five lire. That's one example of what a *spiccia* does, but let me tell you, if I didn't ask more than a hundred lire, I'd be in the red. I'll tell you why. Although *affarismo's* a legitimate business, *spiccie* aren't allowed at the official windows. This regulation, which was made to protect the public against *zuinismo,* is an awful hardship for us *affaristi*—it's the start of our *via crucis* in the struggle against starvation. We can't apply for documents in the regular way, so we have to look for a clerk who's willing to oblige us—for a consideration. We can't transact business with him in the department, so we have to wait till it closes and take him to a café or to wherever we live to fix things up.

Greedy and grasping—that's what our customers think of us. They always suspect us of hiking up the price. Well, if we do, it would only be logical; it would be against human nature if we didn't expect to make a little. A man only becomes a *spiccia* because he's out of work and can't get a job; he's pushed to his limit, he has to do what he can to support his family.

Let's go back to the customer who wants a copy of a birth certificate. Well, if I have to pay fifty-five lire for it and another fifty to the clerk who gets it for me, what's the use of a hundred lire to me? You can see for yourself that I'd be five lire in the hole. So to clear something myself, I have to charge two hundred lire.

It's a nerve-racking, exhausting business, believe me. First you have to find customers; then, when you've found them, you have to hang around a department till you spot a clerk who'll provide you with the papers you want. The next day you pick them up and take them to the customer's house. Quite likely he lives some distance out of the city, which is hard luck since you have to pay your own fare there and back. That's the sort of life a *spiccia* leads.

Some clients employ us because the sight of the endless lines at the windows is too much for them. Government officials don't hurry themselves. Government departments are supposed to open at nine o'clock, but there's never a sign of life till nine-thirty; closing time is one o'clock but the doors are shut exactly at twelve-thirty. Most of our customers are people who can't read or write, but as about 20 percent of them can't afford to pay what we charge for getting a document, they give us ten or twenty lire to fill in an official form for them. About 40 percent of the Palermans engage us to do their business so that they won't have to lose a couple of days at work; 10 percent of our clients are *pescicani*[1] who wouldn't dream of doing anything so unaristocratic as standing in line.

You'll see swarms of *affaristi* outside the law courts, but none inside, because it's the doorkeepers who undertake to get us the papers we need. The Fascists made *zuinismo* illegal, but not *affarismo*. *Zuinismo*'s graft. It's advising the patients of one doctor to go to another doctor, persuading people to transfer legal business to another lawyer, luring away the customers from certain shops and hotels, getting them to patronize others. In 1936 or '37, it was proved in court

[1] Slang for parvenus. *Translator's note.*

that there was nothing criminal in *affarismo*. Caciotto, a certain retired fireman living on a small pension, was brought into court, charged with *affarismo*; the judge was Fazio, who's now dead, but Signor Giovanni Rosano who defended Caciotto is still alive. He argued that *affarismo* wasn't out of keeping with either the spirit or the letter of the law, and proved it was altogether a different business from *zuinismo*. Caciotto was acquitted because the court agreed that *affarismo* was a legitimate business. In spite of that, we're always being arrested, though all we've done is grease the palm of some official.

Until we've reached a better understanding of social conditions, humanity'll make no progress, there'll be no advancement, no co-operation in any field of life.

Most of us *affaristi* haven't had much formal schooling, but we're brighter, more capable than other Palermans, besides which we learn a lot from the officials we're always dealing with; if we do make a mistake, they straighten us out.

Since I depend on what I can earn as a *spiccia*, I have to keep on the right side of my customers. Say you're a client: if you're a Monarchist, I'm a Monarchist; if you're a Christian Democrat, so am I; if you're a Communist, ditto. I can't afford to offend a customer, it'd cost me maybe five hundred lire if I did—I'd be simply cutting off my nose to spite my face. That's why I keep all the party cards in my pocket.

Well, in a few words I've given you a clear picture, a true picture of how a *spiccia* lives. You don't become a *spiccia* by choice—you're driven to it by unemployment. At least you can make some sort of living.

UNCLE ANDREA'S NEPHEW: Yes, but tell him about the times when the cops come along with the wagon and hustle all you *spiccie* away to the clink!

Salvatore R.

I've been unemployed for three years. I used to work in the wholesale fruit business; I packed oranges, lemons, and tangerines in wooden crates, which I stacked on my shoulders and carried.

My wife and I split up because I couldn't find a job—we've been married fifteen years, we've got four kids, but she's kicked me out for good. My sister's a widow, she took me in, and every now and then she gives me a bite to eat, but she can't manage to feed herself and her three kids on her lousy little widow's pension. She only draws five thousand lire a month. I ask you, how can a woman with three kids live on five thousand lire a month?

Time and time again I've tried to get recommended for a job, but no one will ever see me.

At home my wife was always nagging. "Haven't you found anything to do yet?" she'd yell at me. I never had any steady work for more than three or four months in the year, and I used to wear my shoes to pieces tramping all over the place looking for jobs. My wife got more and more fed up; it all came to a head in July when we had a real fight and she slammed the door on me. Now she's trying to get a separation. It's my sister-in-law that's to blame. She paid our rent for us and she kept on and on at my wife: "If you don't get rid of that husband of yours I'll never give you another lira." For three solid years my wife never stopped nagging me; the last year we had the same old argument night after night. Her precious sister'd back her up. "You lazy so-and-so!" they'd yell at me. "You won't even try to find work—you won't do a thing to support your kids!" and they'd call me all sorts of filthy names—I felt like strangling the both of them. At last we came to blows, we had a fight to end all fights, and she threw me out in the street. It wouldn't surprise me if she accused me of hitting her. Lazy, they said I was—lazy! Me! I tell you I nearly went out of my mind trying to find a job, any kind of job. If I managed to pick up a hundred or two hundred lire, I spent it on bread for my family.

After my old lady threw me out I went to the regional authorities and the prefecture hoping to get a job on one of the public-works projects. Then I went to the City Council—I thought maybe I might get taken on as a porter in a housing development. But I had no references. I used to touch a friend for a hundred lire to buy a bite of something to put in my belly. I begged the Honorable G., the Monarchist, for a letter of recommendation; I asked a big contractor to speak for me for a job as watchman in one of the important buildings; I applied at the Montecatini works, but everywhere it was always the same story: "Sorry—there's nothing . . ." or: "We'll let you know . . ."

Every Sunday I meet my four boys in the public gardens of the Villa Bonanno. Giovanni, the oldest, is fifteen. Eugenio's thirteen, Renato's nine and Carmelo's only five. "Why don't you make up with Mama?" they ask, and Renato and Carmelo begin to cry. Sometimes I can't help crying, too. "When I've found a job, we'll see—maybe I'll come home again," I tell them.

The shoes and socks and shirts that I'm wearing were given to me, otherwise I'd have nothing. It's all I can do not to throw myself in the ocean or under a bus. A dozen times a day I feel like making out like I'm nuts so maybe they'd put me away. Often I've been close to stealing, but something holds me back—my whole family has always been honest, we've never been in trouble with the law.

Sometimes Eugenio, my thirteen-year-old, gives me fifty lire so I can buy some bread.

I've lost count of all the employment applications I've filed. Yesterday I went back early to my sister's place because it was raining, and there was a note for me from the Council. I went at six o'clock and handed the note to some official, who told me to sit down. He opened a file, showed me a letter and said that the Honorable G. had written a recommendation for me. Then he asked me my father's full name, my mother's maiden name, my wife's maiden name, the number and the ages of my kids, etc., etc., and when he put everything down, he said: "You can go now. We'll write to you." But they never did. Another time, the regional authorities sent for me and I was given three thousand lire. They issue me an E.C.A. card[1] every month, and I draw a thousand lire relief money. But I don't want relief money, I want work. What do they think I can do with the lousy little bit they hand me? I'm looking for a job. Every time I take fifty lire from my kid to buy a crust of bread with, I feel sick from shame. The second he's out of sight I begin to cry.

Some nights I say to myself: "How can I go on like this? I'll kill myself . . ." I sit around all day long, and when the peddlers that sell food go by, I inhale those rich smells, but I've got no money—I can't buy a thing to satisfy my hunger.

I can't make myself ask people on the street for charity. I'm not a beggar. I've worked all my life, and I'm only fifty years old.

I'm beginning to feel queer in the head. I used to try and figure out how I ever got into such a mess. But now I've stopped thinking—I can't think any more. Work, work, work—how can I find work—that's all that's left in my mind.

I can't rest, I don't remember what it's like to live in peace. I can't even enjoy my kids' company any more. All day long I do nothing but sit or stand around like an idiot, wishing I had something to eat. I borrow comic books from the kids, and read the comic strips to pass away the time. I can't stand it, I'm telling you—it's driving me off my rocker. I'm scared of what'll happen to me. I keep telling myself it'd be better to end it all, and then I remember my kids . . . please God, give me the strength not to kill myself.

If only we had the Fascists back again. There wouldn't be all this misery; we'd be able to emigrate to Africa, or the government would give us jobs on public-works projects. This C.D. crowd we've got now, they're just out to make millions for themselves, and I don't care who hears me say it. They ought to think of the unemployed—start new industries, make some work for them.

Plenty of men have committed suicide because they couldn't find any work. A year ago there was one that jumped off the top of Monte Pellegrino; he was a married man with

[1] *Ente Communale d'Assistenza*—the relief card, usually good for food rather than money. *Translator's note.*

four or five kids and he'd been out of work for I don't know how long. Another one threw himself under a train. I read about them in the papers, and I remember thinking: "Once you're dead, your troubles are all over. One of these days I'll kill myself and put an end to all this misery."

Nicolò A.

Up until the age of thirty, I was strong and healthy. I was out of work, so I joined up with some guys who were dealing in black-market wheat. I lived near Catania. Their lordships the *carabinieri* locked us up and took us to the barracks at Porta Nuova; that was in 1944. They accused me of being mixed up with the bandits,[1] and ordered me to come clean about all the rapes, murders, robberies and so forth that I was supposed to have committed. When I told them I had nothing to confess, they started to bang me around and torture me; they beat me up with their clubs, flogged me with rawhide whips, and forced me to go through the *cassetta*.[2] They finished up by fracturing my spine with a blow from a rifle butt. Just talking about what I went through makes me feel sick. To think I was once a strong, healthy guy . . .

They smashed the leg of one of my buddies, shoved him in a sack and threw him down the stairs. The rest they beat up without mercy. I was in prison for four years.

I'm a married man with five kids. I've been arrested three times for begging in the Via Libertà. The first time they gave me fourteen days, the second time eight, the third twelve. "You know perfectly well that begging's against the law," they said. "It's not my fault that I'm a beggar, it's yours," I said. "I can't even stand up without my crutches. Give me a

[1] This was during the reign of the bandit Guiliano. *Translator's note.*
[2] See the story of E.A. *Translator's note.*

pension and I'll stop begging." "That's not a matter for the courts—you have to apply to the government if you want a pension," they said. It would give tourists a bad impression if they saw people begging in the Via Libertà, they said. A few days ago, some tourists—they could have been French, I don't know—were walking along the street, and the same cops said to me, "If you beg from foreigners again, we'll kick your ass out of here." Every once in a while someone comes along and bawls me out.

I've written dozens of letters to Rome and Palermo for a pension, but never one answer have I got.

I used to live in a dirty hole in the Via Molo. I applied for a housing project, but all I got was: "There ain't any." I had to move out to Bagheria, and I have to take a bus to get here.

Every time I beg, I feel ashamed. Some people stop and give me a few lire, some say: "Sorry—I don't have any change." They can't tell me I ought to be working, they can see for themselves I can't move a step without my crutches.

I start my pitch at ten o'clock, and stay till five. The best times for me are feast days and holidays—Christmas, New Year's Day, Easter, All Souls' Day—because the people have got a little extra money in their pockets and it gives them a lift to be charitable. On ordinary days it's the workers who give me the most—laborers, masons, dock workers and so forth. Once I tap-tapped my way to a car with a dame sitting in it—all covered with gold she was, earrings, necklaces, bracelets, rings. "Can you spare a few soldi, Signora?" I begged. "Go away, I've got no money," she said. Rich people —the nerve they've got! Won't part with a soldo. "You're far better off than we are, you probably eat twice as much as we do," they say.

The working-class wives are much more generous; they give me ten, twenty lire—once in a while one of them will give me fifty. The kids ask their mothers or fathers to give me something—poor kids, I mean. The rich kids wouldn't give a damn if I starved to death.

I don't know how many beggars there are in Palermo—there are so many you couldn't count them, there must be thousands. We'd rather beg than steal. Most of the beggars are old men and women. Some beggars hang around the Via

Libertà and the Via Roma, and as soon as they spot the cops they beat it. I'm not that lucky—they'd grab me right away, rough me up and shove me in jail.

If you go to the Via Molo at night, you'll see men and women huddled there in the doorways, or, if the doors are open, lying on the stairs. Some poor bastards sleep on the benches in the public gardens, but if a cop catches them, he chases them. Some of the others flop on the station platform beside the railroad tracks, wherever they can. It's not only men who sleep like that—it's women too, always old women. What else can they do if they have nowhere to go? The only houses that are being built are for the people with money, who don't need them. It's not so bad in the summer, but the winter is murder for the ones that have to sleep out. They won't even let them use the old air-raid shelters. They found the body of a beggar from Bagheria in the ruins of a bombed-out house—it was frozen stiff with cold. He wasn't the only one that died of exposure . . .

There are kids that are beggars, too. They walk along the streets with two or three plaster statues of saints. "Buy something, lady . . ." Sometimes I'll be eating a crust of bread or a roll, when kids of six or seven come along and say: "Can I have some?" I never say no; I always give them whatever I have; I know what it is to be hungry.

It's no use begging in the wet weather; the streets are almost empty, and the few people that are out rush past in their raincoats, or they catch the bus or hail a *carrozza*. Sometimes it pours for ten days without stopping, and when it's cold, and wet, too, I feel like I'd been turned into a block of ice.

On Sundays we hang around in the church vestibules, but if the cops see us, they call the wagon and in we go. Sometimes the cops get a *carrozza* to take us to the station house; they give the driver a ticket for him to turn in at the Town Hall so he can get his money for the fare.

Bernardo L.

In 1951, my wife (she's the same age as me, twenty-nine) began to feel sick. She had aches and pains between her shoulders, and we thought it must be rheumatism from the change in the weather. Then she started running a fever, and I decided I'd better take her to the clinic. After they examined her and X-rayed her, they found out she had t.b. She was sent to a sanatorium.

I didn't know what to do with my three little babies. I went to the *Pontificio*[1] to find out if they could be put in an institution, but the lady in charge said all the institutions were full. "Please, could you give me a little money to buy some food for them?" I begged, but instead of giving me money, she handed me two bottles of milk. "Signora, I can't look after the children myself," I said. "I can't do anything more for you here," she said. "Go back to the clinic and ask them to help you." But at the clinic they said, "Our business is to cure people, not help them."

So I went back to the *Pontificio*. "Here's five hundred lire for you," the woman said. "That's all you'll get, so don't come again." I didn't know where to turn, so I got a *spiccia* to write a letter for me, and when the Cardinal was leaving the Cathedral after he said Mass, I threw myself at his feet and put my letter in his hand. (It's a wonder I wasn't arrested—no one's allowed to go near the Cardinal, you know.) "Please, please help me, Your Eminence," I begged him, "my wife's in the hospital, and I can't go out to work and leave my three little children all alone." "I'll help you, my son," he said.

But a month went by, and nothing happened, so I knelt down at the Cardinal's feet again. "I'll help you, my son," he promised me, and when I began to cry like a baby, he put his hand in his pocket and pulled out a hundred-lira note. "Take this, my son, and buy some bread for your little ones," he said.

[1] One of the Vatican's charitable organizations, mainly supported by gifts and contributions from state funds. *Translator's note.*

I was so desperate I took it. "Now go home quietly," he said; "I'll see that you get help."

I couldn't leave the kids with my mother. She's a widow, and what's more, she's lame; she has to keep herself alive by begging in the streets. My wife's parents are dead. Another two months went by, and no help came—it was pretty obvious that the Cardinal must have forgotten all about me. I went to the parish priest. "We don't give charity here; we celebrate Mass," he said. "But I'll let you have fifty lire." "Forget it," I said, and I walked away. I waited outside the church door for Signorina L.R.; after I'd been there for about half an hour, she came. I asked her if she knew about my case, and I told her the details and where I lived and all, and she wrote everything down in a book. "I'll send someone to see you," she said. Sure enough, a welfare worker came around to look into my situation. "I've seen all I want to see, so I won't stay any longer," she said; "now that I know how you're fixed, we'll help you." At the end of a month I got ten pounds of pasta. "What good is that?" I said. "If you can't take my children into an institution, at least give me enough money for their keep." I was working as a bricklayer at the time, but the work was very irregular. It was plain as day I wouldn't get any help from the *Pontificio* or the Cardinal, so I went to the Town Hall and told one of the officials. "Well, my friend," he said after I got finished, "we'll arrange to take one of the children, but only one." "Only one?" I said. "But . . ." "I've made you an offer—take it or leave it," he said. I saw it was no use going on, so I said: "If you could make arrangements for my youngest one, then . . ." He sent me to the *Maternità e Infanzia* and my fifteen-month-old baby was put in a home.

Then I asked the doctor in charge of the clinic what I was supposed to do with the other two, and through him they were sent to the *colonia*[2] at Corleone. They were kept there for two years and then they were sent home.

Well, my wife was discharged from the san and I found a job. I was working for about four months when I had a bad fall and dislocated my shoulder. A little while later I began

[2] A state school for needy or neglected children. *Colonie* have been set up all along the coast, and children are sent to them for short periods so that they may have a week or so by the sea. *Translator's note.*

to spit blood and I was told to go see the doctor of the *Cassa Malattia*.[3] "It's nothing," he told me. "You can go back to work."

But exactly a year later, I started to spit blood again. This time the doctor said, "You'll have to go to a sanatorium for treatments—you've got t.b." My employment book was sent in, but it came back with a letter saying there weren't enough stamps in it—I couldn't get help under the *Previdenza Sociale*[4] until I'd done another two weeks' work.

I had to spend the next three months home in bed. We weren't given any assistance, and all we had to live on was the three hundred lire a day the san allowed my wife after her discharge. I got the doctor from the *Cassa Malattia* to visit me, but he said: "I can't do anything for you—the treatment for t.b. comes under the *Previdenza Sociale*."

As soon as I was able to get up, I went back to my job. I don't mind telling you I did some cheating—I gave my boss a certificate that said I was fit to work. I had to work at least another two weeks so my book would be stamped the right number of times.

Well, somehow, I managed to go on working for another two months, but I didn't dare go on any longer. So I went back to the clinic, and I was sent to the San Lorenzo sanatorium for treatment. Though I wasn't anywhere near cured, I was sent home at the end of three months. I wrote to the *Previdenza Sociale* and asked them to let me into another san, but they sent my letter back and said I would have to have another medical exam, and I had to write again enclosing the doctor's certificate. Well, I was re-examined, I got the certificate to say I still needed treatment and I was admitted to the Ingrassia sanatorium.

I spent eight months in the Ingrassia. My wife had to go to the clinic every week, and since it was too far for the children to walk, she had to leave them in the courtyard. The courtyard gets flooded every time it rains because the toilet drains are stopped up and they overflow in the wet weather. There are twenty houses on the courtyard and there are other people besides us that have t.b.

[3] Equivalent to a sick-benefit society. *Translator's note.*
[4] The government medical program. *Translator's note.*

It wasn't right for the children to be cooped up all day in our one small room; the window looks out on a blank wall, so there's no light or fresh air. Once the Cardinal visited our neighborhood; he saw our dark dingy hole and the other rooms in the house, promised us something would be done, and gave us all Absolution. But nothing *was* done. The months went by, still no one ever came to see how we were living.

After eight months I was discharged from the san, but I had to go once every month to the clinic. I was given an allowance of five hundred lire a day, but by this time my wife had stopped drawing hers. Neither one of us can read or write, so I got a *spiccia* to write a letter to the prefecture for me asking for help. The *spiccia* said I ought to send the letter to the Town Hall and that I should enclose our health certificates and my family book. A month later the Council wrote a letter to me telling me I'd been given twenty-six hundred lire a month, plus a three-thousand-lire cost-of-living allowance every three months. But we could never get along on this, so I went to the prefecture to see if they'd give me some extra help. Every now and then they sent me a thousand lire, and they also advised me to write to the Honorable Alessi about the kids. I wrote to him all right, but I never got any answer.

Next I sent a letter to the Honorable Restivo, the President of the Regional Assembly, but I never heard a word from him either. So then I went to the Cathedral for one of the parcels from America.[5] "My dear son, we have no parcels here," said the priest. "Will you please do something to help me?" I said. "My wife and I've both got t.b., we have five little children—Signorina L.R. knows how we're fixed." "Go home, now," said the priest. "I'll send for you in a couple of days."

Six days went by, and when he hadn't sent for me I went back to the Cathedral. I saw a lot of well-dressed people coming out with parcels—parcels from America! "Why did you tell me you didn't have any parcels from America?" I asked the priest. "Those people I saw just now had them—every day I see people with American parcels." "The parcels we have

[5] Parcels of food and clothing dispatched from the United States by UNRRA and sent to the various religious organizations to be distributed to the needy. *Translator's note.*

here are for Rome, my son," said the priest. Then I let loose. Maybe you'll think it was terrible, but I couldn't stop myself. I swore at the priest, I called him every name in the book. "My son, my son, this won't do—calm down," he said. "I'm ready to help you, you know." So he gave me an American parcel, and a voucher for ten pounds of pasta. "Seems like a guy has to make a pig out of himself to get anything out of you priests," I said. He didn't say anything, but he gave me a ticket for free bread and soup that was good for three months. You had to get in line at ten sharp every day, and you got three spoonfuls of soup and three small rolls.

For a month we managed a little better, but then my wife and me began to get worse and worse; at the end of five months we asked to be sent back to the Ingrassia. We were examined again, and were sent to the san for further treatment. We had to leave the five children alone; all we could do was to beg the neighbors to keep an eye on them and give them a little bread and a few spoonfuls of soup.

When I had been in the san for four weeks, I asked for forty-eight hours' leave to see what arrangements I could make for the children. In those forty-eight hours I did everything I did the time my wife was first taken sick to get them into institutions. But it was no good; they told me the Council was short of money and couldn't afford to pay for the board and keep of five kids. "They're too young to look after themselves," I said. "They just can't be left there like that." "Go apply to the Child Care Committee," the official said to me. But I drew a blank there too. "Do I have to kill somebody before I get any help?" I shouted at the director. "If you 'kill somebody,' you'll be sent to prison," he said in a cold voice. "All right," I said, "I have to go back to the san, so there's only one thing for me to do—bring the kids here and leave them."

As soon as I left, the director, a shrewd-looking egg, went around where I lived and asked the neighbors about my case. One of them said how sorry she was for the children. "I'll make you responsible for them, Signora," the director said. "I'm only a poor woman—I'll take them in and feed them, but I can't do it without the maintenance money," she said. Well, she did take them in, but a month went by and the maintenance money wasn't sent to her, so she went to see the director. "If you'd let me have the money—" she started to say, but he never let her get any further. "Go away, Signora," he said, "but remember, if any harm comes to those children, you'll be to blame."

She burst out, "But I'm telling you I can't manage to keep them on my own!" and insisted that it wasn't right till the director yelled at her: "Get out or I'll have you thrown out!" She was so terrified that she did what he said.

Well, she came to see me in the san and told me the whole story. I got another forty-eight hours' leave, got my kids and took them to the Child Care Committee. As soon as he laid eyes on us, the director started to shout at me, and I shouted right back at him till a *brigadiere* who was there nudged me on the shoulder and said, "Calm down, you're in the right." Then the director called up the Council about my case. He was told that arrangements had already been made to place my oldest, a boy, in an institution. "What about the other four?" I asked him. "I'll see what can be done," he said. So the children and I went away, and we all started to sob, and I yelled at the top of my voice that Sicily stank, that it stank to high heaven, and made me sick and disgusted. My youngest child was given a home by his godmother, but the three others were left to shift for themselves.

Then I was advised to go and see Professor M., who was in charge of *Maternità e Infanzia* in the Piazza Bologna. My case was looked into and two more children were placed in an institution.

After ten months, my wife and I were discharged from the Ingrassia. We were both given a year's grant; mine was for five hundred lire a day, but hers was only three hundred because she had to keep on going to the clinic. We hadn't been discharged more than a couple months when the Council sent two of the kids home. I went to the Assistance Board, and I asked them: "Why couldn't you let them stay in the *colonia*?" "You ought to be grateful we've done this much for you," was all the answer I got.

Then I put my trust in God, and brought all the children home. I did what I could to earn a few lire: I went out selling balloons, old iron, rags, any kind of junk. Thirteen days ago my wife had another baby, so we've got six now. I pay forty-five hundred lire a month for this hole, and I can't find a room with a window that's cheap enough for me. We need at least two rooms to keep the kids from breathing in all our germs.

Once some foreigners came here—I couldn't understand a word they said. They made all the kids sit on their potties in front of the door and took pictures of them, then they made them lie down with my wife and me in bed and took some more pictures. They were for the newspapers. Five years ago, that was. The pictures were taken to show the conditions we lived in and were meant to open the eyes of the Cardinal, the ladies in charge of the *Pontificio* and the Cardinal's charities, the firemen, the prefect, the Americans, and of the Communists, to the terrible state of things. Well, the *parrini*[6] party—that's what we call the C.D.'s—and the Communists each tried to outdo each other. The Communists said to me: "Vote for us and two months from now we'll give you a new home. Vote Communist!" And the C.D.'s said to me: "Vote for us. We'll see that your children won't have to play in the courtyard. They'll go to school. We'll arrange for them to be taken care of in an institution. Vote Christian Democrat!"

I took the voting slips and tore them all up. Eight weeks from now my wife'll stop getting her allowance, and in another six months I'll stop getting mine. Then we'll be back where we started, and to get my wife and me into a san for a bare three months, I'll have to go through the whole lousy business once more. And the children—what'll happen to them? I'll go from pillar to post like I did before—it'll be the same old story all over again . . .

---

[6] *Parrini* is a derogatory term for priests. *Translator's note.*

Cortile lo Cicero

"You couldn't live in a worse place than this," say the people of Cortile lo Cicero, yet, although the layout is different, there is nothing to choose between Cortile lo Cicero and slums already described.

From Via Colonna Rotta, a flight of stone steps leads down to number 19. Below is the courtyard, and when it rains heavily the basements of the houses are invariably flooded. The passages are dark and without air, and in many of the rooms it is impossible to see unless the lamp is lit or the electric light switched on.

Twenty-eight homes were picked at random for consideration. They house thirty-six families numbering a hundred and forty-four persons, who live in thirty rooms (plus one cubbyhole). The average number of persons to a room, then, is 4.8.

None of the homes has a water tap. None has

a toilet. All the families use a hole in the corner of their room above an open drain. The smell is terrible!

Eleven of the rooms have electric lights; a few of the lights are unmetered. Four rooms have no windows; eight have a tiny slit overlooking the stairs. One has a single window looking out on a heap of human excrement on the railroad tracks. In seventeen rooms, most of the windows measure sixteen inches square; the rest of the windows measure twenty inches by thirty-six.

Only two rooms have good floors; the rest have floors of coarse cement or broken tile.

There are sixty-one sleeping places. The average number of persons to a place, then, is 4.2.

Among the children from three through six years old, two go to kindergarten; the remaining thirty-seven are exposed all day long to the filth and contamination of their surroundings. Among those from six through thirteen, only seven go to school regularly; ten have never even seen the school. On the average, the people over six years old have finished only a fifth of the second grade. Only three married couples can read and write.

As for the occupations of the heads-of-family, six are hawkers; three are junkmen; three, laborers; two, roasted-seed sellers; one is a street photographer; one, a cowherd; one, a lottery organizer; one, a carpenter; one, a tradesman; one, a streetcleaner; one, a wheelwright; one, a handymen. Five men are in and out of prison. Five families are on relief.

As for the women, thirteen go out daily as houseworkers and the rest stay at home.

Eighteen people (twelve and a half percent) are ill with some form of t.b. Fourteen cases of typhus (about ten percent) are certified. Six of the seven cases of meningitis have recently proved fatal.

Filippo L. R.

Guys like us that run lotteries in the poor parts of Palermo offer for prizes all you could want for a meal, and the charcoal to cook it on: four pounds of pasta, three pounds of bread, an onion, a small bottle of olive oil (150 grams) and a bottle of tomato sauce (100 grams). That's the first course; for the second course we throw in a couple pounds of cheap fish—"poor man's fish" we call it—and a bottle of wine. We arrange it all in a basket so everything can be seen, and we make out the card for the drawing—the numbers run from one to ninety. For a few lire we buy strips of tissue paper that have all these numbers printed on them, stick them on sheets of cardboard, and cut them out as we sell them.

Each section of the city has its own lottery man. It's only the people who live there that play the game—outsiders ticket, you do it in a roundabout way. Like this: I would go up to a woman and say: "Good morning, Signora, how are *you* today? And how's your son?" Then I kibitz with her a while; if I didn't, she'd never buy a ticket. And then:

ME: "Come on—why don't you try your luck with these two numbers?"

THE WOMAN: "All right—I'll take them."

ME: "Thanks a lot—I kiss your hand, Signora . . ."

That's how it's done. If you have a nice little talk with her, you understand, she can't resist buying a ticket.

In the poor sections almost everybody'll buy a lottery ticket, but people that live in the better-class districts never do.

Nearly all the old people with nothing to do, day in, day out, are anxious to try their luck. Many times they don't have the price of a ticket—thirty lire—in their pocket, but they'll take one and say: "Pay you tomorrow, or the day after tomorrow for certain."

Some days a customer'll take more than one number. I walk through the streets, doing my best to stay clear of the ones that won't pay me cash on the line, and in an hour or an hour and a half I've sold all the tickets. Then I stand in the piazza, draw my bag, that's filled up with wooden or bone counters, from my belt, rattle it, and announce: "Attention, please! The drawing's about to begin!" I dig my hand in the bag and pull out a number. "Number 72, Line 18's the winner!" I shout. As soon as I call out the line, a ticket holder can see at a glance where his number is—the card's made out like this:

1	19	37	55	73
2	20	38	56	74
3	21	39	57	75
4	22	40	58	76
5	23	41	59	77
6	24	42	60	78
7	25	43	61	79
8	26	44	62	80
9	27	45	63	81
10	28	46	64	82
11	29	47	65	83
12	30	48	66	84
13	31	49	67	85
14	32	50	68	86
15	33	51	69	87
16	34	52	70	88
17	35	53	71	89
18	36	54	72	90

Of course we know the card by heart, and so do all the regulars, the lottery fans. I change the color of the tickets every day; if I didn't somebody might pull out one that he bought for another drawing and claim the prize. I have them in white, red, green, blue, yellow—every color of the rainbow. I never use black, though—black's unlucky, and we're very superstitious, so superstitious that some players always insist on having one particular number.

"Give me 44," one of them'll call out.

"Wait till I see if I've still got it."

"If it's sold, I won't buy a ticket."

"Why not?"

"Because I'm sure 44's going to win."

Somebody else will ask me for two numbers in Line 17. If they're gone, they won't play. The most popular numbers are the ones in lines 17, 13, and 7; they sell like hot cakes, all the real gamblers go for them. The other numbers go to people that aren't so smart.

Some customers have a liking for Line 3 but they won't take Number 75 at any price; or they may go for Line 5, but they won't buy Number 77. It's because the numbers have different meanings—you can find all of them in the Lotto Book— a very popular game in these parts. We call them out in dialect: "Number 4—do it on the floor!" "Number 9—baby mine!" "Number 45—the half-thief!" "Number 90—the whole thief!" "Number 16—the pimp!" "Number 75—Punchinello, that comical fellow!" and like that.

As soon as I call out the winning number, up comes the holder of the lucky ticket, grinning all over, happy as a lark because he's picked it and won the prize.

The stuff in the basket's worth about eighteen hundred lire —maybe thirty lire more or thirty less. Sometimes I may lose fifty to a hundred lire because a customer'll say to me: "I'll take five tickets if you'll throw in one for nothing." Still, I make up my losses all right, because the prize-winner's so delighted he nearly always gives me a present of a hundred lire.

Women as well as men run lotteries, but they can't cart around a heavy basket, so they give away a thousand-lira note for the prize. In the poorest districts, the Capo, the Kalsa, San Pietro, Ballarò, Briaria, Piazza Incrastone, and like that, it's nearly always older people that run the lotteries. I guess there must be at least two hundred of us, but there may be more— we don't meet up with all of them that's in this line, you understand.

We never run a lottery on Mondays or Fridays—they're un-lucky days. There are other days in the calendar too, quite a lot of days, that are "black"—"excommunicated," we call them. This is one of them, and that's why I'm not working—it's not worth my while, I'd have to go around looking for customers that aren't superstitious, you understand, and it'd take me a good four hours just to get rid of my tickets.

Sometimes, when business is slow, I have to let some of the tickets go cheap—if I didn't get rid of all the numbers, I could be accused of cheating.

When I'm running a lottery I have to keep shouting, and by the time I get home and get in bed, my chest and my throat are so sore I can hardly breathe. You've got to yell for all you're worth; if you don't the people indoors won't hear you, they won't come out on the balconies and buy. Sometimes I can't work—I've got absolutely no voice left.

I don't go out in damp weather. If I did, the rain'd ruin the stuff in my basket, and anyway there aren't enough people around. The women that offer a thousand-lira note as a prize and charge fifty lire for three tickets put up umbrellas and go right ahead as usual; they don't do very well, though; if they clear four or five hundred lire they're lucky.

Running a lottery in one of the big piazzas, let's say the Vuceria, is a very different kind of business. There may be one or two or more of us guys running a lottery in an impor-tant piazza; the prizes we have to give are much better be-cause the people are much more choosy, but then we make a much bigger profit. Here are some of the prizes I give:

A goat; two baskets of strawberries, when they're in season; four pounds of oranges, half a pound of sugar and two bot-tles of marsala; at Easter, a tremendous five-pound brick of ice cream; ten tender young chickens.

In fact, what I do, I offer as a prize anything that'll attract the people's fancy. Right before All Souls' Day I put up great big beautifully dressed dolls, toy cradles complete with baby dolls, kiddiecars, bicycles and tricycles that cost me thirteen thousand lire. Of course I sell the tickets for much more than usual, and I make more than usual.

The drawings take place every Saturday in the big piazzas

—four o'clock in the winter, four-thirty in the summer. Saturday morning we borrow the money we need for the next week's prizes from the moneylenders—two, five, seven, even ten thousand lire. We pay the whole bundle back, plus 10 percent interest, right on the dot Sunday. It's better that way. If we were to hang on to our loot, we'd blow it all very soon.

I've been running a lottery for nine years to support my wife and five kids. When I was a boy I used to watch lottery men at work, and two months before I got married—I had no job, I couldn't read or write—one of them hired me to carry the basket. He gave me five hundred lire and free meals. As soon as I'd learned all the tricks, I went out on my own.

In my line of business you got to be straight, you can't give people any reason to distrust you—if you do, you're through. You pull a fast one on them and it's all over. They'll never buy another ticket from you. It'll soon get around that you're crooked and you might as well pack up. A guy like me with a family to keep has to be as honest as the day . . .

AT THIS POINT A COUPLE OF YOUNG MEN WHO ALSO RUN LOTTERIES COME IN AND SHOW US HOW THEY WORK.

GIOVANNI: Right through August up to the first of November, we dress up in tails and top hats, clown around and do magic tricks in the street to attract customers. We make thimbles and cards vanish right before their eyes. We do a fire-swallowing act, too—we pour some gasoline on cotton wool, tie it to a stick and set it on fire; it looks pretty dangerous, but if you practice the trick enough, you hardly ever burn yourself. My buddy here and me, though, we've got out of practice—we spent a couple of months selling ices, so now we burn our months five or six times a day. When we've finished with the fire-swallowing bit, we do some more magic: we lay an empty bag or an empty can on the ground and—Presto Chango!—we find an egg in it. Then we start clowning around. Peppino, make like you bring out a pear; show it to me, and go into our act:

PEPPINO: "See this? It's the city of Rome!"

GIO (takes it): "That's not the city of Rome—that's a pear." (stuffs it in his mouth)

PEPPINO: "Hey, what do you think you're doing? Take that out of your mouth. You understand or don't you understand, you knucklebrain?"

GIO (takes it out): "Sure I understand."

PEPPINO: "The Vatican's in Rome—"

GIO (studies the pear): "Oh, ah! Yes, here's the dog!"

PEPPINO: "Then there's a cupola—"

GIO: "All right, a couple a' them. [These bits always get laughs, says Gio.]

PEPPINO: "I'll teach you a lesson, you louse!" (slaps Gio around) "Hey, you! Can you make the city of Rome disappear? I'll make a bet with you if you can make it disappear in three tries, I'll give you a thousand lire."

GIO: "It's a deal." (turns around three times, and puts the pear in his left armpit)

PEPPINO: "You ever been in the army?"

GIO: "Course I've been in the army."

PEPPINO: " 'Shun! Did you ever see Mussolini?"

GIO (at attention): "Sure I saw Mussolini."

PEPPINO: "Give the Fascist salute, then. No, no—with your *left* arm—"

GIO: "I can't raise my left arm."

PEPPINO: "Why not?"

GIO: "Why not? Because I was wounded in the left arm at the battle of Pipirito,[1] and I can't lift it up—" (Peppino grabs hold of him, makes him raise his left arm, then grabs the pear!)

PEPPINO (triumphant): "Aha, didn't I say you couldn't make

---

[1] Pipirito—this is a mocking reference to the interrogations at the *carabinieri* barracks in the Via Pipporetto, distorted to incorporate a pun on *pi-pi*. *Translator's note.*

the city of Rome vanish? (Peppino orders him to turn around three more times. After he's turned around, he gets the pear between his legs.) "Ever been in the army?"

GIO: "Course I've been in the army."

PEPPINO: "At ease!" (Gio sits down.) "I said 'At ease!' Forward march!"

GIO (gets up): "Give me something to munch, then—"

PEPPINO: "Idiot! I said 'march,' not 'munch'!"

GIO (aside): "Idiot yourself!"

PEPPINO (furious): "What did you say?"

GIO: "I said you were a good captain." (Peppino gives him a kick in the pants, and the pear rolls out from between his legs.)

PEPPINO: "You've got just one more chance to show me you can make the city of Rome disappear!" (This time Gio orders Peppino to turn around three times, and as soon as he's facing away, Gio starts to eat the pear.)

PEPPINO: "Are you ready?"

GIO (with his mouth full): "Nyum-nyum-nyum!"

PEPPINO: "Are you ready? . . . I said are you ready?"

GIO (after several more nyum-nyums): "Ready!"

PEPPINO (turns): "Did you read the paper today, Vanni? Two hundred people have been poisoned in Rome . . . what did you do with the city of Rome? Did you give it to one of those kids?"

GIO: "No-o-o! I—I ate it—oo-oooh! I'm poisoned! O-oooh, look at me, I'm dying!"

GIOVANNI AND PEPPINO HAVE FINISHED THEIR ACT; GIOVANNI NOW FINISHES THE STORY.

Then I make horrible faces and throw myself down and roll on the ground, and Peppino says: "Come on, get up, there's nothing the matter with you!" He points his finger at a nearby bench where we've laid out our marzipan fruits. "Vanni we've got to give these marzipan fruits away," he says. "Come on, everybody!" But when the people push forward, I say: "No, no, you've got it all wrong! Buy a ticket—ten lire for four different numbers! We'll give four of these delicious fruits to the lucky winner! Only ten lire for four chances!"

Then we start selling the tickets. We collect about a hundred and eighty lire; the four marzipan fruits cost us a hundred and forty, so we clear forty lire.

We change our show every week. Peppino and me squat on our haunches and think up new tricks that'll make the crowd laugh.

When it's getting towards All Souls' Day I offer a special prize of cigarettes, charcoal, wax matches, salt, oil and what we call St. Martin's cookies—the whole business goes to the winner—a real bargain! For a week or so before All Souls' Day I run the lottery on my own, and Peppino goes around selling candy.

I'm twenty-two, and I've got one little boy. I've been in the lottery line off and on for seven years. In the summer I run a lotto game sometimes, or work as a waiter at Mondello. I can't read or write, but I've taught myself to speak in a really fancy style just by listening to the high-class types that spend their holidays at Mondello . . .

PEPPINO COMMENTS ON HIS CIRCUMSTANCES: I'm twenty-four, and I've got two kids: one's a year and a half, the other's just four months. When I go home at night my throat and my chest ache from all the yelling I've done. The police keep after us; every time they catch us they fine us a thousand lire, and if we don't pay them pronto, they shove us in the paddy wagon.

Once they sent me a notice that I was fined a thousand lire, but I didn't have the cash so I let it ride. They kept raising it till it got to forty-five hundred. So I went to the police station and said I'd pay it off at the rate of a thousand lire every two weeks. They asked for a thousand right then and there, but I got them to agree to five hundred. It was rotten weather and I couldn't work, so I wasn't able to pay the next installment or the next one, or the one after that. We'd have starved if it hadn't been for my uncle. He works on the railroad; he gave us the money to live on, and he helped my old man, too. He sells bread and pigs' feet at Porta Carbone. The fine mounted higher and higher, and when it got to seventy-five hundred lire, the *migni*, the cops—sometimes we call them *sbirri* or *spiuni*—came to the house. My wife opened the door and told them I'd gone away—if they'd known I was there, they'd've arrested me, and for every day they kept me in the clink I'd've had to pay five hundred lire.

Well, in the end, I had to go to a loan shark and borrow ten thousand lire. He took my ice-cream bike as security and made me sign a paper to say I agreed to pay him back thirteen thousand lire.

a black-market cigarette seller

I'm one of eleven children. I went to school but never got past the first grade; I was in it three years running. My father was a longshoreman; he draws a pension of sixteen thousand lire every six months, but although he's sixty-seven now, he still works as a laborer.

I was just ten when I started working on the docks. I hoped one day when my father was too old I'd get his job, and I kept going till I was drafted. I used to unload coal, but I wasn't on the regular payroll. One of the men hired me to do his job for him; he split his pay envelope with me, but kept all the family-allowance money for himself. While I was taking his place he was selling cigarettes on the black market.

Work was scarce on the docks, though, so finally I borrowed twenty thousand lire and went into the cigarette game myself. I had to pay six thousand lire interest on the loan every six months.

This was in 1952. I'd been selling cigarettes only two days

when the cops nabbed me and took all my stock, on top of which they fined me thirty thousand lire. After that things went from bad to worse for me. My wife got sick; I didn't have the money to pay for the treatment she needed, and I felt very ashamed of myself. I thought about joining the Foreign Legion. A friend of mine was a legionnaire for five years. In Palermo, young guys who have a record and can't find a job sell themselves to the Legion—that's right, I mean sell. At the end of five years, you see, they become French nationals and then they can find better work.

My family, though, couldn't stand the idea of me joining the Legion. My father pawned his pension book for ten thousand lire and set me up as a fig seller.

But the cops were always after me; I don't know how many fines I had to pay. One day, when they came after me for another five hundred lire, my blood boiled; I heaved the scales at the cops, and before they could grab me I got away.

Well, I went back to the cigarette racket. I got mine from a guy who trusted me and let me have them wholesale. There are thousands of cigarette sellers, from kids of ten to men of forty, in Palermo—too many to count. In one bar alone there were eight of us young guys just past teen-age selling black-market cigarettes.

We get our supplies from the wholesalers. Some of us go around to customers' houses, some have regular spots outside the different government offices, the *Cassa Malattia* and so on where lots of people work and business is good. We go in the banks where the clerks and tellers know us and get us to bring them their favorite brands. We sell in hotels and restaurants, too, but when the cops arrest one of us, and it looks like they're going to crack down, we lie low for a while and only deal with our customers in their own homes.

The cases of cigarettes are brought into Palermo on fishing boats, loaded onto trucks, and delivered to the wholesalers. The customs police know all about these wholesalers, but they hardly ever crack down on them; they call on them all right, but only because they're sure of getting a little graft. But us with our ten or twenty packs—they grab us whenever they feel like it and take our stock.

Wholesalers have got it easy. They're rolling in dough.

They don't even bother to cover up what they're doing by pretending they're in some legitimate business. One day, for instance, I went to see one of them, and there, right in his house, was a police sergeant—I knew him all right even though he wasn't in uniform. Well, the wholesaler gave him twenty-five packs of Swiss cigarettes—he could afford it seeing he had more than two million lire worth of goods in the house! I've gone right into the police stations and sold cigarettes to the cops myself.

There are at least a hundred wholesalers in Palermo. The trucks are loaded at night and the cases are hidden under layers of tomatoes or fodder or straw. A lookout goes ahead on a Lambretta or in a car to make sure the coast's clear, and as soon as the trucks get in they're unloaded at top speed—of course, the whole neighborhood knows what's going on. From time to time, for safety's sake, the drivers deliver the stuff at a different place.

Some wholesalers can read and write, some can't; hardly any of them have had more than three or four years of school. It may surprise you to hear, though, that there are quite a lot of lawyers in the cigarette racket, and a damn good living they make out of it too. Their wives are decked out in the latest styles and covered with jewelry; they've got necklaces worth thirty or forty thousand lire, the kind that only ladies in high society used to wear. They've all got two houses, one that the Council knows about that's supposed to be their regular address, and one that's not on the books. The first one has hardly anything in it—a bed, a couple of chairs, a table, and that's all—but the other one is furnished real fancy and is full of every kind of luxury you can imagine.

Hundreds of cases of Swiss and American cigarettes are landed here and then sent on to Naples and Rome. Palermo's the ideal spot to land them. Everybody in the racket knows the score, and the only ones that get pinched are the ones that haven't paid off the police.

The cases are brought in on Spanish ships. In Rome and Naples they bring a higher price than they do here. Everything is c.o.d.

The Kalsa's the home base of the racket, but it's carried on in every section. A lot of us are skilled workmen; it's being unemployed or as good as unemployed that drives us into this game. You wouldn't catch me doing it if I was offered a regular job. "Get lost!" I'd say to the lousy cigarettes.

The competition's really awful. A wholesaler who's not making as much dough as another wholesaler'll turn him in, or else he'll cut his prices. He keeps on selling at a loss till he's forced the other guy out of business—then he's top dog.

When I first went out selling cigarettes, I felt guilty as hell. I'm young and healthy and able to work. It's no kind of job for a man. But I had to buy bread for my kids, so I forced myself to do it; I didn't have any choice.

I'll never forget my first day. I had a couple of packs in my pocket, and I walked along, singing out: "Cigarettes, cigarettes—who wants American cigarettes?" A man came up to me and said: "Give me twenty." I don't know why but I thought he was a cop in plain clothes, so I said: "I'm not selling cigarettes." "What made you say you were, then?" he asked me in a surprised voice. I could see he was okay, so I fished out a pack. "I can let you have this one—it's the only one I've got," I said. Well, he bought it, and I went home with three hundred lire. I've been a cigarette seller ever since. I don't dare work a regular spot, though; I have to keep walking so the cops won't pick me up and take away my seaman's ticket—my name's down on the fishing-fleet register, but I've never had a call.

Some cigarette sellers get hit with big fines; they get a summons, and if they can't pay they're sent to the can. It's the only way I can buy food for my family, but I'm scared stiff all the time I'm out. Six times I've had a summons—I've had to find the cash to pay six fines. The cops came up on me from behind once and took me by surprise; they frisked me, found ten packs or so on me and grabbed them all.

I keep walking to avoid getting caught. What makes it tough is that some guys can sell cheaper than I can; they save by buying a whole case at a time from the wholesaler, and even though they only charge a hundred and forty lire a pack, their profit is much bigger than mine. I can't afford to buy more than ten or twenty packs at a time, and I have to ask a hundred and fifty. A lot of us sell flints and lighters too. Sometimes the customs police look the other way; they know we've got to live. Lots of the cops and the *carabinieri* don't interfere with us—they buy from us. Occasionally, though, the customs men dress up in rags, the word goes around, and they move in on us. Of course, some of us get away. The kids who sell cigarettes give all the money they make to their mothers; they only do it to help out at home.

There's a profit of twenty lire on every pack we sell, and we make from five to eight hundred lire a day. In a good spot it's possible to clear as much as fifteen hundred lire. We sell more Swiss cigarettes than American because they're scarcer; the duty on them's so high that cigarette stores never order a big stock.

The wholesalers make the most, of course, but they also risk the most; if the revenue agents got wise to them, bang! would go their stock, their dough, their trucks and their cars. But most of the wholesalers fix things with the tax collectors.

Yesterday a wholesaler was bumped off in Piazza Marina. He just got back from Naples, where he cleaned up, and because he wouldn't split with the guys who were in the deal with him, they shot him dead, snatched one of his bags and beat it; in the other bag the cops found over a million lire and six gold bracelets.

A little while ago some cigarette sellers settled an argument in the Via Roma; it was some mess.

The cases are brought ashore by fishing boats and other small boats. So many cases are landed that even if a whole boatload of cases is grabbed at sea, the price doesn't go up. As I already told you, there are thousands of us in this racket; as long as there's no work men'll be forced to make a living by dealing in black-market stuff. Even if the Cangeloso jail was a hundred times bigger than it is, there still wouldn't be anywhere near enough customs men to stop it.

People buy Swiss and American cigarettes from us because they're better and cheaper than those in the stores. Half the smokers in Palermo buy black-market stuff from us not only because it costs less, but also because they know it does us some good. They can't see any sense in throwing money away on the tax which goes to the government.

the Kalsa

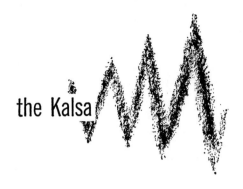

The Kalsa is the section which stretches from Via Lincoln to Via Alloro right down to the sea, and is intersected by Via della Vetriera, Piazza S. Euno (most of the organ grinders live near here), Piazzo dello Spasimo, and Via del Pallone. Bordering on the Kalsa and forming part of it is the "Scoparia," with some three hundred and fifty houses. There are some seventeen hundred and fifty houses in the Kalsa itself, and apart from a few small dwellings in fair condition, there is nothing to choose between them; all are in the same sordid state, both inside and out.

Here, the hundred and fifteen families studied, numbering eight hundred and fourteen persons, live in a hundred rooms (plus thirty-five cubbyholes measuring four feet by five). The average number of persons to a room, then, is 8.14. The homes of all these families happen to be one-room homes. Seventeen people live in one of them. In three, fourteen live; in six, thirteen, etc. This crowding is extreme.

At night, mattresses are laid on the floors, all floor space in some rooms being completely taken up by mattresses. There are two hundred and fifty-five places, so that the average number of persons to a place is 3.19.

Nearly all the rooms have electric light, but only eighteen have water taps. There isn't one proper toilet; that is, a toilet that is partitioned off and can be flushed. Only eleven rooms are in decent repair. Seventy-three have floors of broken tile; the remaining floors are fairly good, though.

Among the children from three through six years old, twenty-six go to kindergarten, forty-four do not. On the average, the six hundred and sixteen persons over six years old have finished only a third of the second grade. Thirteen married couples are literate.

As for the occupations of the heads-of-family, thirty-eight are fishermen, seven are dock workers (they unload coal), six are laborers, and five are porters in the fish market. The fishermen and most of the others just mentioned work only about six months in the year. Only four heads-of-family have regular work. One of these four is a mailman, one is a streetcleaner, one is a chauffeur, and one is a doorkeeper. Seventeen families are on relief. One completely destitute family is not on relief. ("We have no soldi to buy the relief book.") Over a quarter of the men have been in prison, some for years.

As for the women, ten are domestic servants, one is an embroideress, one is a post-office clerk, and one is a seller of rolls. The rest stay at home. ("It isn't the custom for us women to go out to work . . .")

Hardly any of the youngsters have a trade. They earn a living by dealing in black-market goods, chiefly cigarettes and saccharine.

There are a hundred and five cases of t.b. (about thirteen percent), forty-two of typhus (about five percent) and seven cases of meningitis (approaching one percent).

a fisherman

Since we always fish in the same water, it's becoming harder and harder for us to make a living. We destroy the roe with our dragnets, and the men who go out after sardines and anchovies do almost as much harm by catching the small fry. We're ruining the breeding grounds and ourselves in the bargain.

There's a three-mile limit, but we don't bother about it; sometimes we don't go out more than a hundred yards from shore. The Fishery Board doesn't give a damn. We draw the family-allowance money, but we have our food on the ship. By saving that much we can just manage. It's tough, though, if you've got a kid that's sick—one of mine is, something to do with his glands.

The fish are scarce, so nearly all the fishing boats and lots of smaller boats go in for landing black-market cigarettes. They head for the open sea, about a hundred miles from Palermo, and wait for the Spanish ships. The wholesalers fix everything with the owners of the fishing boats; if there are a thousand cases, one boat a day goes out to bring back a load; every boat can carry from two hundred to two hundred and fifty cases, so it takes from four to five days to land the whole works. We could carry as many as five hundred cases if we could count on a clear run, but we can't. A case weighs over twenty-eight pounds, and costs the wholesaler forty thousand lire cash that he pays aboard the Spanish ship. By the time it's landed and loaded onto the truck, the price is up to fifty thousand lire, but as he sells a case for anywhere from sixty to seventy-five thousand lire, he does okay. Each case holds five hundred packs of cigarettes. I figure that fifty cases are smoked every day of the week in Palermo. Also, every day thousands of black-market cigarettes are sent to Catania, Rome, and other cities—it'll give you some idea of the amount when I tell you that two hundred and fifty cases are sent from here to Naples alone.

We fishermen pray that the goods won't be grabbed when we get them ashore; if that happens we're not paid. But when everything goes okay, we get three thousand lire for every case, so if we bring in two hundred cases there's six hundred thousand lire to divide among us. The owner of the boat gives us thirty-five thousand lire for every million he clears. We can figure on roughly twenty thousand lire a run, and we may make a couple of runs a month.

We start out by taking on the cases from the Spanish ship around noon in order to get them ashore by eight o'clock. As soon as we're loaded up we send a message to our lookout on the coast so that the owner of the boat'll know we've got a good "catch." Then we stand by the radio waiting for him to send a message back to us. A guy who drives back and forth along the coast between Santa Lucia and Foro Italia keeps him informed about the movements of the customs fleet, and the minute the coast lookout knows whether it's putting out or not, he signals to us in code: "Calling fishing boat X. Can you hear me, fishing boat X? I have a message for you: There's hardly anyone in the piazza. I repeat: There's hardly anyone in the piazza. Over." In other words, it's safe for us to proceed. If the message we get is: "The new net's ready," or "The naphtha's been delivered," we know that the customs fleet's on the move and we reverse the engine and head straight back for the Spanish ship.

If only there was enough work for us and we could make an honest living, we wouldn't be risking our necks in this racket, believe me. If we don't stop right away when the customs fleet hails us, they open fire on us while we're dumping the cases overboard. If we're arrested and put in jail, we never get hired again.

When we're fishing inside the three-mile limit in the Gulf of Castellammare off Trappeto, we're warned by radio if the Fishery Board boats are out. When they do catch us, though, they let us off with a very small fine, and it doesn't worry us much.

We land the stuff at certain deserted spots on the coast where there aren't any houses; we put out all our lights, lower a small boat, load it with as many cases as it will hold, and row ashore in the pitch dark. We know these places so well that we don't need to see. When you're home, if you want a glass you can lay your hands on it without turning the light on, right? After we unload all the cases, they're loaded onto the trucks—a truck can carry a hundred cases—and they're hidden under a layer of tomatoes or some green vegetables. A lookout in a car or on a motor bike goes ahead to make sure the road's clear, and then the trucks start off, with other cars and motor bikes right behind them. There are thirty engine-powered fishing boats in Palermo, and there can't be more than two of them that haven't made these runs sometime or other. Fifteen make regular runs. There are only five or six of us aboard a boat that's smuggling in cigarettes, but eighteen of us are used for the searchlight fishing trips in Tunisia. I've been in this racket for the past two years. Occasionally we manage to bring ashore four hundred cases in a single run, and when we do, we get paid in cash as soon as they're on shore.

The Palermo customs fleet has eight cutters and one speed-boat good for thirty knots.

There are thousands of cases of cigarettes in Palermo, and more and more of them arrive every day. There's no end to them . . .

an organ grinder

I was born in Favara in the province of Agrigento. My mother died when I was two, and when I was five, my father, who was a tailor by trade, married again, and we moved to Palermo. I didn't hit it off with my stepmother, so I ran away and wandered all over the place. After a while, though, I gave up, came home, and went to school. I got as far as the fifth grade, then I ran away again, and made out on my own. When I was thirteen I had my first taste of prison; they kept me inside till I was seventeen. When they turned me loose I met some old buddies of mine, and it was through them I started grinding a barrel organ. But when my father heard what I was doing he said I was a disgrace to him; he made me stop and come home. But I couldn't get along with my stepmother, so a little later I cleared out for good. That's when I first got to know what it's like to be without a soldo, to have a belly rattling from hunger, and get eaten alive with fleas and lice. I couldn't find anything better, so I took up organ grinding again, but I hardly made anything; I was always half-starved. Then I was drafted, and I stayed in the service eleven years.

I got a little money when I got out, and I started to sell black-market cigarettes. At the end of two months I was caught and put in the jug for thirteen days. My stock was gone; I had no more dough; I was half out of my mind. I went back to organ grinding, and for eight weeks I tramped from village to village trying to make a little here, a little there. I was cold and hungry, and whenever I hit a village where organ grinders weren't allowed to play, I'd almost go down on my knees to the cops as if they were saints. "If you don't let me play, I'll starve," I'd say, but all I ever got was: "That's your business. Get yourself a decent job."

Well, I got so fed up that I sent the barrel organ back to Palermo—lucky for me it only cost seven hundred lire. Then, in Palermo, I met a young dame who had five kids, fell in love with her and asked her to marry me. "You don't have a soldo, we'd all starve," she said. "I'll make a living organ grinding and singing," I said. "You'll see." I had a good voice in those days, you know; it's nothing now. Well, I didn't do so bad, and we got married.

Things went all right for a while, and then the *signori* on the Council, who call the shots in Palermo, stopped us from playing in the city and took away our organs. There were about a hundred of us—we went with our families to the Town Hall to see the councilor. We were hungry; we had no dough to buy food, but when we asked him to give us back our organs, he refused.

"We can't have you playing in the streets and annoying people," he said.

"Look," we said, "we all hold permits as street musicians. We've got as much right to work as you have; if you stop us from working, we'll all die of starvation. Either let us go on grinding our organs or find us jobs."

"Come back and see me in three days," he said.

Well, we got no satisfaction. Months went by and nothing happened. With all those mouths to feed, I was desperate—I don't know how I kept from stealing—I felt like doing it enough times, believe me. As soon as it was dark I tramped all over the place looking for cigarette butts—I was too ashamed to hunt for them while it was light—and this way I managed to make four hundred lire a day. Four hundred a day—I had a wife and five kids to keep, and for two solid months that was all I had coming in.

We were starving, us organ grinders and our families, and we couldn't stand it any longer. We all went to the mayor, but he refused to see us, absolutely refused.

Our only hope was Councilor X. We prayed to him for help like he was all the saints rolled into one, but when we could see that he wasn't going to do anything, we said: "Look, Signor Councilor, you wouldn't be where you are now if we didn't all vote for you. Is this the way to treat us?" I nearly lost my temper. "You moved up a notch; you're all the same once you're promoted," I burst out. "Have you forgotten what you promised us? You promised us that if you were elected, you'd give us all new barrel organs, and now you won't even let us play our old ones!" Then he had a fit. "Granted you did vote for me, what do you expect me to do?" he shouted. "I can't go against my superiors, and that's that!" But three months later, when we'd all paid a fine of three thousand lire, they gave us back our barrel organs. Mine's one of the best. It plays first-class music and songs. I love them, and the rich people give me money because they enjoy hearing them.

By the time I got my barrel organ back I was sixty thousand lire in debt. I lived on nothing but bread and onions, and little by little I managed to pay back all the money I owed. But I hardly had my organ back four months when it was grabbed again. I was forced to pawn all our linen; I got four thousand lire on it, bought some fruit wholesale, and started peddling it in the streets.

Three days later the police came with the patrol wagon and took all my stock. I began to cry like a baby. "If you take it away, I'm done for," I said. "My wife and kids'll starve— For the love of Christ . . ." But I might just as well not have said a word; they took no notice of me and went off with everything. I was desperate. I borrowed three thousand lire from a neighbor and started all over again—this time I sold candy and pastry. I made about two hundred and fifty or three hundred lire a day.

But it wasn't nearly enough, so I swallowed my pride and went to see my old man. I begged him to help me, but no—he was through with me. Just at this time my grandmother died and left me three hundred thousand lire. After I paid off all my debts I had sixty thousand. I bought a second-hand Lambretta and went from village to village, selling earrings, needles and pins, socks, combs, necklaces. It was a real rough business though, and if I cleared a few lire I felt lucky. Sometimes I'd come home soaked to the skin without selling one single thing, and my wife would give it to me. "Why don't you do some work instead of riding around on your Lambretta?" she'd shout.

I changed my line of goods, and instead of the fancy stuff I sold weather forecasts, fortunetelling books, calendars, and sheet music. Things went a little bit better until one day I had an accident—I fell off my bike, fractured my ankle, and had to spend three months in bed. We were starving again and I had to keep going to this moneylender or that; I borrowed ten thousand lire, twenty thousand lire, and naturally had to pay interest on every loan.

But I didn't even think about that; I couldn't think of anything but my kids. It nearly broke my heart to see them shivering from the cold, and to hear them crying from hunger —poor kids, all they had to eat was a mouthful of pasta before they went to bed. Even when I got up, I couldn't work; I could only hop around on one foot. I don't know what we would've done if it hadn't been for my parrot—I rented him to a kid who told fortunes. I had bought the parrot and the cage for four thousand lire. There's only one thing an organ grinder can do when his organ's taken away from him and that's buy a parrot or a monkey. A monkey costs anything from thirty to fifty thousand lire, but you buy it on time. Of course, you pay more in the end because the interest's added on. You'd think we'd be allowed to earn a living with a parrot or a monkey, wouldn't you? But no, the cops won't let us alone. The day before yesterday they took my buddy's parrot. Sometimes they fine us five hundred lire. They also grabbed the monkey that belonged to another one of my buddies. If you don't pay the fine, you go to jail. A year ago monkeys were a novelty and the guys who had them did real good; lots of people had never even seen a monkey before, and crowds used to gather around. The parrot earns his keep, too. "Pick out a slip for me, Ciccio," somebody'll say to him, and the parrot picks one with his beak. It may be a horoscope or a football pool. A parrot that's been tamed and trained costs a lot; you can buy a cheaper one, though, and tame it yourself.

Some of my friends sell sheet music and sing in the streets through an amplifier, but this is against the law too. They get fines that come to thirty-six thousand lire a year, and when they're paid up, they can go sing in the poor neighborhoods; in the center of Palermo, Via Libertà, Via Maqueda, Ruggero-Settimo, it's strictly forbidden. Neapolitan songs are the most popular; my barrel organ plays seven Neapolitan songs and three Italian songs best, but Neapolitan songs have much more feeling and people like us that live in the poor sections would rather listen to them.

Organ grinders make the most money on Sundays and feast days. On ordinary weekdays we get very little, and if it rains we don't take in a soldo.

Well, to go back to my story. We couldn't get along without our barrel organs, so we went back to this Councilor X and begged him to let us have them.

"All right," he said, "but on one condition. You're not to

play them in the center of the city. It simply won't do; it's disgraceful, and it gives the tourists a very bad impression of Palermo."

"The tourists like our barrel organs because it reminds them of the old days," we said. "They stop and take our pictures, and even though we never ask them for money, they give us fifty or a hundred lire."

"That's just what we object to," he said. "It's another form of begging."

"Then why do the police call us street musicians and make us pay five thousand lire a year for a license?" we asked him. "Every time we've been hauled up before the judge he's said right out that grinding an organ is no offense. Is Palermo such a great city, the greatest in Italy? Go and see for yourself—in all the big cities there are organ grinders and nobody ever interferes with them. It's only here in Palermo you treat us so lousy. If you stop us from playing, how are we supposed to feed our families? Get it straight, you'll drive us to stealing."

At last he agreed to give us our barrel organs back when we paid a fine of two thousand lire, but he stuck to his condition: we could only grind on the outskirts of the city. We yelled: "Who are we going to play to, the olive trees?" "There's nobody around there in the winter." "It costs us five hundred lire a day to rent our organs, and on top of that we have to buy the songs we sing." "I give a kid five hundred lire a day to turn the handle—maybe you think a barrel organ runs on a motor—well, it don't. You have to keep turning!" "If you won't let us play in the center of the city, a lot of good our barrel organs'll do us; we'll be just as hungry with them as we are without them!"

But it was no use: he made us sign a paper saying we could only play in the outlying streets. I hardly earned a soldo, and with us starving and one of my kids sick and my wife pregnant I went right into Palermo and played in the places where I could make the most money. I took one of my boys with me—I wish I could send him to school where he could learn a trade, but I can't do it; I can't get along without him. Well, I made enough to pay a doctor, and my kid began to get better—she's okay now, and my wife's had the baby, a girl. But last Sunday a week ago they took my organ away again for the third time. I'm right back where I started, and who's going to pay the rent? Seven thousand lire a month—that's what they stick me for this crummy hole which is all we've got for a home—me and my wife, and all the kids . . .

a mother's story: All Souls' Day

I'm thirty-five and I've got five children. My husband was born in 1913; he gets work off and on as a laborer. I never went to school. None of my kids have ever been to school—not one of them can read or write. The oldest is sixteen; the baby's nineteen months. None of them have jobs; they spend all their time in the street. You can imagine the sort of things they learn there . . . See that little girl? The other day she asked her mother where she was going. "I'm going to the brothel," her mother said straight out. All the kids use filthy words: "You whore! You bastard! You shit!" they yell at each other. Sometimes they play mothers and fathers and they come out with the things husbands and wives shout at each other when they're having a fight: "You bitch! You're sore as hell because you're itching for it. Your old man don't satisfy you, eh?" Then they fool around with each other . . . what else can you expect?

I wish I could buy my kids some new shoes—they're all barefoot—I wish I could buy them a few decent clothes instead of the rags they've got on. I'd like to buy toy cars and dolls for the younger ones. I'd like to buy them one of those baskets filled with figs, and nuts, and chestnuts, and a sugar doll—it's not a real All Souls' Day basket without a sugar doll.

All Souls' Day is the only day in the year when all kids get presents. On All Souls' Eve we make them go to bed at seven, but they're so excited they won't settle down. "If you don't shut your eyes and go to sleep," we say, "you know what'll happen—instead of bringing you presents, the dead'll come and scratch your feet!" We make believe to the children that it's the dead that bring them presents—the dead belonging to the family, I mean; Daddy, maybe, or Grandma, Grandpa, Uncle. We tell them that in the night they come in through the keyhole, the window, the cracks in the wall. When anybody dies, the kids are sure that they'll come back on All Souls' Night to bring them a present.

Well, finally the kids quiet down, pull the blankets over their heads and go to sleep. Then the mothers go out, and if we've got the money buy presents for them at the All Souls' Fair. At midnight we fix up the baskets. If one of the kids should wake up and call out: "I want a drink of water," or "I want to pipi," we say: "Get back in bed and go to sleep. You know what'll happen if you don't. The dead'll come and scratch the soles of your feet with the cheese grater!" Sometimes, if one of them is moving around, we sneak up and scratch his feet. When I was little, I was so scared the dead'd scratch *my* feet I used to hide the cheese grater in the bed and lie on top of it. Our mothers told us so much about the toys the dead'd bring us that we called the presents we got "the dead ones."

It's All Souls' Eve now and I don't have any money. When the kids don't find any presents in the morning, they'll burst out crying. They'll see the other kids playing with the toys the dead brought them: cars, punchinellos, drums, swords, pistols, candy dolls. The mothers go around and visit each other to see what the kids got; when my neighbor comes over to see me, I won't have anything to show.

Sometimes we put the presents on the table, sometimes we hide them under the bed. "I've got a trumpet!" one kid'll yell; he blows on it as hard as he can and runs out to play with the other kids. Some of the boys and girls get dolls with beautiful dresses and bicycles and rocking horses, and candy dolls —Paladins—every color in the rainbow they are—and I don't know what else. "Look what the dead brought us!" they shout, and the poor little kids who haven't got any presents burst out crying. "Beat it. You haven't any toys and you're not going to play with ours!" the other kids say, and it makes the mothers who haven't been able to buy anything feel awful. Maybe a few of the lucky ones'll let them share their toys, but most of the time they chase them away. The older kids play a game with stones; whoever throws the farthest is the winner, and the prize is a candy doll.

There's All Souls' Day for the rich and All Souls' Day for the poor. For the ones like me that don't have a soldo there aren't any living and there aren't any dead. My kids'll cry something awful because they got no presents, and then I'll slap them. Like I did today. My neighbor bought her little boy a pair of shoes, and he came around a few minutes ago to show them off. "Look at my new shoes. Daddy gave Mommy the money to buy them for me," he said. "Why didn't your Mommy buy you new shoes?" My next to the youngest started to whine. "Why can't I have some new shoes, Mommy?" he asked me. "Because I haven't got any money," I said, and he burst into tears. He went on and on till I lost my temper and smacked him. I wish I hadn't; it makes me feel terrible. That's him out in the street . . .

The six-year-old who's just been smacked, red with rage, yells at his mother: "Go to hell! Go to hell the whole lousy bunch of you!"

"by the mighty archangels Gabriel and Michael and the great prophet Samuel..."

When there was a thunderstorm, old people living in the country used to ring a bell that had been blessed by the priest to make it go away. Some of them wouldn't treat their vines with sulphur; they believed it would make God angry with them. "He sends the blight; it wouldn't be right to go against His will," they said. When Lent came, people who were fond of their food paid a tax to the Church—the *bulla*, it's called —which gave them a dispensation from fasting and allowed them to eat as much meat and as many eggs as they wanted.

I made my living playing cards. For two months of the year I'd go to private card parties to play *zicchinetta*.[1] I always won. I was taken to these parties by different pals of mine, and I split my winnings with them. My own share I gave to my mother. I began playing cards when I was twelve. Sometimes I played in the city; sometimes I'd go into the country and play in different villages; I played in the part of Palermo where the slaughterhouses are, in all the shady dives, and in the poorest sections, where the ragpickers and the junkmen hang out. As hard as they tried, none of the guys I played with could ever manage to beat me; they never could spot what I was up to. The deck wasn't marked—it was the quickness of my hand that fooled the eye! I could fix the cards any way I wanted. I creased the corners of some of them very slightly; this way I made sure of getting the ones I wanted. When I shuffled, for instance, I'd place four cards on the top; I only had to feel them to make sure that the fourth card, which would come to me, was the winner.

Sometimes there'd be as many as fifteen or eighteen of us playing. It didn't matter which card they bet on, I always won. They kept hoping to get back their losses, and the game would go on till I cleaned them out.

Zicchinetta used to be very popular. They played it in every town and village in Sicily. It was just as popular outside Sicily too. I've played it in Rome, Reggio Calabria, Naples, Milan, Turin, Trieste, Venice, Florence, Pescara, Chieti, Aquila, Bari, Lecce, Brindisi. But I got known as a cardsharp—people won't play with me any more.

When I used to go to a private card party, the friend that had brought me always introduced me as a relative of his, a nephew or a cousin. *Zicchinetta's* a gambling game, so it can't be played in the open. There've been times, though,

---

[1] *Zicchinetta* is much like poker. It is played with Sicilian cards, which differ slightly from the ordinary deck. *Translator's note.*

when I've seen *carabinieri*, even sergeants and corporals, sit down to a game.

Players, after they kept on losing, would wind up getting sore. "You put that card on top of the deck," they'd shout, or "I saw you put that one on the bottom." They were sure I was cheating, but they kept on playing just the same, and every time I won they'd bang their fists on the table and accuse me of rigging the cards. Trouble was they couldn't see how I *could* be cheating them. "It's not like we were playing with his deck," they'd say. "The cards aren't marked, and besides, they're shuffled every time." They just couldn't figure out how I always dealt myself the winning hand.

Before the war, we usually played in the evenings, and I always ended up two or three thousand lire to the good. I kept half for myself, and split the rest among my pals—there might be sometimes as many as five of them—who got in the game. As I did the fixing we'd arrange it in advance that I was to have the biggest share. Sometimes we'd play *scopa,* and I'd make sure that I won at that, too.

Every once in a while I'd be invited to play baccarat at one of the high-class clubs.

Sometimes I'd get a shock. I'd see sharps I knew playing with marked cards and actually cheating one another. Talk about your diamond cut diamond! One night one of them asked me to play. I knew they meant to clean me—they thought they'd make damn sure of winning. But instead of them cleaning me, I cleaned them. They couldn't understand it, seeing how they marked the cards. "You're an *operabolica!*" they said. "An *operabolica*—what's that?" I said. "The devil's master!" they said. "You beat us at our own game—how the hell did you do it? Come have something to eat with us and tell us your secret." Well, I studied quite a lot of magic (I bought a book once on magic by a sixteenth-century writer Rudilio Benincasa), so I told them I had a good-luck charm that made me a sure winner. They pricked up their ears.

"A charm—what kind of charm?" they asked me.

"It's a piece of pure parchment with the movements of the planets and all the phases of the moon on it," I said. "If you keep it in your pocket, you can't lose."

Naturally, they all wanted to have one.

"I can get them for you, but they'll cost you fifteen thousand lire apiece," I said. "Very valuable ingredients go into them: powdered coral, powdered amber, and the dust from St. Rita's bones. You add a little myrrh and incense to them, and at midnight you set the mixture on fire. While it's blazing you say: 'By the mighty archangels Gabriel and Michael and the great prophet Samuel . . .' and then you repeat the spell. It brings you luck in love and in business, as well as cards. It also protects you against accidents and the evil eye."

So they gave me fifteen thousand lire each for a good-luck piece. That was a long time ago, though, before the war.

Another unusual thing happened after the war. I was with some friends of mine in Rome and some armed bandits held us up and took all our money. "Wait a minute," I said to one of them, "give me back my money; you must know where the gambling dens are in Rome. Take me to them, and I'll show you how to make plenty of cash without having to use a gun." They saw I was a hep guy, so they agreed. They told me where to go, and I shared my winnings with them. They learned from me how to make a lot of dough the easy way without using violence. You might say I showed them a better way of life.

I played *zicchinetta* for two months of the year—from the beginning of December to the end of January. Wherever I played I made a name for myself. There wasn't so much gambling during the rest of the year, and I stayed home and worked as a stonemason.

I had a little taste of school and got as far as the second grade, but I was too much for the teachers, so they kicked me out.

When I was fifteen, I had my first broad. It gave me a real craving for tail, so to satisfy it I started lifting dough from my mother. She had a little store and sold ice-cream cones and toys. We lived next to a real low section that was crawling with hustlers, and there was a private cat-house—I couldn't go to the licensed houses because I was under age—so I went there and slept with the same girl five times. Then I began to feel lousy; whenever I went to piss I got this awful burning pain. I told some guys who were older than me about it. "The bitch gave you the clap," they said. I went to the hospital; the doctor wanted me to stay there so his students could study my case; he said he'd pay me for every day I spent in the ward, but I refused; I didn't want my mother to know what was wrong with me. He told me to wash myself and gave me some stuff that looked exactly like wine when it was dissolved in water. I hid it away, but one day my mother found the bottle, and she thought it was wine, so she took a sip of it. It tasted horrible, and she spat it right out. I was scared stiff, thinking she had poisoned herself, so we hurried to the doctor. He calmed her down. He said she hadn't swallowed enough of it to hurt her. That was how my mother found out I had the clap.

I kept going to the hospital until one of my pals told me to forget it; he said he'd looked after himself and that he'd show me what to do. It got worse, though, and finally I had to go have an operation. I came out cured.

Once during the gambling season I met a guy that used to lose night after night, and yet never seemed to be short of loot. I grew kind of curious about him, and one day I asked him where all his money came from. "I'm a con man," he said. "See, I buy a pack of Turmacs at the cigar store, show them to a likely prospect and tell him I can get him any foreign brand of cigarettes he wants. As soon as he hands me the money for a pack I go into a doorway making out like I'm getting them for him, and that's the last he ever sees of me— I come out another way." I worked with this guy for a while, but the spies put the cops wise to us. A plainclothes cop asked me to get him a pack of cigarettes and I fell right in the trap. I did four months for attempted fraud; that was my first taste of jail.

Now that I was eighteen, I needed a regular woman, so I decided the best thing I could do was to get married, so I asked my mother if she knew of a girl that would make a good wife. "I know the very one," she said. "She's the daughter of that schoolteacher that used to teach you; she hasn't had a very happy home life, poor girl." I remembered the girl; we used to play together when we were kids, but I hadn't seen her for years, not since her parents had separated and she'd gone to live with her father. Well, we met, and it was a real case of love at first sight; I was crazy about her, and I told her so. Of course I was mad to sleep with her, but my mother guessed what I had in mind and put a stop to it. "Stay away from her if you're not going to marry her," she said. "I have no doubt she'll have you if you ask her; she's been a neighbor of ours all her life. She's had a pretty tough time, as I've told you before, and you'll be doing her a favor by marrying her—she'll be so grateful to you that you can be sure she'll do everything she can to make you happy."

The girl was living with her grandmother then, so I went and had a heart-to-heart talk with the old lady. At first she wouldn't consider me because she'd heard I was a gambler, but as soon as she learned I only played cards a couple of months in the year and that when I did play, I always won, she changed her tune. Then she was all for the marriage; she saw me as a good, steady breadwinner. So my girl and I got engaged.

I could only make a few lire a day as a stonemason, not nearly enough to support a family, so I quit my job and started out on my own. I bought a supply of yard goods and a season ticket on the railroad and went from place to place selling my goods.

My girl's mother did everything she could to make me give her up. "I warn you," she said, "if you knew my daughter as well as I do, you wouldn't have anything to do with her." I didn't take any notice of her, and at the end of three months we got married. I can't describe to you how happy I was on our wedding day; my wife was artistic besides being beautiful and good; there was no one to equal her. I looked forward to taking care of her with all my heart, and she was very happy because now she'd have a home of her own and because my mother and my whole family loved her. We had a wonderful wedding feast; the table was covered with cakes and sweets and all kinds of good things to eat; every one of my relatives was there, and we kept the party going till one in the morning.

I didn't want to be a drifter any more; I wanted to settle down and work hard. Two days after the wedding I went out in the country to sell my goods. We managed to stay happy for two years; oh, sometimes we'd have an argument, but we loved each other and I never left the house before we kissed and made up.

I took her to the movies a lot, and when the first shoes with unbreakable glass heels on them showed up in the stores, I bought her a pair because I knew that with her eye for beauty she'd love them. Two months after our wedding she was pregnant, and in 1936 our first child, a girl, was born. In 1937 I was peddling my goods from door to door in a village. At one house a woman came out when I knocked on the door, and as soon as she saw me she said: "Go away. We're in terrible trouble here. One of my children's been bewitched." "Calm yourself, Signora," I said. "Let me see the child; I may be able to heal it." From what she said I thought the kid was possessed by evil spirits, but the minute I laid eyes on him and saw that his head was twice as large as a normal kid's I knew he was an idiot. Just the same I said: "I'll cure him for you, Signora, if you'll give me five thousand lire to buy the magic ingredients I need." It happened to be a Saturday, so she said: "Come back on Monday, I'll raise the money by then." Well, I went back on Monday, but only to find a couple of *carabinieri* waiting for me. I was arrested, and I got thirteen months for attempted fraud.

While I was in jail my mother did whatever she could to help my wife: she took her in and baked bread for her and looked after her and the baby.

One of my brothers was a soldier in East Africa, and he sent me fifty lire every month. Out of this I bought three airmail letters so I could write to him; the rest I gave to my wife. I was glad to do without things myself for her sake. But I'm sorry to say that she didn't behave well at all to my mother; things went from bad to worse between the two of them, and one day she walked out and went to live on her own. Unfortunately she got acquainted with two women that lived in an alley nearby. One of them led a kind of loose life; the other one worked in a medical laboratory. They saw she was down on her luck, so they offered her a little friendly advice. "What good is a husband in prison?" they asked. "Why don't you do yourself a little good? Come on with us to one of the licensed houses; you'll make a little dough, too." Some of my wife's neighbors found out what sort of company she was keeping.

They sent an anonymous letter to my mother: "Keep an eye on your daughter-in-law. She's going around with a couple of sluts. If she's not careful she's going to come to a bad end."

I was let out in 1938. My brother met me at the gates, and the first thing I asked him was how my wife had behaved while I was away. "She's been wild as hell," he said, "but she's never done anything really wrong." The minute I knew my honor was safe I calmed down, but I took a dislike to our new place as soon as I was in it. The room was very small and so low I felt the ceiling was pressing down on my head. There was hardly enough space for the double bed and one chair. I couldn't stay there, so I went right out and got another room close to where my mother lived; it just had a packed-dirt floor, but it was pretty fair sized.

My wife got to be more and more of a problem. I couldn't forgive her for the rotten way she'd treated my mother. After all, my mother'd done everything for me from the time I was four when my father died. I worshiped her. We had one scrap after another, and she'd yell and answer me back; she wasn't afraid of standing up to me.

I was only home thirteen days when a *carabiniere* came around and told me to report to the barracks; somebody had spread it around that I had dodged the draft. I said I'd been in prison at the time of the call-up, and I was sent to do my military service at Rivoli. Those born in 1917 and 1918 had just been called up, about two thousand all told. The Piedmontese were separated from the Southerners, but just my luck, they put me in with the Piedmontese. Nearly every night they almost all got loaded; the guy in the bunk over me used to vomit his dinner and wine all over me.

I told the lieutenant about it, and asked him if I could be transferred to where the Southerners slept; I said I couldn't stand the *polentoni*,[2] they ate like pigs, got blind drunk and threw up everything all over me. I didn't know he came from Piedmont himself. Christ, was he mad! "You skunk, you lousy *terun!*"[3] he shouted, "let me tell you this company here's too good for you. Stinking Southerners—when Garibaldi landed in Sicily and offered them soap, they thought it was cheese!"

[2] The *polenta* eaters, North Italians. *Translator's note.*
[3] Southerner. *Translator's note.*

I felt so desperate after that that I took off my belt, fastened it to the bed, put my neck through the loop, and pretended I was hanging myself—it was just to get moved to another company, that's all. A couple of the guys that were playing cards looked up and saw me; they took me down and carried me to the post hospital. While I was there I hit on an idea: I wrote home and asked my mother to send me a pound of that very soft soap that looks like marmalade and is a specialty of Palermo, and three pounds of that very fine powdered sugar you put on cakes and candy. As soon as the package came, I untied it, mixed the sugar with the soap, and then tied it up again. Well, a little after that I was suddenly sent back to the Piedmontese, and I brought out my package. A couple of soldiers gave it the eye. "Hey, he's got a package from Sicily, you guys!" one of them yelled. "Let's have it," said the other one. "We'll open it for you."

They all gathered around while he untied it. "Jam!" he said (his mouth was watering). "How about giving us some?"

"I can't touch it; it gives me a toothache," I said. "You can have it all."

The "jam" was divided among ten of the Piedmontese; they spread big gobs of it on pieces of bread and ate it like they were starving. They couldn't taste the soap for the sugar. About an hour later they were all screaming with belly-aches and had to go to the hospital. The lieutenant in charge of it, a Sicilian like myself, sent for me.

"You haven't poisoned these men, I hope," he said.

"Poisoned them? No," I said, "but the company commander told me that when Garibaldi gave us Sicilians soap, we took it for cheese, so I gave the Piedmontese a little soap. I guess it didn't agree with them!"

Well, from that time on the company commander and the sergeant let me have it. The sergeant made my life so miserable that I made up my mind to get even with him. One of my pals tailed him for me and found out he was having a thing with a gorgeous blonde; there was an out-of-the-way spot where they used to meet every night. One night about seven o'clock I went to this place and there, sure enough, was the sergeant waiting for his chick. You should have seen the look he gave when he saw me. "You skunk!" I yelled at him.

"I've had enough of your doghouse! All that punishment I took from you—will you stop it?" And he said, "Remember that he who makes you cry makes you laugh, and he who makes you laugh makes you cry." And then I beat him over the head four times with the butt end of my bayonet, and he slumped down like a log. He passed out cold, but he was still alive. I didn't wait around for him to come to, though; I beat it.

As soon as I got back to quarters I got into my bunk and started snoring loud to make out like I was asleep. But it wasn't very long before the M.P.'s came and shoved me into the guardhouse. I cracked up under the treatment I got; I was given a bottle of ink so I could write home, and I drank it all, hoping it'd made me sick and I'd be taken to the hospital. Instead, I was taken to a loony bin and kept there for two months under observation. Then I was brought back to the guardhouse and court-martialed; the prosecutor said I ought to get an eight-year sentence for the assault on the sergeant, but as there weren't any witnesses, they gave me the benefit of the doubt, and I was acquitted. I had piles bad, so I was sent to Verona for treatment. I was there six months.

I went home on sick leave, hoping things might be better between my wife and me, but she wouldn't listen to a word I said; she treated me like dirt. I had to go back to Verona for an operation for the piles, and it was another six months before I was discharged from the army as unfit. This was in 1940.

I started to work again, selling materials in the piazzas like the street Arabs. My wife behaved so bad to me that one night I made up my mind to put her to shame by going out with another girl. I went to the movies and sat next to a couple of girls, started talking to them about the picture and got so friendly with one of them that she gave me her address and asked me to come and see her the next day. Well, I went and she told me she was married and had four kids. Her husband was fighting in Africa, and she hadn't had any news from him for months. So she was forced to sell herself to be able to buy food for her kids. When I realized it was necessity that had driven her into that kind of life, I couldn't touch her.

Finally, though, she forced me to make love to her. I didn't know I'd caught syph from her and I passed it on to my wife. We began to feel so rotten that we went to the doctor, and he told us what we had. I burst out crying to think I'd passed it on to my wife. Both of us had to have treatment.

Life at home became one steady fight. I couldn't make enough selling materials, so I did some magic once in a while, and for two months of the year I went all over the place to play baccarat. *Zicchinetta* had died out.

One day my mother heard that some ugly little bastard was bragging all over the place how he slept with my wife when I was in jail. She was in a horrible state; she broke down and cried like Our Lady of Sorrows. "My son—I've lost him! There'll be murder committed for this," she sobbed, and begged my older brother to help her. "He'll kill the two of them," she screamed. "You've got to save him. You've got to." My brother did his best to calm her down, and at eight o'clock in the morning he came to my place. My wife was busy with the housework and the radio was on full blast. "I've got something to tell you," he said. "Get your book of magic and a deck of cards and come with me."

As soon as we were out in the street, he turned to me and said:

"Listen, some bastard's been spreading the story that he had my wife while I was fighting in Africa. I want you to go to his house and tell his wife's fortune. You've got to get even for me; you've got to make her."

The thought of our family honor being stained made me shudder.

"But he may be lying," I said. "Do you really think your wife would do a thing like that?"

He didn't answer me. He pointed out the house to me, and I went in. A woman was doing her wash in the courtyard. As soon as she saw me she turned pale, ran inside, hurried into her room and shut the door. "What's the matter with her?" I asked myself. "Maybe she knows who I am." The door to the next room was open a crack; I could see a woman grinding coffee beans. I knocked, and when she looked at me I had a story all ready for her.

"Do you know the signora with a sick child who sent for the doctor?" I said politely. "Are you the doctor?" she asked me. "No, I'm a fortuneteller," I said. "Will you tell my fortune for me?" she said. "I'm afraid I can't pay you, though; I have no money." "Don't worry about that," I said, and followed her in. "Excuse me," I said, "the signora next door—I could see from her face that someone's put the evil eye on her. Tell her to come in, and I'll get rid of it." "Oh, her!" said the woman. "She's my sister-in-law. We don't speak." "Which side of the family does she belong to?" I asked her. "She's my husband's brother's wife," she said. This was all I had to know. There was no need for me to go any farther: I could get revenge for my brother's honor on this woman.

I started off by reading her palm. "Signora, I fear that someone has cast an evil spell on you," I said as I looked closely at it. "We'll soon make sure." I shuffled the cards, laid them out, made her place her hand over one of them, and mumbled: "In the name of the mysterious center of the Church of St. Paul in Rome, if this woman is bewitched, I command you let the card beneath her hand disappear!" Naturally, I made it disappear, and now that she was certain she was bewitched, she turned deathly pale and trembled all over.

"You see, I was right, Signora," I said. "Your veins are full of quicksilver, and if it isn't removed at once, you will be struck by paralysis in the next three days and you will lie helpless in bed for thirteen whole years." "Help me—get rid of the quicksilver for me!" she cried in a terrified voice. "Save me—save me!" "Trust yourself to me, Signora," I said, and put my hand up her skirts and started stroking her. Pretty soon I had her so excited that I went all the way with her; our passions became like one, and I enjoyed her and gave her French kisses. "I've never kissed anyone like that, not even my husband," she whispered, and she lay back completely satisfied. I took a pair of scissors and cut off a few of her pubic hairs. I told her I needed them for the exorcism. I also made her give me a photograph of herself.

I admit I was a little scared at first that her husband might come and catch us, but by this time I was ready to face a whole army and face death to wipe out the stain on our family honor. If her husband had shown up, I'd've killed him.

As I was talking to her she caught a glimpse of the picture of me and my wife that was set into my wedding ring.

"Whatever made you take a fancy to me?" she asked. "You've got a girl friend who's much prettier than I am, and she knows her way around too; she's played lots of games in bed!"

What she said shocked me. While I was away, then, my wife must have had a lover. I managed to hide my feelings, though, and said like I didn't care:

"It's nothing to me. She's only one of my dames. So she had fun while I was in Africa—"

"You weren't in Africa, you were in prison," she said.

I thought she might be mixing my wife up with my sister-in-law because they're the same height, so I showed her my wife's picture on my identity card.

"That's her all right," she said.

"Maybe you've made a mistake," I said. "I'll tell you what— I'll bring my wife past here for a walk. You look through the window and nod your head if it's her."

I hurried back, told my wife I was going to borrow some money from my brother, and asked her to come with me. When we passed the house where the woman lived, I looked up, and she nodded her head. If she had known it was my wife's picture in the ring, she'd have kept quiet, naturally. I made some excuse to send my wife home, and then went to see my brother. "Thanks for all you've done for me," I said. "You were as slick about the whole thing as an American cop. I never dreamed it wasn't your wife, but mine! Mine! Tell me straight—what's the name of the bastard that had her?"

"Easy," he said, "don't do anything till you've got proof. If you find out she *has* cheated on you, get out fast."

Before I had time to say any more, my mother came in, flung her arms around my neck and burst into tears. "My son, my darling son," she said. "Think of me, who brought you up, don't lay a hand on her. If she's wronged you, leave her, leave her to cry her eyes out over what she's done."

"I'm all confused. I need time to think," I said. I didn't know for certain yet whether my wife, who was nearly seven months gone, had cheated on me; maybe she'd been true to me all the time, maybe someone had tried to seduce her and had bribed this ugly little bastard to blacken her name.

"Look," I said to my brother, "before I do anything, I'd like to meet this guy that's spreading it around that he slept with my wife."

Well, some friends of the guy told him I wanted to see him, and he came. The minute he set eyes on me he yelled: "Forgive me—have mercy. It's not like I ever knew you. I—it was your wife—she asked me to come in, and—"

He came right out with it. His friends had told him I was no fool. "He won't touch you," they said. "He'll understand all right that the door don't open from the outside, but from the inside."

"I won't lay a finger on you if you can prove that she was the guilty one," I said. "If you can't, I'll finish it for you and your wife and your kids—the whole bunch of you."

"But how can I prove it?" he asked.

"Get her to invite you in again," I said.

"But it happened more than two years ago," he said. "Maybe she won't have anything more to do with me."

"We'll see," I said. "Now listen to me. I'll tell my wife I'm going to the country for three days. As soon as I'm gone, go around and tell her she has to meet you at such and such a place because you've got to talk to her about what happened between you. If she agrees, I'll know she's guilty. I won't touch you, but as for her—I'll kick her ass good and hard and send her packing. She can go and live with that precious mother of hers."

At home, I behaved like everything was the same as usual; my wife's pretty quick on the draw, and if I had shown in the slightest way that something was wrong, she would have noticed it fast. "I'm going away tomorrow," I told her. "Won't be back for three days." The next morning I said good-by to her and went straight to the house of one of my aunts. I told the guy to come there as soon as he'd arranged with my wife where and when to meet him. But he never turned up. I found out later that he rushed to his mother and blabbed out the whole story to her. She howled and pulled her hair as though he was already dead. "Are you crazy?" she shrieked. "Don't go near his house! Think of all the brothers he's got! They know how to kill a man and keep themselves in the clear— they'd never get caught, not them!" Then, to save her precious son's life, she sent someone to warn my wife what was up.

My wife knew what sort of man I was and how much I prized my honor. She snatched up our little girl, rushed into the courtyard, and screamed to the owner of the house: "Signora, Signora, my husband is going to kill me. I'm done for. I'm innocent, I swear I am. Save me, save me!" My brother was watching my place, and he went up to her and said: "Someone's warned you, eh? Go pack whatever you need and clear out right away. If my brother finds you here, he'll kill you for sure."

She ran upstairs, rolled up all the clothes she'd made for the baby she was expecting, and ran like crazy to her mother.

I'd bought a revolver and a knife. I'd planned to slit her belly open, tear out the baby and fling its body beside hers; I'd made up my mind that as soon as I'd finished her, I'd go to the cemetery and shoot myself on my father's grave.

I can talk about it calmly now. I'm older, and more experienced, and through having studied magic for twenty years, I know what a woman is and what she's not. I've learned a lot about the female sex. If I'd had as much knowledge about it then as I've got now, I wouldn't have suffered like I did. I wouldn't have been forced to go into crime out of desperation. If the same thing happened to me today, I'd just shrug my shoulders and say: "Good luck! Who needs you? There're plenty more fish in the sea."

But to get back. My brother hurried around to tell me my wife had cleared out, and as soon as I knew she was with her mother, I rushed over there intending to strangle her. I sprang at her and clutched her by the throat. "I—I—I'm innocent!" she said, gasping for breath. I'd have killed her right then and there if some of her relatives hadn't pulled me off her and forced me out the door.

A few days later she found out through asking questions which guy it was that had been smearing her name. She dressed herself up in her father's suit, pulled a beret down low over her face, took a knife, smeared the blade with onion juice to poison it and followed him into a cigar store. She went straight up to him.

"Look at me. Do you know me?" she said, pulling off her beret.

"No, I don't," he said in a hurry. "My sister-in-law's been gossiping about you, but—"

Well, before he could finish, she grabbed hold of his hair and drove the knife over and over again into his balls. "Get out!" the owner yelled. "Get out." (She didn't care what happened as long as it wasn't in her shop.) The guy collapsed, and my wife dragged him into the street, bleeding and unconscious. "Police! Police!" she screamed. "Lock me up. Do whatever you want with me!" The cops took her to the police station and locked her up in a cell.

A couple of months later she gave birth to a boy, and she called it after my father. Some friends that went to visit her in prison told me she acted like she was nuts; she kept on shrieking and calling out my name and yelling: "I'm innocent; I'm innocent! I've proved my innocence. I've restored my husband's honor!"

There was a certain baroness who was well known for being kind to people in trouble. To animals too. She persuaded the judge to try and bring me and my wife together. After six months, she was released on probation, and as I still couldn't make up my mind whether or not she was innocent, I told the baroness that if my wife would agree to live quietly with her mother for two years, at the end of that time I might take her back. In the meantime, I said, I was willing to pay for her support.

I sold materials like I always did, then I went to Foggia to play cards. From Foggia I made my way to Pescara, where I had an affair with a married woman. It wasn't the first one by any means—I'd had any number of them since my home was broken up. To get back at the world, I purposely made love to married women; I gave them syph, and they passed it on to their husbands. I stopped having treatments just so I could get revenge.

I left Pescara and went back to Foggia. My wife followed me there; she hid in an alley and watched for me, and as soon as she saw me coming, she fired a couple of revolver shots at me—one grazed my leg. The police arrested both of us. "You won't stop me from doing what I'm going to do!" she screamed. "I'll kill him if he doesn't kill me first! He's got a woman in Pescara—I won't let him get away with it. Treating me like I was a whore—me, an honest woman!"

Well, they put her in prison, but they let me go.

I went straight to Milan, where I sold cloth and played cards. After which I returned to Sicily and I had to stay because the Yanks had just landed. This was 1943.

It wasn't long before I was arrested for selling cloth without a license, all my stock was taken away and I was thrown in jail. My brother went to see a signora who had certain connections with the judges, and he asked her if she could get me out. She said it would cost him a hundred thousand lire, and after he raised the dough she went to work. She asked a beautiful hustler if she'd like to make ten thousand lire. "I'd do anything for ten thousand lire," the girl said. The signora told her my name. "I want you to pose as this man's wife," she said. "Put on a cheap simple little dress, and I'll take you to the judge. Plead with him to release your husband—you know how to act the part." Well, they both went. The signora was on very good terms with the judge and she really poured a sad story into his ear. "Such a sad case," she said. "His wife's such a sweet girl, hardly more than a child—you will see her, won't you?" He agreed, and as soon as my "wife" was alone with him, she begged him with tears in her eyes to let me out. "There, there, you mustn't cry," he said, "I'll see what I can do, but it's a serious matter, you know—the sentence may be anything from three to seven years." She cried harder than ever, and he began to pet her and stroke her. "Now, now, my dear, you mustn't upset yourself—I told you I'd see what I can do," he said and he put his hand up her skirts. On her second visit, he went the whole way with her. "What a shame it is that such a little darling as you should be married to a black-marketeer, a good-for-nothing idiot!" he said to her, and then, out of the kindness of his heart, he presented her with a thousand lire! As soon as he was sure the tomato would sleep with him whenever he wanted her—she got another ten thousand lire out of the signora for being so obliging—he saw to it that I was let out provisionally.

For the last few years, things have been going better for me. I'm more at peace with myself now because I'm living with a woman I think the world of—she's given me what I never had from my wife—love and affection. I'm happy and contented now that we're together. She's one of the real old-fashioned kind: obedient, gentle, proud of her house, and thrifty. She caught syph, from me, and because of that she had a miscarriage, but we both had treatments, and now it's not active any more.

For some time now I've been a fortuneteller. I've got a permit for predicting the future with cards, and so on. I renew it every year. It's valid for every city in Italy except Rome. The Pope looks after his own; the priests don't want any competition!

I cure people who've got manias; sometimes I heal the sick. I cured one woman of hernia; she'd been to see one doctor after another, and none of them had done a thing for her. I told her to wear an elastic belt, and in a very few weeks she was all right.

When some bad luck hit a family, I'd say: "Signora, someone's put the evil eye on your house!" "The evil eye?" she'd say. "Are you sure?" "Very sure," I'd say. "Give me a piece of cotton wool and you'll see for yourself." I'd place the cotton wool on the floor, and quick as a flash, while she wasn't looking, I'd put a little metallic sodium inside it. Then I'd take a bottle of water and I'd mutter: "I command you in the name of the Prophet Samuel and the Archangel Gabriel . . ." and I'd pour the water over the cotton wool, which would instantly burst into flames. Naturally, this convinced the signora that somebody had put the evil eye on her house, and she'd beg me to remove it. Of course, I was paid to drive it out.

If I was called in to cure anybody of a mania, I'd ask the patient for half a bottle of vinegar. I brought three packages of bicarb with me that I'd colored red, yellow and green, and that I said was powdered coral, powdered amber and the dust of St. Rita's bones. I mixed some of each one together, and recited a spell that began: "I conjure you, evil spirits, I command you to rid this house of the quicksilver with which you have bewitched it . . ." Then I poured the bicarb into the vinegar and put the cork back. Right away the bottle glowed with a light like phosphorus, the cork shot out with a loud pop, and the vinegar foamed up and overflowed. "There goes the quicksilver, Signora," I said. "Now take this bottle, and every day for the next thirty-three days, sprinkle a few drops of the vinegar that's left in each corner of the room, and recite as you do it three Credos, three Our Fathers and three Hail Marys. At the end of these thirty-three days, all the quicksilver will be gone from your house." Sometimes, just to impress my customers, I'd drape a priest's stole around me and finger a rosary, but naturally I had to do this in secret; if the priests ever got wind of it, they'd have had me arrested —like I said, they won't tolerate competition.

Men believe in magic just like women—not only the ones that live in the country but the ones in the city, too, educated ones as well as ignorant ones. One time a man came to see me and begged me to get rid of a spell that a neighbor of his had put on him that made him impotent. "My wife's kicked me out because I can't be a good husband to her," he said. He was crying. He wanted me to kill the neighbor with my magic, but instead, I used my power of suggestion on him and pretty soon he was potent again. A little while after that he came to thank me, brought me all kinds of presents, and gave me two thousand lire in the bargain.

I went from village to village with an assistant. As soon as I arrived in one of them, he'd paste up posters with my picture on them and underneath it the words: "The Great Professor of the Magic Powers of Science."

Through practicing my art, what tragedies I've learned about! I found out, for instance, that a father was sleeping with his daughter, a brother with his sister, a son with his mother. I discovered that plenty of young girls had been had by their fiancés and that lots of married women had lovers.

Some people would ask me for harmful potions or they'd want me to cast evil spells on somebody for revenge; some came to me for love potions. I discovered that a lot of girls tried to poison themselves when an affair they had went wrong; but as soon as they were all right again, bang! they started up with somebody new.

When I was staying in N., a girl that looked just like Venus herself came to me to have her fortune told; she was seduced by the prefect, so she asked me for some kind of charm that would make him marry her.

When I was staying in V., the wife of some good-looking

guy that owned a bicycle shop begged me to put a spell on her husband that would make him die in thirty-three days; she had a boy friend and she wanted to be free.

All these things I saw made me think that they happened because priests mix in politics and play all kinds of dirty tricks instead of doing their jobs: preaching to people, teaching them how to lead better lives. We need somebody that'll set us an example, because we're all sinners.

As I got to know more and more about people, I realized that men and women are just figures in life, figures that pass like a breeze, as light as feathers. And I realized too that a man, the wild animal that he is, becomes just like a lamb in a woman's presence.

I think if people could only understand, even a little, that we're only on this earth for a very short time, then maybe they'd cherish every hour, every day, every month, every year, because as the hours and the days and the months and the years passed, they'd realize that it was their own lives trickling away. We ought to love each other, do what we can for each other, live in peace. But we don't do anything of the kind. The rich mistreat the poor, they want to keep them down, make slaves out of them so they can surround themselves with luxury, lounge around in easy chairs and drape their wives in jewelry. They've got big cars, chauffeurs, beautiful mistresses sparkling with gold and diamonds like statues of the Madonna; the world's full of these selfish, wealthy men that never give a damn about anybody else. My father died when I was four, and my life's been one long struggle; I've never been able to give my kid a chance—that's why he went wrong and had to be put in a reformatory. It's through telling fortunes all over Italy I've gained so much knowledge and experience. The poorest and the richest, princes, barons, counts, have revealed the secrets of their hearts to me. I've learned what men are like by talking to strangers in trains, talking and listening to people of all kinds in cafés, bars, hotels and so on, all over the place.

If I could have foreseen my own future, I would have made sure not to be born; once a man's born, he serves a life sentence.

If we're sent to prison, who offers us work when we come

out? Who gives us a chance to make good? Wherever we go, we're kicked out. Once a man's been in prison, he goes back over and over. He may be a criminal, but all the same, he's a member of the human race, right?

I'm too old now for a laborer's job. I'd like to own a small grocery store with a counter and scales; I'd give credit to the poor, and at the same time I'd manage to make a living for my girl and myself—I'm ashamed, I'm sick as hell of roaming around; and if I had a store, I'd be able to give it up. Or I wouldn't mind being the foreman of a gang on a big public works project. I'd rather do anything than what I do now; if anybody buys me even a cup of coffee, I know it's only because he wants a favor out of me, maybe his fortune told free, gratis and for nothing.

Men are so ignorant they always want the forbidden pleasures, the innocent ones don't interest them. Like—if a guard leaves the door open in a prisoner's cell, the idiot doesn't even want to step outside into the corridor, but if he's locked in, his one thought is escape. That's the way life goes.

Since I've been in prison I've let my beard grow. When I come out I won't be able to push cloth—I can't pay back the money I borrowed to get a permit. I'll have to go on with the magic, that's all. I'll pass out handbills in the villages and get fresh customers. I charge two hundred or one hundred lire for fortunetelling, but the fact is a hundred's not enough. I have to use certain tools—a pair of glasses, for instance, to impress people.

When I was traveling around and I heard there was another well-known magician in the neighborhood, I always went to see him. I never let on I was in the same line, of course, I made out I was an ordinary customer. I wanted to hear his patter—patter's even more important, you know, than the book of magic and the cards. "I see things are going badly for you, especially in the way of business," he might say. "I can let you have a charm that'll fix everything right away, but it'll cost you fifteen or twenty thousand lire." Then I'd tell him that I was a magician, too. "Are you sure your charm would be any good to me?" I'd say. "I've got one of my own, and I'm under the protection of good spirits." I'd be on the verge of thinking that maybe his charm was better than mine, and he'd be asking himself whether maybe mine was more powerful than his!

By the power of suggestion, a magician can make people do anything he wants. The women who come to him for help —girls that've had their engagements broken off, mothers that believe their daughters have been bewitched, wives with unhappy married lives—they'll let him do anything with them; he can twist them around his finger. Plenty of married women are anxious to bewitch their husbands to death—for three hundred thousand lire! When I want to impress my customers, I roll my eyes up, close them, make believe I'm in a trance, and use all kinds of different voices so they think it's the spirits speaking through me.

Once, when I was in Gela, I mesmerized thirteen men and women! I made them kneel down on the ground. People there were so amazed at my powers that they gave me a real feast and a place to sleep free of charge.

If you're a well-known fortuneteller you get streams of customers. I used to pass out handbills that said that anybody that wanted a sitting had to make a reservation twenty-four hours in advance, and that I wouldn't handle more than ten sittings a day. Sometimes a customer would come to make a reservation and say he preferred not to give his name, so I'd hand him a numbered card with my signature on it.

I'm an outcast now; I've got a record, and nobody will give me a job. I can't start a business because I've got no cash. Magic's the one business that can be carried on without any capital. I can't afford posters and handbills, but it doesn't matter; I go from house to house to foretell the future, remove the evil eye, and so on.

Sometimes a customer that's well off and demands my services will send a car to pick me up . . .

the witnesses in the province of Palermo

Rosario T.

Five or six different kinds of greens that are good to eat grow wild in the country; no one sows them, they seed themselves.

When I go out gathering, I leave home at three or four or five in the morning—it's all according to what time of year it is and how far I have to walk. I trudge for ten or twelve miles before I start looking for greens. There isn't anything to be found on the roadside, everything that grows there is covered with dust, besides which people who've passed that way have already picked anything worth having and the cows have trodden down or eaten the rest.

When I reach the woods, I may have to walk another four or five miles before I've filled my sack with enough greens to make two hundred tiny bunches. Usually two or three of us go picking together and help to tie up one another's bunches. Sometimes we land in trouble. The owner of a field will accuse us of trespassing, or else he won't let us gather any of the plants growing in it—"I need them myself," he'll say.

When two of us go together we arrange ahead of time to pool everything we pick and to share whatever we get for selling it. That's all right, but if I'm out on my own and another fellow's out on *his* own, we keep watching each other out of the corners of our eyes. He's thinking what I'm thinking: "Is he filling his sack faster than I am? Has he come across a better patch than mine?" You worry all the time, especially if you can't find enough to fill your sack. It's exactly the same when you're hunting for snails. Once you've found a good spot, you have to keep a sharp lookout on the other fellow who's after them if you want to pick up twelve or fourteen pounds before he does. You stoop down, grab a snail, make sure he isn't catching up on you, and rush around here, there and everywhere.

You've got to make sure when you're gathering greens that they're not full of worms—some of them are so small that you can hardly see them, so you have to look very closely. This time of year, almost every bit of fennel's crawling with them. There are two kinds of wild fennel, valley fennel and mountain fennel. The fennel that grows in the valleys isn't eatable, it smells too bad. It looks just like mountain fennel, but we can tell the difference because its leaves turn color and fall off about now.

I gather all sorts of greens in the fields and woods: chicory, small wild cabbages, some fruits, orachs, fennel and asparagus that grow in the brambles. When my sack's full to the brim, I go home, my wife brings in a basin of water and I give the stuff a thorough soaking; if it's not properly washed, no one'll buy it. Then I sort it out and make it into bunches. I sell the bunches to a wholesaler at three or four lire the bunch. If I took them to market myself, I'd get fifteen lire for two bunches, but I'd lose a day's gathering, so it's not worth my while.

I can make six or seven hundred lire a day—it'd come to more if I didn't have to pick twenty or so bunches for nothing. I go picking right through the winter up to the end of March, but in April the winegrowers start spading up the vines and there's nothing left but a few scraps of chicory and the berries that grow in the stubble.

Sometimes we go out to pick on a Sunday, but if it rains before we start, we hunt for snails instead. If it begins to rain while we're actually in the fields, we keep right on, that is unless it pours; still, even a shower's enough to wet us right through. But we can't let the weather stop us—either we'd have nothing to eat, or we'd have to buy food on credit, and where would we find the money to pay the bill?

There are twenty-five thousand people living in these parts; fifty of them are regular pickers like me. When the farm hands are out of work they go picking, too, and even the owners pick every bit of eatable greens that grow on their land.

In March, it's hopeless—to gather enough to make a hundred bunches, you have to walk all day. So we go on bicycles the twenty-two miles to Balata, where everything's later than it is here. It's a much smaller village than ours, and only a handful of people who live there are regular pickers. We leave our bikes at the side of the road and climb up the mountains. As soon as we've filled our sacks we have to make the long, downward hike to the road, half-falling under their weight. We peddle our weary way back, and by the time we get home it's so late and we're so tired that we can't do another thing—the sorting and cleaning has to wait till morning. We make these trips to Balata right through April, till the greens have gone to seed and taste so bitter that no one'll buy them. There's nothing left worth picking but a few bits of chicory.

When you go out snail hunting, you start very early, not later than two or three o'clock—you have to reach the fields while it's still dark, because the minute the sun comes out the snails disappear underground for the rest of the day. If it's a heavy, cloudy morning, you may find them creeping in the grass till about eleven, but after that, good-by, snails! There aren't any snails in the vineyards because the vine-dressers hoe the earth four or five times a year; you find them in fallow land and in bean fields and wheat fields, mostly on the banks and close to water. When the grass is wet with dew you find plenty of them. But these new fertilizers they use nowadays are killing off the snails; they sprinkle ammonia and salt all over the land, and you can walk for miles and never come across a single snail. Then all of a sudden you may chance on a place where there are heaps and heaps of them. When the first rains fall, crowds of people go snail hunting: hunters, peasants, small boys, all carrying baskets— yes, when the first rains fall, it's *ghiotta*[1] time. "Go get as many snails as you can and I'll make *ghiotta* for you," my wife says to the children, and all four of them race off into the fields. They may get four or five pounds of them, and then we sit down to a rare feast.

I hunt snails for a living, to buy bread for my family. There are three different kinds: *babbaluce, attuppatedde* and *cras-*

---

[1] The snails are boiled into a kind of thick stew which is eaten with tomato sauce. *Ghiotta—ghiotto*, a tidbit. *Translator's note.*

tuna. The *crastuna* are the biggest, but you don't find many of them. The commonest are the *attuppatedde*. The *babbaluce* hide under stones, where they glue themselves, and if there's a shower they put out their little horns. They don't go underground, they just stay fastened to the underside of a stone like this one—see, there are two of them coupling. Sometimes the *babbaluce* creep into a crack in the rocks underneath a bridge, and when the hole is crowded, the ones that can't get in glue themselves one on top of the other at the opening—they form themselves into a ball as big as your fist. We poke our fingers or sticks in the crack, and shake the stones and turn them over, and there are the *babbaluce*. It's no use looking for them under a single stone, though; you've got to look for them where there's a pile of boulders. If you want *babbaluce*, go to Lo Zucco—the mountain is one of their favorite places. They taste much sweeter than *attuppatedde* or *crastuna*.

You can eat *attuppatedde* raw or cooked. *Attuppatedde* go underground, so when I'm hunting for them I use a little hoe; sometimes I accidentally cut one of them in half, and when I do, I clean it and eat it right on the spot. In summer, when it's so hot that the earth cracks, the *attuppatedde* lie in the shade under the stones that give them a little moisture and coolness and save them from being roasted alive. Six months of the year, snails don't eat a thing, they just sleep. In March they start sealing themselves inside their shells; they spit out a sticky liquid that dries into a whitish skin. At first, it's just like a very thin onion-skin, then in April, as the weather gets warmer, it grows harder and harder until it's almost as hard as the shell itself. We have our problems hunting for them, though, because lots of the owners won't allow us to go and look for them on their land. Don Ciccio grazes his cows in this field, for instance, and he says we cut up the grass with our hoes.

In September and October, when the first rains fall, the earth gradually begins to soften. The seals the *attuppatedde* have used to fasten themselves into their houses soften too, and out they come again. In the autumn, the owners don't interfere with us—they let us go wherever we like on their land.

When the *attuppatedde* first begin to stir after their long sleep, they're delicious to eat, but as soon as they start feeding on grass again, they have a bitter taste. We take it away by putting them in a tub or a bucket and sprinkling bran over them; in two or three days the bitterness has gone. *Babbaluce* are always juicy and sweet.

Snails often get killed and eaten by *crasentole*, long worms that wriggle into their shells. The *attuppatedde* see their enemies in front of them and draw as far back inside their houses as they can, but they can't draw back far enough—they're too big. The *babbaluce* are smaller, so they usually manage to save themselves, but sometimes they're not quick enough and then the *crasentole* kill them and eat them too. In the summer, though, when the *attuppatedde* are sealed up, the *crasentole* can't get into their shells and they can't get to the stones where the *babbaluce* have fastened themselves, either —they can't crawl on the hard, dry earth. In blazing summer weather, *crasentole* stay near manure heaps or on any soft, damp patch they can find. How do I know all these things? Through keeping my eyes open. We use *crasentole* for bait when we go eel fishing at Corleone. These last few days I've been there with some other fellows. When we're halfway between Contessa and Corleone we get the baskets ready; we thread ten or twelve *crasentole* on wires, each one on a separate wire, and then put them in the baskets. We throw the baskets into the edge of the river after we've tied them to the bank. Eels don't eat in the daytime, they only come out after food when it's dark. So we stretch ourselves out on the grass and go to sleep; then, as soon as it's light, we look for our baskets—sometimes we spot them right away, sometimes we have to grope around underwater for them. We may find five eels in a basket, or even six or seven; there may be a basket, though, with not a single eel in it. The eels we catch are tiny— none of them weigh more than a half a pound. Our baskets are too small for the big eels. Pretty soon, though, there won't be any eels, little or big—nowadays fishermen throw poison into the river to catch them and it kills the unhatched eggs.

When there's a stretch of water that hasn't been poisoned and the river's very low, we catch eels with ordinary table forks; we lash the forks to sticks, turn over the stones and stab them before they can wriggle away. But they're as quick as lightning, you know, so some are too fast for us; when we lose sight of them, we go a few yards further and move the stones a little downstream; eels when they're trying to escape always glide along with the current. You can't go eel fishing alone, it takes two or three; we can only fish for them in summer when the river's shallow—in winter it's a flood, and then it's no good.

In June, July and August, up to the time when the first rains fall, we catch another kind of *babbaluce*, little tiny things that fasten onto a blade of grass or a bramble twig. They stick themselves one on top of the other and seal up their shells. As soon as we can find the big snails again, we don't bother about them. These little *babbaluce* stay wherever they've fastened themselves and they always keep moist. We cook them the same way as we do the large ones, and suck them out of their shells.

We go wherever the wind blows us, we take whatever we find. Walking through the fields, we learn quite a number of things about the snails. We've learned, for instance, that when they creep underground to hide from the light, they don't go any deeper than an inch—that's where they lay their eggs, too. If we catch sight of a little mound of earth, we dig into it with our fingers, and there, sure enough, is a snail that's just dug himself in with his nose. Snails' eggs are about the size of a grain of rice. They couple together just above the ground; when you see a pair stuck together, you can't tell which is the male and which is the female. Sometimes I've pulled them apart and had a good look at them, but I've never been able to see the slightest difference between them. Sometimes you find four or five snails pairing off side by side—it's easy then to pick up eight or ten at a time!

In March, the snails hatch—tiny little things with soft, shiny flesh almost as clear as glass. Sometimes when I'm out snail hunting, I look all over the place and can't see one, then I catch sight of a trail of silvery slime on the grass and I follow it; it may vanish underground, or it may lead me to a stone, but I always find the snail in the end. At night, especially in winter, they creep around all over the place; that's why we get up so early to catch them before the sun drives them underground. I think they see better in the dark, but they can see in daylight too—the minute we put a hand out towards them, they draw in their horns. If there's a little wind blowing or it's bitter cold, they disappear inside their shells—they hate the wind more than anything else, and unless it dies down or a few raindrops fall, they won't come out. They don't like heavy rain, though, they won't move in it, but if it's just a light shower, they begin creeping around again . . .

Do you know what river crabs feed on? Worms and dead animals—you'll see thirty or forty of them feeding on a carcass. They look like sea crabs, only they're not hairy. You can eat them, but they're nearly all bone; still they're better than nothing, and they make delicious soup. During some months there's much more meat on them—they change with the moon.

Frogs eat worms, too, but only tiny ones. How do I know? Because I take out their insides after I've skinned them, and so I can see everything they've had to eat: worms, ants and other small insects. I watched the black adders that live in the river, too. I've seen them fix their eyes on a great big toad, just squatting there unable to move, and letting itself be swallowed whole. In these parts we have real big toads—they often weigh as much as a pound.

I'll tell you a little more about frogs. We can tell the sex of a frog before we skin it. How? Because a male frog's got a kind of beard on his chin. When we've skinned it, there are its tiny balls—it's got everything we men've got. A female frog has a smooth chin, and when we've skinned her, we know whether she's been fertilized or not. If she *has* been fertilized, she'll have two clusters of eggs inside her—she lays loads of eggs. She doesn't lay both clusters at once, though. When we grip the neck of a female frog that's ready to lay one of her clusters and turn her over on her stomach, the eggs drop right into our hands, but the second cluster doesn't break—if we hadn't caught her, she'd have laid it in a month's time.

When we're getting the frogs ready for market, we cut off their heads and their feet with scissors, skin them, and clean them out. Then we break their legs to make them swell up— they look so tasty with their nice plump thighs and bodies that people say: "Give me a couple pounds of them." Even after we've cut off their heads and their feet, and skinned them and broken their legs, frogs still move. We put them in water for a couple hours, and then they're ready to be sold—we get about a hundred lire a pound. We catch them in the daytime and clean them that same night—if we didn't, they'd all go bad before morning.

Watching all the different creatures in the woods and the fields and rivers, I get to thinking a lot of times they're no different from us. We all eat each other up—you do, I do. An animal's life is just as hard as ours.

When I look up at the stars, specially those nights when I'm eel fishing, I often wonder if the world's real—maybe it's not. I do believe that Jesus came down on earth to live—I'd kill any man who spoke against Him. But there are times when I don't even want to believe in God myself. "If He is really up there, why doesn't He send us work?" I say to myself.

If I only had a good job. Sometimes I get so desperate I feel like hanging myself. But then I think of my wife and children—what would become of them without me? All the same, though, when I let myself think about the work I can't find, I go crazy. . . .

I feel miserable when I'm skinning frogs—miserable because I've killed them. I wish I didn't have to kill them, but it's part of my living, I can't help myself. As soon as I get hold of a frog, the frog knows it's going to die. I'm certain of it. What makes me certain? Because the minute I grab hold of its legs and get ready to cut off its head and its feet, it empties it bladder just the way a man does when he's afraid. So I'm sure it knows it's going to die. Some animals start to tremble all over as soon as you've caught them. When I take a bird from its nest, I can feel its little heart beating like a bell in my hand. It knows its time is up—it has the same feeling that you and I would have if someone pressed a revolver against our head. I believe that every single creature, even including a snail, which you might call nothing, thinks in its own way. I'm sure that every single one of them knows when it's going to die.

When you land an eel, it opens its mouth, gasps for air and tries to bit you with its tiny white teeth. It thrashes about all over the place because it can't breathe out of water. We cut two slits in its head in the shape of a cross and through the slits we pull out its insides.

My two cousins come along to help when we're skinning frogs. We all stand around the basket, and one cousin snips off their heads, and the other one cuts off their feet, my wife skins them, and I clean them out and break their legs. Sometimes, just to pass the time, we play a game of judge and jury; my cousin, the one that cuts off their heads, gets thirty years because he's the murderer; my wife gets twenty years because she only does her work when they're dead; the other cousin that cuts off their feet, she gets twenty years too; and me, I go to prison for life, because if it hadn't been for me, the frogs would still be alive.

When you've sliced the head off a frog, its eyes seem to go on watching you, just the way the eyes in a painting seem to follow you. When all the heads are cut off, it's like a real massacre—if we lined them up, one behind the other . . .

I can't tell you how bad it made me feel the first time I put the scissors to a frog. But . . . last year, I killed three hundred pounds of frogs. I've got so hardened to it that I fly into a rage if one of them tries to jump out of my hand when I'm in a hurry to get the cleaning done; I either bite its head off or smash it down on the ground. The rich people that keep all their land and money for themselves, and never give us a thought, and let us starve to death—they ought to dream at night about a basket full of heads—not frog's heads, but the heads of all the men and women they've killed—yes, they ought to dream about all those eyes in all those faces just watching and watching them . . .

Well, now I've told you what I have to do to scrape together some kind of living for my family. I've tried my hand at every trade. I was eight when I left school—I got as far as the second grade—and ever since then, I've managed the best I could. Thank God, I've never been in trouble with the law— I've always earned my bread honestly, by the sweat of my brow. I work much harder than any laborer or factory hand, and I've got to use my head all the time.

If I didn't use my head, I'd never make a living. I have to

know where to go and when to go—I plan everything out in the night. I enjoy what I'm doing, that's true, but I'm tired, you see, I can't ever let up. I'd like to have a job and go to work regular every day. I won't let myself lose hope, but it's hard to believe I could do something better—I've got a brain, though; I could learn. Of course, it would take me some time, it wouldn't sink in all at once, but after a couple weeks or so I'd begin to understand. When I came out of the service five years ago I was hired as a manual laborer; I had three months' work in the first year, four months' in the second, six months' in the third, three months' in the fourth, and five months' in the fifth. In between times I went picking greens.

Sometimes I even pick capers. They grow out of the rocks. You split the round seeds in two, sprinkle them with salt, and lay them out in the sun to dry.

When I was seventeen, I used to go out after coal and charcoal—I went on doing it till I was nineteen. I'd climb up in the mountains till I came to a place where the charcoal burners had just finished work. They let me poke around in the earth with a stick for pieces of charcoal, and they let me carry thirty pounds of them away. When I couldn't find any charcoal I'd go to the railroad tracks and hunt for coal there. Engines always leave a trail of coal behind them. Sometimes when a train pulls into a station, the fireman will shovel out the hard coal; it's no use to him, but it's just the thing for us because it makes no smoke. I sold the good coal I picked up on the tracks to blacksmiths; they have to have the best coal because it gives off the most heat.

These last few years we've been going out looking for lead. The police have target practice nearby—listen! you can hear them shooting now. They're at it the whole month of May, they bang-bang-bang from morning till night—throwing money away when there's none for us. There are scraps of lead all over the place, but we have to dig into the earth to find them. Sometimes they shoot heavy bullets and we spot them easy by the holes they make in the ground. We line up out on the range and search every inch of it—nothing escapes us, not even the pieces of aluminum from the grenade casings. Sometimes we pick up a few live cartridges that they overlooked. We make a few lire by selling what we collect. Lead for bread—that's how we scratch out a living . . .

A gust of wind blowing through the Church, that's what's needed, but not the sort of wind that would put out the candles and blow away the altar . . .

four braccianti

FIRST BRACCIANTE:[1] This kind of thing only happens because of the estates. Some people think the motive for my brother's murder was revenge, a few people think it was envy —envy of the position he held for a year. I myself, though, believe that he was killed for political reasons and that the killers were really gunning for me. I'm the secretary of the local C.P., so if they'd liquidated *me*, everyone would have known why, and the murderers would've been brought to trial. They probably decided it was easier to knock off my brother. His movements were known; he was the overseer at Conte Raineri, and he went there without fail every day.

He was killed just five days before the elections, and people were so terrified they were afraid to vote for us. The comrades were horrified and confused. "What does it mean?" they asked each other. "Are they going to come after us? Will they steal our animals, damage our crops, cut down our vines and our fruit trees?" My brother's murder might have been the work of the Mafia, and the Mafia was a hundred percent behind the Baroness. The same question was in everyone's mind: "If the Communists win the elections, won't somebody else get bumped off, won't there be more killings?" The police have kept quiet about my brother's death; the authorities haven't made a move, they're still waiting for orders, and

[1] Agricultural worker. *Translator's note.*

they won't take any action till they get them. It's nothing new. There've been armed robberies around here, but they've never been investigated. No one knows anything, no questions are asked—everything's kept quiet.

We've seen some pretty sights, let me tell you. Three years ago, at Contessa Entellina, a band of unemployed farm workers, men and women, went to the Mole estate to glean in the wheat fields. The owner told them to clear out, said he needed the ears to fatten his cattle, but they wouldn't go away. One of the owner's men fired at them, and one of the gleaners fell down dead. The killer got off scot-free—far from being arrested and sent to jail, he wasn't even questioned. The trial was a farce—it seems that he fired in self-defense, and he was acquitted. Anyone would have thought the poor bastard planned to steal the cattle, instead of which all he went to the estate for was to glean in the stubble. But every one of the witnesses to the murder gave evidence for the owner.

They won't give us land, they won't give us work, and they shoot us down like dogs if we dare pick up a few miserable ears of wheat.

SECOND BRACCIANTE: The estate's always there, but we're kicked off the land. It's supposed to be sold to us peasants, but there's an amount of money over and above the purchase price that has to be paid under the table before the sale goes through, and we just haven't got it. They say the government's on our side—on our side, yeah, I'd like to know who's on our side! I wanted to buy a *salma*[2] of land, but the terms were too steep; I had to put down four hundred thousand lire, a third of the purchase price, in cash, and I didn't have it. I tell you it's the owners that get favored every single time. We peasants get chased off the land. There are plots for sale at Campofiorito, but they go to men from other districts that've got the cash. As for us, we can starve, and there's nothing we can do about it. Once the harvest's over, I give you my word that I'm clearing out of Sicily for good. I hate to think of what I might be forced to do if I stayed here . . .

More often than not, the people are for us Communists, but

[2] A Sicilian measure—approximately 6½ acres.

they always vote for the Right. It's this present system of the preferential vote that turns the tide against us; the ballot's supposed to be secret, but actually it's nothing of the kind. "If we don't vote for them, we'll be really stuck," the peasants say. They're told to vote for a certain combination of numbers, you see, and after the vote, these numbers are rigged so that all the candidates they stand for get elected. The leaders can tell from the slips if anybody hasn't voted or if he's voted against their party. Then they persecute him. "Don't come to us for work, you didn't vote for us," they say to him, and if he puts in a claim for something he has a right to, the only answer he gets is: "Go ask the Commies to give it to you—you voted for them, go collect your pay!" It's a real reign of terror, I'm telling you.

A couple of days before the elections, two men came to see me. "If the system was different, we'd vote for you," they said, "but as it is we can't help ourselves—we have to vote for the Right." They'd just gone to work in a lumber yard, and they knew that if they didn't vote the way they were told they'd get the sack. It's a rotten setup. The ones who control the ballot sometimes reward the men who voted for them. They told one man, Pino: "If you vote for these numbers, we'll give you five thousand lire," so he came to me and asked me: "Do they always know which numbers we vote for? They told me to vote for two and five, but I'll take a chance—I'll say I did even if I didn't!"

Just before the elections, the estate overseer invites all the *mezzadri*[3] to a friendly gathering. "Which party are you voting for this year?" he says with a smile, as if it didn't matter to him one way or the other. Maybe one of them who's taken in by his friendly manner will say: "I'm going to vote for the workers' party," and that's the end of him. The agent arranges to have him evicted, or else to leave him with so little land that he'll be forced to quit. He won't find another plot in these parts—he'll have to take himself off and look for one somewhere else!

Some *mezzadri* are Communists and they do their best to hide it. "We've got to make Don Ciccu believe we're C.D.'s,

[3] Sharecroppers.

that we're on the master's side. If we don't, we'll all be evicted next year." One of them even said to me: "Don't come and see me, because if Don Ciccu finds out about it . . ."

If only people would speak their minds when they're told what numbers to vote for, if only they'd say: "Don't bother to pick them out for us—we know how to vote, and how we want to vote, and we'll vote for the numbers we like." It would soon put a stop to this system—they wouldn't dare to point out any particular numbers to us. But where will you find men with enough courage to come right out with the truth?

There ought to be a law that would make it illegal for people that are directly interested in the elections to stand behind the teller when he unfolds the slips, and examine the results for as long a time as they like . . .

THIRD BRACCIANTE: I've been to the woods today in order to pick asparagus. The right time of year for them's April and May; they're few and far between now, and I only managed to find enough for three bundles. I wouldn't go picking if I had regular work, but two or three day's hoeing in the vineyards, or in the bean fields and wheat fields is all I get in a month.

I climb up the mountains, and go way into the brier thickets where the wild asparagus grows. I start out as soon as it's light. I walk three or four miles—it's no good going nearer home. Many times I get to the place I've been heading for only to find out that some other picker's been there before me; and I have to go deeper into the bushes. I may come across two or three sticks of asparagus in one spot, and none at all in another. It takes from a hundred to a hundred and fifty asparagus stalks to make a bundle, and we sell them to people on the road or to passengers on buses that stop here.

There are about twenty of us that go out all the time to pick asparagus, and if we can't find it, nobody can. Our clothes get torn to shreds by the briers, and by the end of the day, with our hands all scratched and bleeding, we look like so many Jesus Christs. Sometimes we come home soaked to the skin, but we haven't got anything to change into, so we get into bed as soon as we've stripped off our rags and wait for them to dry off. Our shoes are falling apart and we have to hold them together with wire. If we paid to have them fixed, we wouldn't be able to buy anything to eat.

Many a morning I start out without a bite of food inside me; I haven't got the money for a loaf of bread till I've sold my bundles of asparagus, and many times I don't manage to sell them until six in the evening when the last bus stops here. If there's a crust left over from the day before, I take it with me, but there hardly ever is because I've got five children.

At the end of May the asparagus begins to go to seed, then there's nothing else to do but wait and hope for a day's hoeing. In June we go reaping; the reaping goes on for about ten days—maybe a little longer. Last year I did a couple of weeks; I got fifteen hundred lire a day and my keep, but I had to work from five A.M. till seven P.M. with only short breaks for meals (maybe an hour and a half altogether). I worked a twelve-hour day, and on top of this, since it was too far for me to go home, I had to sleep out in the open. "The inn of the moon," we call it. Reaping's the only regular work I get in the year; out of what I earn then I pay the rent on my place for a year. I also settle the year's bill with the barber and pay off the small loans I have to make when I don't have money to buy food. I've always got a bill or two hanging around my neck, though, that I can't pay till after next year's reaping, and so it goes—I'm never out of debt.

After the reaping comes the threshing. We take our families with us, even the children five years old and younger—there are hundreds of us. When the threshing's over, more and more peasants come to glean, and we all join together. As soon as there's an acre or so of stubble, we line up one behind the other and start gleaning—we rush around like crazy, each of us trying to outdo the others and pick up the most. When there isn't a single ear left, we move on to find other work.

The villagers from Missilmeri and Partinico come here to glean. They come in carts that are drawn by mules or donkeys, and they camp in the fields.

The sun's so bad that lots of people are taken sick. Last year it was too much for my wife; she got dizzy and fainted, and I had to carry her to the water hole. There are lots of pregnant women and others with small babies, some of them no more than two months old. The babies are left in charge of a seven- or eight-year-old while their mothers work. The heat curdles their milk sometimes, and the babies break out in a sweat and get colic because they can't take it—some of them die from sunstroke.

There are old people, too, that go gleaning. Last year my mother-in-law, who's seventy, came with us. Sometimes, all of a sudden, a big black adder that looks a mile long'll rear up its head at us from the stubble, and give all the children and the grownups too a terrible scare. They're harmless, but they can give you an awful fright.

Oftentimes, after I've been gleaning for half an hour, the *mezzadro* whose land I'm on will come around and tell me to clear out, or he may order me to give him half of what I pick up—the *mezzadri* consider this their right. What can I do but go halves with him? Some *padroni* won't let us glean in their fields. "Get off," they shout. "We need the gleanings to fatten our stock."

Sometimes we go gleaning in the afternoon. The families that live far away spend the night out in the open. When there's a big crowd of us, and the *padrone* wants us to clear out, he starts firing his gun in the air to scare us and make us go away. Lots of times we sing while we're gleaning—hymns or "Red Flag," it depends who's leading the singing. If a few shocks have been left in the field, some gleaners'll loot them, and pull out a handful or so of wheat. We may get two or three weeks' gleaning, never any more. The last few days, there's very little stubble that's left uncleared, and we wander all over the place looking for ears that might have been over-looked—usually there aren't any to be found. The few stray ears that we haven't picked up already have been eaten by field mice or crickets.

Sometimes we go home with our sacks full—sometimes they're only half full. We pound the ears with a wooden mallet, and winnow the chaff away by fanning with our hands. We get about twelve to eighteen pounds of wheat, and we take it to the miller and he grinds it for us right away. It's the only time of the year we have both bread and pasta to eat.

August is a very bad month. A few men, ten at the most,

are hired to crush sumac leaves; their juice is used for staining leather. There's no work at all for the rest of us.

In September, when the first rains start, we hunt for snails and *crastunedde*. Even before the rain has started, though, the peasants from Corleone come out to look for *babbaluce* under the stones. We go to Bisacquino to sell our snails; this is only a tiny village, and almost all of us are snail hunters, so there are no buyers here. About two or three hundred of us laborers that can't find regular jobs try to make a little this way.

In the Campofiorito district, there are the estates of San Giovanni, Ridocco, and Conte Raineri—about thirty-two hundred acres all told. Only a hundred and seventy acres are cultivated by a co-operative. The Baroness used to lease the land to smallholders that had to give her a hundred pounds of wheat for every four acres they rented; then she fiddled around with the leases, got rid of the smallholders and gave the land to *mezzadri*. Two years later she evicted the *mezzadri* and leased the land to the smallholders again, only this time, for each acre, she took nearly two hundred pounds of wheat—roughly half the land she leased out was fit for plowing, the rest was pasture land. We're still waiting for something to happen from the land reforms.

In November, we may get four or five days' work, maybe a week, sowing wheat. We may get a little more going over the olive trees for any olives the regular pickers have overlooked. Other people still go over them after us in case we've left a few. There aren't many olive trees in these parts, though.

In December the fennel begins to sprout. We gather it and a little wild chicory and sell it in Bisacquino.

In January we start making charcoal. We cut down briers and cover them over with dirt, light a fire over them, bake them very slow, and moisten the dirt with water. We sell the charcoal to villagers, and they kindle it with a few sticks; the well-to-do people with good stoves don't use charcoal. Sometimes, during the winter, there's a regional training center set up here to teach us a little forestry, roadbuilding, and so on. January and February are bad months for us—if we get eight or ten days' work we can count ourselves lucky. A few of us try to make something as criers,[4] but it's a business that's out of our line; some of the others go to farms and clean out the stables for a half-pound of pasta or bread; and still others climb up the mountainsides to cut down *disa*. *Disa*'s used for making brooms, but when it's dry it's no good for that, so we sell it to poor people. They always burn *disa* and straw in their stoves. For eight bundles we get the price of four pounds of bread; that's all we make for a hard day's work. We have to have a donkey or a mule to carry the heavy bundles, and the *disa* grows so far from here that we can't make more than two trips a day.

It's only when we have two or three weeks' regular work that we can afford to buy ourselves enough to eat. There are seven of us, and we've got half a room and even that is halfway below the ground, it's no better than a stable. When we want water we go to the fountain; when it's dark we light wicks that are soaked in paraffin. The owner won't bother to put in electricity. I'd put it in myself if it were my place. My oldest boy, who's twelve, helps in the bar when he gets out of school; he gets three thousand lire a month. My second boy, who's nine, always comes with me to give me a hand when I'm gathering greens.

Just after the war we had a Leftist administration. They sent a commission here to see what could be done for us, and started a few projects. But at the end of one year the elections were held, and the Baroness promised us that if we voted for the Civica party, there'd be plenty of work for all of us. Well, the Civica party got in, but we never heard any more about the work. Nothing comes our way but a little help, a little charity in the winter and that's all. Five years ago, Rizzotto, the secretary of the *Camera di Lavoro*, was murdered—nothing's ever come to light about the crime . . .

FOURTH BRACCIANTE: There are at least twenty-five hundred of us in Corleone, which is the biggest village in these parts. According to custom, we all gather around the lamp-post in the piazza at four every morning; it's the market for

---

[4] To announce political meetings, etc. (not advertising). *Translator's note.*

flesh and blood. There we stand waiting, all us men that are for sale, waiting for the half-dozen landowners to come by and pick out the four or five that each of them wants to hire. As soon as they get to the piazza the auction begins.

"You—how much do you want?" an owner will say to one of us.

"Eight hundred lire," may be his answer.

"What! eight hundred lire!" says the owner. "I never heard of such a price!" and he walks off, goes over to somebody else and says, "What about you? I'll pay you five hundred," or whatever he feels like paying at that moment.

The man thinks of all the times he's stood in the piazza, of his children, of his wife's nagging when he comes home, after waiting and waiting for nothing: "I can't figure out why you're never able to get work any more. In the old days . . ." He thinks of it all and he says in desperation:

"All right, I'll take five hundred."

It's harder than ever for us to get work these days with so much machinery being used. Machinery's all right, it saves a lot of energy, but it takes the bread out of our mouths—something ought to be done about it so that we and our families could live.

Quite often four or five owners will come to the piazza together, after they've agreed that they won't offer any more than four or five hundred lire.

I'll tell you about the hiring market at Alcamo. At three A.M.—maybe a little earlier or a little later, according to the season—the men are all gathered in the piazza. Lots of them haven't got clocks at home; they jump out of bed the second the cock crows—probably it's no more than half-past one. It's pitch dark, so they know they'll be way too early, but they don't dare go to sleep again—it's better to be too early than too late.

The overseer has his breakfast in peace, and then makes his way to the piazza, where he's surrounded right away by the men. He stands there and looks at them with his hands in his pockets, then he lights a cigarette or a cigar. "Are you hiring any men this morning, Don Peppino?" the men ask him, and he shakes his head short. "Have you pulled up the vines at such-and-such a place, Don Peppino?" some men will ask him that have already worked for him, hoping to get into his good graces. "No," he says, discouraging them. Probably he'll walk a few steps, and as soon as he stops another bunch of men gather around him. He looks at them like he's annoyed, walks some more, stops again, and once more he's in the center of a circle. "Have you pulled up the vines yet, Don Peppino? . . ." Every time he stops, the men do their best to get his attention.

At last he makes up his mind. "I want four men," he says. He looks them over from top to toe, picks out four strong, well-built young fellows who'll give him something for his money, taps them on the shoulder and feels their muscles. Once he's sure he's got hold of a man who's really good with a hoe, he'll say: "Well, my lad, you're hired—go and stand over there," and he pushes him to one side. As soon as he's picked all the men he needs, the fun begins. "Now then, I'll pay you so much," he says. (The prices change according to the season, but an overseer'll fix his own price.) If one of the men he's picked won't accept it, another one plucks the overseer's sleeve. "I'll take it," he says. Sometimes, none of the men he's picked is willing to work at the low rate he's offering. "Very well," he says, and he turns his back on them. "If any of you others want to be hired, you'd better follow me." Ten or fifteen of them rush after him, and he stops once more, takes his pick, and away he goes.

The overseers have another trick. If one of them's hiring men for a day, he gets to the piazza very early, but if it's a question of a week's work, he takes his time. He knows that the man that's been waiting there for hours with two hundred or so other men, out of which no more than twenty have been hired, has lost heart and is thinking of the angry reception he's going to get when he gets home. "You didn't get hired, then," his wife'll say, and it's no use trying to quiet her down by saying "Neither did Pierino, neither did Ciccio . . ." It's the same story day after day. But to go gack. The overseer shows up in the piazza the minute the men have lost all hope of getting hired. As soon as they see him, they push around him. "It's too late in the day to hire workers," he says, but suddenly he picks out a few of them. When they ask him for the fixed rate, he refuses to consider it. "Look what time it is!"

he says, and he offers them one or two or three hundred lire less. It's take it or leave it, and if they complain at the end of the week about the cut price, all they get is: "You lost half a day's work on Monday."

What are we supposed to do? "We better take what's offered—lousy as it is, it's better than nothing." That's what we think, and so we sell ourselves dirt-cheap.

Of course there are a few decent overseers, but only a very few. If one of us tries to talk the rest into agreeing that they won't work for less than a certain rate, the police get to hear about it and they keep their eyes on the "agitator." They send their plainclothes men into the piazza to watch out for any signs of trouble, and these birds make very sure that the "agitator" doesn't get us united. "Bad egg, that guy," one of them'll say to somebody who hasn't the slightest idea that he's a spy, "he'll be arrested before long." Of course, the story spreads, and we're scared to go near him.

By the time a laborer's forty or forty-five, he's got very little chance of being hired. The strong young fellow who's standing next to him is taken, and he's passed over. It happens to him morning after morning, but he goes to the piazza just the same, hoping that his turn'll come.

A trusted man that works all year round for an owner and gets a lower total wage, often is given two or three eggs to eat when he has a hard day's hoeing ahead of him; he has to set the pace for the rest, so he needs his strength. The faster he goes, the faster the men behind him, with their backs bent over their heavy, short-handled hoes, have to follow.

Sunday is payday. The laborer goes to the owner's house to get his wages, and quite likely he finds that he's out, that he's gone around to his club. But he may be home. "Is Don Turiddu in?" the laborer asks the servant that opens the door. "I'll go and see," she says, and leaves him standing there. "There's someone to see you, Don Turiddu," she says. "Who is it?" says the master. "A laborer, Don Turiddu." "Ask him what his name is," the master orders. Well, the servant goes and comes back, and probably the master'll say: "Oh, him! Tell him I'm out!" Oftentimes an owner will keep a man hanging around a whole day—it never occurs to him that the poor bastard needs the money to buy food for his family. Sometimes, before he pays him, he'll make him do an odd job—he'll get him to run a few errands or clean out the stables.

Of course, the *mezzadri* that exploit their workers get exploited themselves by the owners of the estates.

By eight o'clock, or nine at the latest, the men in the piazza know there's no hope of being hired. They go home in despair, and have to listen to their children crying with hunger. To make a lira or two they go out in the country to pick greens, or they gather kindling wood which the baker gives them a little bread for. Many times they're in such a state of mind that they just wander around aimlessly and trespass on somebody's land; if they get caught, they're fined or maybe sent to prison. Some unemployed laborers are driven to becoming thieves and lose everything that a man should value: honesty, decency and self-respect. There are plenty of murderers that walk around unsuspected, but the poor bastard that's forced into stealing a few lousy sticks of firewood is branded a criminal for life.

In Palermo you can always make a little money on the sly in some racket or other, but you can't do that in the country.

Sometimes when I go out to glean, the *padrone*'ll say: "All right, I'll let you glean if you'll carry some straw for me, winnow a little wheat." The villagers from Modica come here for the gleaning. They come in small groups and the overseers allow the women and children to glean provided the men agree to give them a hand with the heavy work. Whole families of them come and sleep "at the inn of the moon" (in the open fields); some of the men don't even mind their wives taking care of the overseers.

As for the landowners, they treat the *mezzadri* so bad that the *mezzadri* don't take any interest in the land they hold for only twelve months at a time; they don't even bother to clear it of stones and weeds or pull up the ivy spreading all over the place. When I was a *mezzadro*, for instance, there was some trouble over the sharing of the harvest. The owner of the land was furious when I refused to give him more than the 40 percent he was entitled to by law. He was carrying a gun and his son followed him with a pistol. He walked onto the threshing floor. He wouldn't listen to reason, and when I reminded him that he owed me for two days' pay, he shouted at me: "Go to the Rubina!" (The Rubina estate belonged to Baron Cammarata, who filled the courtyard with beautiful peacocks.) "Go and get your pay from the *pay*cocks!"

If a *mezzadro* sticks up for his rights, the owner calls him a no-good scoundrel, and gives him such a bad character in Corleone that nobody will lease him a scrap of land. All the landowners in the district blacklist him and his family.

Bernardino Verro and Giovanni Zangara were assassinated in Corleone just because they upheld the rights of the *braccianti;* that was a good while before Placido Rizzotto was murdered for the same reason on March 10, 1948. Two more syndicalists, Nicolò Cianciano and Luciano Nicoletti, were killed on their way home from the fields. The *mafiosi* are trigger-happy. A hundred and nine men from Corleone lost their lives in the 1914-18 war; the list of those that've been murdered in these parts since the end of World War II already numbers a hundred and thirty-eight . . .

Vincenzo C.

Three nights ago I dreamed about pigs. I dreamed about cows, too, chewing their cud in the fields. Every night I dream about cows and mountains and goats and sheep and lambs. Sometimes I dream I'm tending my animals. Last night I dreamed I was tending them in the fields where I always go and I saw somebody coming towards me. It was my father, and he was carrying a ewe and two lambs in his arms. He put them down in the grass, and a cow suckled one of the lambs and the ewe suckled the other one. Then along came an old man and killed a lamb, and a hen began to cackle and she laid an egg. The old man took the egg, sucked it, threw the empty shell down, and started to run away. I picked up a stick and ran after him, to hit him with the stick, but I couldn't catch him. So after a while I stopped running and my mother came up to me and said, "Who broke that egg? Who killed that lamb?" and I told her the old man and that he was bad. "We'll cook the lamb and eat it," my father said, but I said: "No, let's carry it over to that olive tree and leave it there because it's so small." So we carried the lamb over to the olive tree and laid it down in the grass and left it there.

Once I dreamed we were in a truck, taking some pigs to market to sell at the fair. The pigs had leather collars around their necks.

I had another dream last night. I dreamed I was in the mountains and I was taking a herd of cows, three hundred perhaps, to drink. There were other cows in the mountains. But there wasn't any water, so I went to see if I could find some. Ever since I've been shut in by these walls, I've dreamed about animals and fields and mountains . . .

One dream was about my uncles. "Don't be a coward, you must be brave," they said to me. I dreamed I saw a stake outside a door, and fastened to this stake was a chain, and behind another door, fastened to this chain, was a pig. The pig grunted and grunted, and I didn't know what it wanted. There was water there, but the pig didn't want water. Then a man came out of the door and said: "Did you bring any broccoli tops?" "Yeah," I said. Then I walked along with him a while, and in my dream he said to me: "Why don't you go away?" "I won't go away because you haven't paid me for the work I did for you last week," I said. "I won't go away till you do pay me." Then he said, "All right," and he gave me a thousand lire. "That's not very much," I said. But he thought that three hundred lire a day was much too much to give me—he didn't want to give me more than two hundred lire. "I'll pay you a thousand lire or nothing," he said, and I took it and went away.

Once, in February last year—which month of the year is this, February?—I dreamed I was galloping on a horse at the seashore, with a machine gun in my hand, and I saw two bulls goring each other with their horns. The next morning the man brought the summons (this wasn't a dream, though the bulls on the seashore were a dream) and they put me in prison and punished me because the police sergeant called me a bastard, so I called him a bastard. I don't know what bastard means, but it must be a bad word. Then the priest came (I did not dream this either) and he said that if anybody called me a bastard, I shouldn't say bastard, I shouldn't answer. So I said: "Why shouldn't I answer?" and he said: "If they hit you, you must turn the other cheek." Then I said: "By the horns on your head and the horns on the sergeant's head, didn't you both say bastard?"

Sometimes I dream about girls I've seen, I dream of lying with them. Once I dreamed about a girl I saw going to Mass with her friends. I dreamed she called me, and I went to her house and shook hands with her father and mother, but she wasn't glad to see me and wouldn't let me shake her hand. Then I dreamed I was in bed with a girl—she was my cousin. Another time I dreamed I saw that other girl coming out of church with two of her friends, and I just came out of the stable and they both stopped and looked at me. I was wearing a beret and a thick coat, and the girl came closer and closer and said: "What! Are you still here?" And I was still there . . .

I always dream of animals—animals out in the fields—because ever since I was five years old I've looked after animals. I was born among the animals.

I was the first one to get born. My brothers and sisters came after me. I was five when I began to look after animals, not our animals, though—my father was hired for a year, or half a year—how many months make a year?—and they gave him four thousand or five thousand lire a month. I don't know how many months make a year. I don't know if I'm seventeen or eighteen—we could get a letter written to the place where they know when people are born. I can count up to fifty, but I don't understand soldi because I was always in the fields and I never went to the villages and I never saw Christians. Sometimes I was with my father, but not so often. My mother doesn't understand soldi either, and she can't count at all. I used to cook herbs and roots and wild cabbages and eat them. I can count up to fifty lire, but that's all—I can't add them up with any other soldi.

If you don't have any work, you eat herbs. When you're hungry, funny things happen to you. You can't see out of your eyes. Being hungry makes you kill yourself, it makes you do awful things. If you got work, you got everything. If you get paid good wages, then you do your work right, and you talk right to people—you don't say bad things to them. No mistake about it, we all kill each other. If a man knows how to go get a job, a boss'll hire him and trust him. But me—who'd trust me? My head's always going round and round and round, and I don't know what I'm doing. What was I saying? Yeah, we all kill each other. If us two, for instance, stole some other man's bread and soldi, and wanted to make sure he wouldn't talk, what would we do? We'd kill him.

Once I fell off a horse and broke my arm. It was my master's horse and I was taking it to the water trough to drink. I should have got some money because I broke my arm, but nobody ever gave me any.

Sometimes, but not too often, there'd be six of us kids together in the fields; none of them could understand soldi or how to count. Nearly always, though, I was alone. The rich men don't care anything about us—they just go on tramping around the country in their leather boots.

All of us in here—we're headed for prison, just like we're headed for the graveyard. We fight, we kill each other, and we either end up in prison or in the graveyard. When a man comes out of prison he's more wild than when he went in. "You ruined my honor," he'll say to his enemy. "Now you're going to pay for it!" and he kills him. He'd get away with it, too, if there weren't any spies. Take us; if I killed you or you killed me, nobody would know anything about it unless somebody squealed. It's the spies that get us; if the police didn't have any spies, crimes could be committed right under their noses and they wouldn't even know it.

I used to be away from the village for six months or a year, and when I came back I was so wild-looking that the kids didn't know who I was and they were so scared they threw sticks and stones at me till I ran away. Once, one of them hit me with a lot of scraps of colored paper, and I grabbed hold of him and bit his finger.

I've got a brother that's thirteen and a brother that's

twelve—they don't understand soldi, they can't count. I've got a little brother five and a little sister six—there were two more but they died. Then there's the sister that came after I did, but I can't tell you her age. Maybe she's twelve, maybe she's sixteen, I don't know—she's married, she got married when I was in prison.

When I was real young, the *sbirri*[1] came and took us all to the barracks—my mother and father and all of us. We cried and cried and cried. My father jumped off the cart and ran away, and they couldn't find him. They put my mother in prison and she kept the baby with her because she was nursing it; and they sent the rest of us away. My mother was in prison six months, then they caught my father and let her go.

After that I went and lived in the fields and looked after cows and goats and sheep. I didn't take my clothes off at night—I just used to lie down in the straw and I pulled it over me, I didn't have any covers or anything. A lot of times I didn't have any shoes to wear, and sometimes I had nothing to eat. I was covered with fleas. I milked the cows, but the *padrone* wouldn't let me drink a drop of it—if I did, he used to beat me. In the morning I had bread and whey, and at night bread and onions, or, if there were any olives, bread and olives. Sometimes I ran all the way down the mountain to where the houses were, in the valley. When I went to a house the dogs barked and snapped at me, but I went past them and knocked at the door and said I was hungry and asked for some bread. Some people gave me a crust, and some people wouldn't give me anything. When they didn't give me bread, I stole it.

One day I was coming back from the fields holding onto my father's hand when all of a sudden he saw the *sbirri* coming, and he ran away for all he was worth and left me by myself. The *sbirri* fired at him, and he dived into the river. Some of the *sbirri* were riding, some were walking, and they fired ninety-one rounds at him with their machine guns. One bullet hit him just between the shoulders if it'd hit him a little higher or a little lower, it would have killed him. He got out of the water and hid behind a hedge, but the man that owned the field saw him and yelled to the *sbirri*: "There he is!" So

[1] Police.

they got a hold of him by one foot like he was a ewe or a lamb and they pulled him out. One of them said: "Is he alive or dead?" "Dead," said another one. Then my father opened his eyes: "Dead, am I, you cuckolds?" he shouted. "Not half as dead as you are, you lousy bastards!" And he spit at them.

They put him in prison for three years, one month and fifteen days—my father added up the time. When he was let out he wasn't allowed to go outside the village for three whole years. I worked, but I was very little then, and I couldn't do much work, so we were always hungry. I looked after four cows for a man; he went halves in one of them with me and gave me a share in the other four.[2]

I washed myself in the summer; when I took the cows and the sheep down to the shore, I washed myself with the sea water. I didn't go in the ocean, I couldn't swim. In the winter I never washed. Once I took the cows into the man's field where my father hid from the *sbirri*, and he ran after me with a stick, shouting that he'd beat me, but I got away. Another time, when I went into his field he pulled out a knife and said he'd cut my throat, but I got away that time too. I left the cows behind me, and I met my uncles and they said: "Where are the cows?" So I told my uncles where I left them, and my uncles saw the man driving the cows towards the village; he was going to keep them, but my uncles took them away from him. Another time, my uncles had a fight with him.

I never went to school—I never even went to school for one single day. Nobody in my family ever went to school—we can't read or write, any of us.

Last night I dreamed about my uncles. They were dressing a white sheepskin. I dreamed about cows, too—the cows were chewing grass.

What are stars? I know what stars are. The sun and the moon make the stars. I look up at night and see I don't know how many stars. It must be smoke, all the smoke in the world,

[2] Instead of paying him, his employer gave him half the milk money of one cow, and so much of the milk money of the others. If the cows were sold, he was given a proportionate amount of the money. *Translator's note.*

that makes the sky—sometimes you can see the smoke, sometimes you can't. The moon's made out of the sky, the sky's made out of smoke—all the smoke rises up from the earth. Sometimes, in the morning, you can see the sun and the moon both together in the sky. The stars never stay still, they move around in the sky all night long. Then when it gets light, they go away; just like the cows go in their stalls, the stars go in theirs. All of us human beings and all the animals, too, are just like the stars.

I dream a lot about fire. What does it mean to dream about fire? I see a fire and I'm afraid and I run away. But it's only in my dreams that I'm afraid of fire. When I'm awake, fire doesn't scare me. Sometimes I dream people are pushing me under the water and trying to drown me and I scream and then they beat me.

The earth is an island, there's water all around it. I know because before I was in Trapani, I was in the Colombaia jail, and I got quite sure that the earth is the earth, and that we're planted in the middle of an island. When I was in the Colombaia, I said to myself: "If there's sea all around here and the sea's at Castellammare, too, then for sure, the earth's an island." When they took me in handcuffs to the Colombaia I understood what an island was, because Colombaia is an island.

What's Italy? Italy's an island, too. Italy's here, Italy's in the Ucciardone too. There's jail here and there's also Italy. Italy's in Sicily, too. What's the difference between Sicily and Italy? When they say: "*Giornale di Sicilia*," they mean the newspaper of all the different parts.

In the world, there are different countries, and lots of houses; the world looks just like half a pumpkin. Since I've been in prison, I have lots of things I never had before: a bed with a mattress, pillows, sheets and a blanket. I never had any of those things. I know I was born in the country because they told me, I remember my father telling me. I've stood outside houses, but I never went inside. What would I do there? Was I the master? When I knew the *sbirri* were coming to catch me, I used to hide with my cows, and whenever I saw them I ran away.

I know how to shoot. If I shot at a Christian, I'd get him.

I met a man who taught me how to shoot. He was carrying a long stick and it went bang-bang. "Will you give me that stick?" I said, and he said, "It's not a stick, it's a gun." "Will you show me how to make it go bang-bang?" I said, and he let me put my hand on the gun and I made it go bang-bang at two branches of a fig tree and they fell on the ground. He taught me how to shoot; he held the gun and I pulled the trigger.

In the summertime when the rabbits hide in the rocks, I used to catch them with my hands. I used to break their necks, skin them and clean them out, and cook them on the fire. I ate them just the way they were, without any salt or oil. Who would've given me oil? To light the fire, I rubbed two stones together and they made sparks—we call the stones that make the sparks fire stones. Well, I put the rabbit on the fire, and as soon as it was brown on one side, I turned it over, and when it was done, I ate it. Sometimes I ate the rabbit raw. I used to eat snails raw, too; sometimes I ate whole snails, shells and all. I ate asparagus, and I ate orach, roots and all, whenever I could find it. I like orach. Whenever I was near water, I caught frogs, skinned them, and cooked them on the fire. I caught foxes, too; there are big foxes and little foxes and I set traps for them outside the caves where they lived. Once I caught a great big fox that sank its teeth into my shoulder—I picked up a big stone and bashed its head in.

I ate wild dogs whenever I could catch them. If I managed to get ahold of one, I killed it by flinging it to the ground; if it wasn't killed right away, I kept throwing it down till it was. Then the crows would come down and start pecking at it, and I'd throw rocks at them to scare them away. I sucked the eggs of goldfinches and robins, and I ate porcupines, too. I put straw outside their holes, and when they came out they got trapped in it and I hit them with a stick and killed them. Porcupines are very nice to eat—they taste like rabbits. They're hard to skin with all their bristles, but I did it with my bare hands and cooked them on the fire. I used to eat a whole porcupine at once.

When I was in the Colombaia, they gave me a few school lessons. They showed me an egg—"O for Ovo," they said, and then they showed me a small o with a little leg on it and told me it was a. Then they made a noise like a cow: "Uuuu-uuuh!" and that's how I learnt U. Then they taught me E, and that's all.

What would I like to do if I had a choice? I'd like to look after animals. I'd like to be able to count. I'd like to understand what money's worth. I'd like to work hard and buy things and sell things and earn a little money. I'd like to buy a pair of shoes for one hundred lire, for instance, and sell them for two hundred lire. How much does a pair of shoes cost? I've only had four pairs of shoes in my whole life. When my father came out of jail, he gave me the first shoes I ever had and when they split open he gave me another pair. The rubber ones I'm wearing now one of my cousins gave me; I had another pair but they had hobnails and I kept on slipping and falling on the cement floor and the stone steps; every time I fell, the guards stared at me, so I sent them home and went barefoot. Then my cousin gave me these.

Is there any way to make the world a better place? *Puttana*, sure there's a way! Want me to tell you what it is? The way to make the world a better place would be to do away with the jails. But, somebody would say, if there weren't any jails, we'd all start fighting and killing each other. Well, maybe we would, but we'd use common sense and only kill the people that deserve to be killed.

Is there anybody the head of Italy? Sure there is. Who? Mussolini, I think. There's others over us, too: the lawyers and judges that gobble up the money and keep us down. We ought to kill all the people that hurt us—it's because of them we haven't got anything to eat.

What difference is there between my life up in the mountains and life in the city? Well, I grew up wild—men in the city wouldn't look at me, wouldn't have anything to do with me. We're different, you see. They can read and write, they've got work, they know how to behave. They're used to being with each other, but up in the mountains you're always alone. It would be all right to live with Christians if you knew how to talk to them, but if you can't talk to them, if you can't act like they do, they don't want to have anything to do with you—they throw stones at you so you'll go away—they kill you. They do some horrible things to you—lock you up, put you in jail, put you away. If you're a scarecrow like me, they won't pay any attention to you, but they all run after the rich and important big shots. They're the ones they ought to kill, not us poor people.

If I had a chance, I'd like to learn to read and write, but I'd never leave my animals—never. They can't talk, but they've got their own way of speaking—when I called them, they said, "Uuu-uuuh!" and they were in such a hurry to turn around that they bounced into each other, and some of them got hurt. You should never be rough with animals; the *padrone* used to hit them between the horns with a rock or a stick if they didn't obey him right away; they never forgot it, and after that they never came when he called. You should always be gentle with them, and see that they get what they need. In May, for instance, and right through the summer, the grass is so dry that they're thirsty all the time; they can't tell you they're thirsty, but when you're tending them you ought to know it, and take them to a place where they can drink; if you don't, they start to get thin and weak. I understand much more about cows and sheep and goats than I do about Christians. When I look after a cow right, she pays me back, she gives me milk; I'm good to her, so she's good to me. But Christians aren't good to me; instead of helping me, they do me harm. I know what to do when I'm with animals, but with Christians—no. My animals, they've showed much more love for me than Christians have. Some of them always stayed close to me. I had a kid and a lamb that used to follow me wherever I went. If I had a little bit of bread, I used to share it with them. They got so tame they'd even eat pasta and tomato sauce. If I went into the barn, so would they, and if I went down to the seashore they'd come with me. Whenever I called them, they always answered me in their own way—they'd rush up to me and dance around me. When I'm in the fields, I'm happy, but I'm unhappy when I'm with people because there's so much hate. It's true there are some animals you take a dislike to—a bull maybe, or cows that get on your nerves. There was one cow, for instance, that always kicked at me, and another one that messed up the fig trees and wouldn't come when I called her, and another one that was the greediest cow I ever minded—she had a calf that was as greedy as she was, and was always straying away to feed.

Still, even though some animals are a pain in the neck, they're better than Christians. Some of them go wild and have to be killed; if you can't trust them not to turn on you, they're sold for next to nothing, and they're slaughtered. But if you can't trust a Christian not to turn on you, it's much more dangerous to get rid of him. Suppose, for instance, I killed you or you killed me, we'd have to pay for it. Cows can't think, they can't all get together and do me harm, but Christians can; they can all join together against me to take the food out of my mouth, and take away my freedom.

I've never had any real friends except the lamb and the kid. I hardly ever saw my father—he was either away in the army or away in prison, and when they let him out he wasn't allowed to leave the village. My mother and my brothers like me, but nobody, not even God Himself, has ever cared about me as much as that kid and that lamb did. I watched them get born, I looked after them when they were little and lifted them up in my arms so they could suck the cow's teats. I really loved them—they were real good, they followed me around just like puppies.

I wish maybe I didn't love them so much, but I couldn't help it. My brothers had each other to play with, but I had nobody—nobody except that kid and that lamb that used to leap and jump all around me.

I wish I didn't love them because, you see, I had to have money to buy bread with, so I had to sell the kid. For a whole month I just couldn't do it—I wanted the money, but I wanted the kid, too. "Shall I sell it or shall I keep it?" I kept asking myself—I didn't know what to do. The kid had a white coat, but its head was red, and it had splotches of red on its neck. Its eyes were just like a human being's, like yours and mine, and it had a little hairy tail. Its horns had started to curve in. I loved that kid so much I couldn't stand the idea of parting with it, but in the end I forced myself to sell it. With the money I got, I bought a couple pounds of bread and a couple pounds of fish, but every mouthful I ate, when I thought about the kid, the food stuck in my throat. I couldn't eat anything for two whole days, and I couldn't stop crying. I went back to work, but for eight months I kept thinking and thinking about the kid, I've never stopped thinking about it . . .

My mother loves me. Whenever I left home to go up in the mountains, she'd say: "Be careful, now—be sure not to fall and hurt yourself. Be sure to be honest, and keep to yourself —don't have anything to do with people that'd hurt you." Then she'd kiss me, and I'd go far, far away—sometimes it would be six months before I'd see her again. She would always give me bread when she had any; I only went without when she didn't have any.

I've spent two Christmases and two Easters in prison; when I was free, I had some Christmases and Easters home, and some up in the mountains. They've started showing us movies; I never saw a movie till I came here, and when I saw one the first time I couldn't make out what it was all about—men waving swords and galloping around on horses all over the place. One picture was about a circus: there was a lady that balanced herself on this great big ball and a horse that walked on a tightrope. The first time I rode on a train, I was eleven. We were going to visit my father in the Colombaia, but when the train stopped, and we got out, the sea was so rough the boat couldn't cross, so we had to go back. The second time I rode in a train was when I fell off the horse and broke my arm, and the third time was when they took me to prison.

How many parties are there? Three or four, I think—the Socialists, the priests' Democrats, the Monarchists and the Communists. They ought to cut off the heads of all the Democrats and play ball with them. The Monarchists are the richest of all, they've got the most; they hang onto people's throats and strangle them. I've got no use for any of the parties, I don't belong to any of them—I can't vote because I've been in prison. If I had my way, I'd stand the whole lot of them up against a wall and shoot them. They're all sons of bitches. None of them that have anything to do with the law tell the truth—pigs, that's all they are. When it's election time they give presents to the people—clothes and stuff. I know because I heard some Christians talking about it, and I caught a few words here and there.

What sort of government have they got in America and Russia? The same kind of government that we have. What's Russia? Russia's a little island. What's China? Is it a kind of grape? I never heard of China.

It's just on account of two bunches of herbs that I'm here in prison. I was picking herbs in a field when a boy saw me and whistled. The *padrone* came running and I threw a rock at him, and ran like hell with my cow ahead of me. The first time the *sbirri* came to get me, I was in the barn; I was raking out the straw when I heard the sound of horses' hoofs. I put up a fight when they got ahold of me and tried to handcuff me—I didn't want them to take me to jail.

Another time, the *sbirri* came when I was milking; I hid in the middle of the cows, but they saw me and caught me. They made me walk between them, they rode on both sides of me and took me to the barracks. When we got there they threatened me with their knives and beat me and kicked me and wrote down what I said, not with pens, though—they tapped on something that went tin-tin-tin—I don't know what kind of a son-of-a-bitching thing it was. When the tin-tin-tin was over, they made me put a cross on the paper, and then they let me go.

But four months after that, they came and arrested me and put me in prison. Then they sent me to the Colombaia. Then they tried me and sentenced me to four years and twenty days. They tried to make the judge give me six years. The judge asked me if I wanted to appeal; I was crying so hard I couldn't see out of my eyes. Ever since I've been here in the Ucciardone I've been waiting for my appeal to get heard. They keep fixing a day for it, but when the day comes, the man that brought the case against me, the man I picked herbs from, doesn't show up, so it has to be put off till another day . . .

Campofiorito

Campofiorito, which is more than two thousand feet above sea level, is a typical inland village between Bisacquino and Corleone. When the 1951 census was taken, it had a population of twenty-two hundred and twenty-five. Campofiorito is linked to the neighboring villages by a daily service of six buses, but the farm lands are so far away that a farm worker can hardly exist unless he has a mule or a donkey to take him to work. The tracks are much too narrow for carts, hence the manure cannot be brought back to Campofiorito and has to be burned in the fields.

The fifty families considered were picked at random. They live in forty-seven rooms. The average number of persons to a room here is 4.17. Thirty-seven of these rooms have recesses for beds. The average number of persons to a sleeping place is 1.87.

Thirty-two families share living space with their animals. Four families have pigs, twenty-two have hens, ten have mules, six have donkeys, one has a cow and one has a goat.

Twenty-seven families have radios, four have toilets, fourteen have gas, sixteen have water taps and twenty-seven have electric light.

Among the children from six through thirteen years old, twenty-six go to school, eleven do not. On the average, the people over six years old have almost finished the second grade.

As for the occupations of the heads-of-family, nineteen are farm workers working about seventy days out of the year, six are *mezzadri*, four are smallholders, one is a carter, one is a vendor and one is a mailman. There are fourteen disabled men of whom four own a little land (in no case more than five acres) and ten own none.

La Patata

Where do we get our leeches from? There's a man catches
them in the springs at Canicattí and comes here to sell them,
but we mostly buy them in Palermo. We've just sent for a
hundred—we need a good supply because some won't fasten
on, and two or three die every day before we use them. They
die when there's a hot wind—none of them live more than a
couple of months. We keep them in glass bottles filled with
water, and change the water every day—we're very particular about that in summer. They cost us a hundred lire apiece,
and we charge a hundred and fifty for every leech we put on.

On what part of the body do we put the leeches? It's all
according. Between the shoulders and on the chest for bron-
chitis, behind the ears for meningitis and sunstroke. When
we use leeches on a child with diphtheria, we throw them
away the minute they drop off—the blood they've sucked is
poisoned, and it often kills the leeches outright. Usually,
though, we can use a leech several times. We apply leeches
for sprains too. They do much more good than injections,
they're the best cure of all. We put them on children with
chest trouble, we even put them on week-old babies. When
people get ill in Valleldolmo, Alia, or anywhere else in these
parts, they always call us in, no matter whether they're rich
or poor; there are two or three of us in every village, more
if it's a big one.

There's nothing like a leech to help the sick. Wonderful
creatures, they are. When they drop off, we just stroke them
with our fingers and milk the blood out of them, or we give

them a saucerful of wine to drink; it makes them tipsy, and they throw up the wine and all the blood they sucked. Then we wash them and put them into fresh water.

We put leeches behind the ears of anyone who's got typhus; as soon as they drop off, we cut them in two and throw them away to make sure we don't use them again. When a leech has fastened on, it makes an opening with its sharp little teeth and through it it sucks the blood, and as soon as it's full, it drops off of its own will; we have to milk them or give them wine to drink right away, otherwise the blood'd curdle inside them and they'd die. We can't make any profit unless we can use a leech more than once. When it drops off, it's all swollen up, it's just like a little bottle, and so much blood comes out of it when it's milked that it gives some women a real scare.

How many leeches do we put on at a time? Sometimes up to six or seven. For meningitis brought on by the heat, though, we put on twenty; the person gets over the meningitis, and even though he's kind of hard of hearing for the rest of his life, what's that? We also put lots of leeches on people with too-rich blood, on people who've been kicked by a mule while they were threshing. If we haven't got enough leeches we send for the barber. He opens a vein in the sick person's wrist and lets out a stream of blood. We hardly ever call the doctor; it costs too much. He charges five hundred or a thousand lire for a visit, but you don't have to pay the barber, you just give him a present—one hundred lire maybe.

If a woman has milk fever, we put leeches on her stomach. Or if a mother's milk won't flow, we put them on her breasts. For piles, we apply them to her back parts. We also use leeches to cure toothaches. These cures we use have been handed down from mother to daughter, for I don't know how long. "Look—this is what you do," a mother will say to her daughter, and that's how she learns. The other day I cured a woman—her navel cord was dropping. I made her turn around and around while I wound it around my finger three times, and then she was cured.

I can rid people of worms, too. I rub the person who's got them, and while I'm rubbing I recite this charm:

Monday is holy,
Holy, most holy,

[and so on through all the days of the week till Saturday.
Then:]

On Easter Sunday the worms will fall
Onto the ground so kill them all,
Chop head and tail off each that squirms
And free this living creature from worms.

The minute I've finished saying these words, the worms
come right out of the person's body.

If a woman washes her breasts in cold water, her milk'll
curdle and the baby can't digest it. While she's crying with
pain, I say this other charm:

I met a man bound with a cord to a maid,
Mighty St. Martin, come to my aid,
With this clear water as pure as dew,
Come forth, evil, I conjure you
In the name of the Father, the Son and the Holy Ghost.

Then I say a Credo to the Sacred Heart of Jesus and a
Salve Regina to the Madonna of Altomare and pray that the
woman's pain will be taken away. I repeat the Credo and the
Salve two or three times, and then, all of a sudden, her
breasts get soft and she stops crying. Sometimes a woman's
milk'll curdle in the night and she'll scream with pain; I rub
her breasts and say these prayers and very soon she's all right
again.

Doctors don't know about these cures, or if they do know,
they don't believe in them. At harvest time the hard work
often makes a man's wrist swell; we rub them with foxes'
grease and the swelling quickly goes down. We can remove
the evil eye from people too; we sprinkle salt on the head of
the bewitched person and recite prayers.

What sort of work do the village women do? The housework, of course, and after that, the most important thing is
gleaning. Whole families go off to glean, and at night they

sleep in the *pagliari*.[1] There are *pagliari* at Tudia, Vicarietto, La Niculiddia, Berboncando, Susafa, Mattarieddu, Belice and Polizzello, and people live in them all year round. There are *pagliari* in other places, too. A man with a *salma* of land who can't afford to build a proper house—he'll put up a *pagliaro;* his laborers help him and the women gather things.

Last year, R. and his wife left one of their children inside a *pagliaro,* and their other two playing nearby, while they were out in the field gleaning. There was a glass bottle in the *pagliaro,* and the sun's rays shone down on it so hard that it set the whole place on fire. The mother saw the flames and rushed over; her hair caught fire, and her face and hands were badly burned as she tried to save her baby. She screamed and sobbed, and her husband and the overseers they came running, but there was nothing they could do. We all just stood there crying, helpless. Poor people—a few ears of wheat cost them the life of their little one. They had nothing left but the clothes they stood up in—everything else was burned to ashes.

The notaries came and wanted to know all about the fire. *Pagliari* are always catching fire, and always, somebody's burned to death. Not long ago the gleaners were out in the fields and a storm blew up, and two brothers took shelter with their horse and their two mules inside a *pagliaro.* Another young fellow wanted to come in, but they said there wasn't room for him, so he ran off and took shelter in a shack close by. The storm broke, and while he was watching the lightning zigzag across the sky, he saw it set fire to the *pagliaro.* He rushed over to it, but in a moment it was a mass of flames, and the brothers and their animals were burned to death. If they'd made room for him, he'd've lost his life, too.

In our village, a man won't marry a girl unless she has some linen to bring him. I've got daughters of my own, and they're all engaged to be married, but I have no linen to give them, so the promises won't come to anything. Love's love, but linen's linen . . .

[1] Conical huts of mud and straw. For further details see "A Country Woman." *Translator's note.*

Salvatore G.

When a farm hand's unemployed, he's still got to feed his family. It's no good for him to hang around the piazza in hopes that something'll turn up, because if the police sergeant and the *mafiosi* see him standing there day after day, they'll say: "There's a fellow that don't like work." So he goes into the country, picks up sticks and sells them for a hundred or a hundred and fifty lire a bundle, the price of two or three pounds of bread. Or else he goes gleaning or picking wild asparagus, fennel, chicory, orach—whatever he can find.

The men in Campofiorito make out by selling greens, but their village is much smaller than ours. Nine thousand people live in Bisacquino, and twelve hundred of them are farm hands like myself, unemployed for the best part of the year. We're much worse off than the farm hands in Campofiorito because, though Bisacquino's surrounded by estates, not one of them comes within the boundaries. There are four stone quarries nearby, and in the winter we shape and square the stones that'll be needed for the road building when it starts up in the summer just before the elections. The trouble is, too many of us are doing the same thing; there are always anywhere from thirty to fifty of us trying to sell stones to the contractor, and so he can force down the price; by rights we should get five hundred and fifty lire for a cubic yard of stone, but we have to take two hundred and sixty, or at best two hundred and eighty. The total we receive works out to something like four or five hundred lire a day. What makes things worse is while we're preparing the stones, we have to borrow money from the contractor in order to live; he has us by the throat and we're always in debt. The cost-of-living allowance? We get it for a couple of months before the elections, but after that—no more.

The quarry owners take advantage of us too. In the first place, they employ a great many children—little kids ten and twelve. Sometimes you see as many as thirty of them working all day long in the thick dust from the crushing mills—presses, we call them. The dust gets inside their lungs and a lot of them get chronic chest diseases. Child labor comes cheap. The owners don't hire men like me, adult, married, registered at the labor bureau—it would cost them much more in wages, not to mention family allowances. But they do have three or four insured men on steady work. Their names are kept quiet; if an accident happens, this allows the owners to claim compensation. Accidents occur quite often in quarries. Instead of loosening the stones at the top, quarrymen will loosen those at the bottom because it's quicker; it's dangerous, though, because they may dislodge a boulder that'll crash down and bury one of them. Even if a man notices a heavy slab about to topple, he may not have the time to jump clear, so his leg or his arm'll get crushed or his back'll be seriously injured.

The kids' job is to carry the stones to the crushing mills. They hoist them up on their shoulders, or pile them in baskets, and stagger along doubled up under the weight of the loads. Their bones haven't yet had time to harden, so the work they do deforms them for life. You can see the poor little kids with one shoulder higher than the other, or with humped backs. They can't hold themselves straight, they walk with their heads poked out forward or else all twisted to one side. By rights, the stones should be fed into the crushers through an iron funnel, but this would mean employing a man as a feeder. So, no iron funnel. The kids have to dump all the stones from their baskets straight into the crusher while it's grinding away; they have to do this with one short, sharp heave and then get back fast or else they'd get struck in the face with flying stones.

You can't mistake kids from the quarries—one look at their poor little backs is enough. They go from six in the morning till six at night, with an hour's break for a little food: eleven hours a day. Even at Custonaci there are boys twelve, thirteen and fourteen working in the quarry to help out at home: they earn from three to four hundred lire a day. While the skilled men shape and square and polish, they shovel the pieces of stone and loose earth into iron baskets; they hoist them on their shoulders, carry them away, empty them, and come back for another load. They do it all day long.

Actual quarrying's a different matter.

The owners usually employ unmarried men or men without state insurance to do the real blasting. It's difficult and dangerous work and the maximum pay is one thousand lire with no allowances, and if there's an accident, if one of the men gets killed . . . well, the owners and the labor bureau always see eye to eye about the compensation, and in a couple of hours it's all settled to their satisfaction. Once in Bisacquino the official from the labor bureau was attacked by some angry workers and beaten with sticks. A man that's been injured can go to the police station and complain he hasn't been given enough compensation, but it doesn't do him any good. "We can't do anything, it's not our concern," they'll tell him. Machinery *is* the concern of the police, though; they were called in, for instance, over that business of the bulldozer. One fellow, when he saw it could do the work of a hundred men in a single day, went crazy; that night he smashed up all the spark plugs, and wrecked the engine for good.

As for family allowances, wait till you hear how we get cheated out of them. A quarryman has just as much right to a family allowance as a streetcleaner, but does he get it? He either has to agree to divide it with the man that's hired him, or he gets swindled out of it by the management. The family allowance of a married man with two children is twelve thousand eight hundred lire a month, but instead of giving it to him, the owners pay him a monthly wage of fifteen thousand lire—subtract twelve thousand eight hundred from fifteen thousand, and you can see that all the owners spend in a month is twenty-two hundred lire—in other words, they pay the man at the rate of about eighty lire a day. A man with five children might find thirty thousand lire in his monthly pay envelope, but the management is pocketing his family allowance money of twenty-eight thousand lire a month.

The farm hand gets cheated, too. When a landowner with several men on his regular payroll makes out his returns, he'll either leave out the names of some of them or else he'll state that they're only temporary, and that they haven't done more than fifty or sixty days' work for him in the year. In this way he gets out of paying the state tax—forty-five thousand lire per man—and the workers lose their family allowance. On top of which, of course, they can't claim any benefits under the social insurance.

The local authorities, far from supporting the rights of the workers, help the landowners. The fixed rate of pay for a hand is nine hundred and eighty lire for an eight-hour day; what he actually gets, though, is five hundred to six hundred lire (he can count himself lucky if he gets seven hundred lire) for a thirteen-hour day. In the past, it used to be he could count on getting between eight hundred and a thousand lire a day, plus his keep, but now they've cut out his keep and cut down on his wages too.

Things are going from bad to worse. In 1947, when Fausto Gullo was Minister of Agriculture, and the peasants started to take possession of the uncultivated or badly cultivated land, the occupation was peaceful and the *carabinieri* came down to protect the *contadini* from the Mafia. The estates of Licia, Gibilcanna and Balatelli became co-operatives, and they were collective until 1952. The owner of these three estates brought an action immediately against the peasants' co-operative. In 1951, when he was unable to evict the peasants, he had a deed of gift drawn up which stated that fifteen persons were to hold two of the estates in what they call perpetuity. Through this deed of gift, he took the land away from the co-operative, and in that way forced ninety-two men and their families off the estates.

In 1950 we occupied the estate of Santa Maria del Bosco. It took us just under a week. The first day was a real holiday; laughing and yelling to each other, the peasants marched out of the different villages—men, women, girls, children, mothers carrying their babies—and they joined up with each other till they formed a line a mile long. As soon as we set foot on the land, we set to work clearing it of stones; we pulled up the briers and weeds, and began to hoe. That land hadn't been cultivated for sixty years. The villagers from Bisacquino, Contessa Entellina, and Giuliana formed three separate groups, and the air was loud with the music of accordions and guitars —it was just like the feast day of a patron saint. While we hoed, the boys and girls and the women too cleared away the stones. We sang while we worked, the children played together, and our banners that we fastened to the trees made quite a colorful show. The ones that had bread shared with the ones that had none—and plenty of us had none. Next day, still more peasants came, some on foot, some riding horses or mules.

On Wednesday, the *carabinieri* arrived and ordered two of our leaders, Sicula Vincenzo and Ferina Castrense, to step forward; as soon as they were well clear of the rest of us, they were arrested, put into the wagon and taken straight to the Ucciardone. Later, when it was time to go home, all of us went to the barracks to protest, and when the *carabinieri* saw the thick crowd they got their machine guns out onto the balcony. The lieutenant, with a grenade in his hand, ordered us to break up. "If you don't leave at once," he told us, "I shall order my men to open fire." Two of the *carabinieri*—one was behind a machine gun, the other was shouldering his rifle— were so sorry for us they cried. We couldn't do a thing by staying there, so we broke it up and went home.

The next morning there were twice as many of us. We were happier than ever when we marched onto the land, yet our minds were full of bitterness when we thought of the arrest of our two leaders. When we got back to the village we held a mass meeting; the piazza was black with people, and all around it were squads of *carabinieri.*

On Friday still more of us set out for the estate. The day went by pretty peacefully, but on our way back, when we came to the Convent of Santa Maria del Bosco, we saw the *carabinieri* approaching our rear and we split up to let them pass. "Long live the *carabinieri!*" somebody shouted. The lieutenant that had threatened to open fire on the crowd on Wednesday had called the *celeri* from Corleone; they arrived on foot just as we reached the outskirts of the village and the women and children were running out to welcome us. "Drop those banners!" the sergeant in charge ordered. "Never!" a woman shouted.

"Drop those banners!" the sergeant ordered again, and then all hell broke loose. The *carabinieri* tried to snatch them away from the women, the women hung on to them for all they were worth, the *celeri* began to get rough, and some of the men, when they saw their wives and their daughters, their mothers and their sweethearts struggling and being roughly handled, picked up rocks and flung them at the *celeri*. The other men quickly joined them; in one second, it was a regular hail of stones.

The *carabinieri* started away, but as soon as they got out of range they opened fire. Tamburello Giuseppe (at the time he was the secretary of the local C.D. party, but now he's not in any party), was wounded in the wrist and the foot. A burst of machine-gun fire hit Bortino Salvatore in the hand, and another burst caught Catalano Salvatore in the back and broke the leg of a mule. Seventeen more of us were hurt; some were struck by bullets, others were clubbed down with rifle butts.

Thirty of the *celeri* were hurt by the flying stones. The *carabinieri* lined up right along the main street and started firing their machine guns to frighten the villagers. A first-aid station was set up, and warrants were made out. They arrested thirty-five of us, thirty men and five women, and hauled us onto a truck; the lieutenant jumped on and handcuffed La Torre and then the rest of us; later, when La Torre was tried, this same lieutenant said such filthy things to him that his father fell on the ground half-fainting. They drove us to the Ucciardone, and after an hour or so some of us were allowed to go home. Sixteen months later the rest were tried; altogether one hundred and eighty-one persons were accused of rioting. I was put in prison for one year, eight months and fifteen days. La Torre, though he was only sentenced to three months, actually served sixteen months. La Russo got twenty-three months, and of the rest, some got twenty-six months, some got three months, and some fifteen days.

Since 1950 we've not only stopped going forward, we've actually gone right back. There are groups sprung up in the villages whose sole purpose is to frighten the peasants into voting for them by keeping the threat of unemployment over their heads. The estate system hasn't been changed at all, and it's no wonder the people are losing heart. They sympathize with the workers' party, but they don't dare vote for it. On the eve of the elections, my brother heard shots; he leaned out the window and a bullet whizzed past him and only just missed him. There are certain marked men that for two weeks before election day stay away from their homes, wisely so ... People are afraid, not so much the ones with strong political beliefs, but the ones that are dissatisfied with the present state of affairs and have only the haziest notion of politics.

Angelino P.

In these parts, ninety out of a hundred of us use mules to thresh our wheat. Before we start threshing, the oldest member of the family says: "Let us turn our thoughts towards God," and we all pray. We usually have two or three mules. One man stands in the middle of the threshing floor, holds the reins and makes the mules trot around; they crush the wheat with their hooves, and he crushes it with his feet. After half or three-quarters of an hour, the work is over; he halts the mules, and we all stand perfectly still and listen while he recites the thanksgiving:

One and all, now take your ease,
Breathe the sweet, refreshing breeze,
And with mine your voices raise,
In thanksgiving and in praise,
To the Blessed Sacrament,
And Jesus in the firmament,
To his saints all gathered there,
And his maiden Mother fair,
Who of earthly stain was clear,
Let us praise her spouse most dear,
That the angelic hosts rejoice
At the music of his voice,
And all the souls in purgatory

Turn to hear his song of glory.
Holy Mary, thou art here,
Blessed Gabriel, thou art near,
Present is the One in Three,
Of the Blessed Trinity.

Then he stops, makes the sign of the cross, and says the rest of the thanksgiving, which ends up like this:

Turn three times, for you have heard,
I have given you the word.
In the wind we all must spin
In the pains of mortal sin.
I'll be lightened by God's grace,
You'll be saved in little space.

He tells us, you see, that we still have work to do—the wheat still has to be winnowed. When he says, "Turn three times," the mules understand, and around they go. "Once, twice, three times," we count, but the mules don't need any help from us—as soon as they turn around three times, they stop on their own and their heads begin to droop. They've finished their work patiently and now they're anxious to leave the threshing floor. Their flanks are so streaked with sweat and dust you can't tell what color they are any more. We tug their ears gently because, according to the old belief in these parts, it stops them from feeling giddy and catching sunstroke.

When the mules are ready to begin threshing, we say to them:

Turn around in peace, strike while the iron's hot,
Nothing will harm you—turn and fear not.

"Head to head!" we shout to them, so they'll all move together. If the mule on the outside doesn't complete the circle as quick as the other two, we call out, "Two are hot, one's cold!" and encourage him to go faster: "Put your best foot forward, your other three feet will follow it!" we say, and:

Press down the wheat for all you are worth,
Wheat is the father of all things on earth.

Then the mule turns fast, and we praise him. "Best of all
mules!" we say, and when we see the threshing's almost done,
we say:

Tread the wheat with all your might
Till it turns from gold to white.

Sometimes the wind begins to blow, the sky gets dark, and
the thunder starts to growl. We've got a name for a thunderstorm that blows up while we're threshing: we call it the
Black Dragon. Only a left-handed man can make the Black
Dragon go away. This left-handed man must never breathe a
word about his magic powers to another man, he must pass
on his secret to a woman, who then must pass it on, not to a
woman, but to a man. Twenty out of a hundred peasants believe that the left-handed man can charm the Black Dragon
away. This is what he does. He takes a scythe, he points it at
the sky, looks up and says to the darkest cloud of all:

Tell me once, tell me twice, what is this awful thud?
Why, it is the stormy beat of living creature's blood.
If it be yours, sweet Jesus, then may your head be blest,
But should it be a man's blood, a man like all the rest,
My scythe will be red for I'll chop off his head!

and he slashes down the scythe, making believe to cut off an
imaginary head.

In the winter we pick greens in the mountains and hunt
for snails; in summer we go gleaning. There's so little water
around here that oftentimes we don't wash for weeks. When
it's reaping time, there's not room enough for all the harvest-
ers in the *pagliari* so some of them sleep in the village piazzas. Families come from far away to glean here—crowds
of us gleaners, there are. The villagers from Modica camp
out in the fields. They make tents for themselves—twenty,
maybe thirty—with white sheets. They come in donkey carts;

nearly all of them bring their hens, and sometimes they have other livestock with them, too—chickens in coops, a suckling pig, a goat with her two kids.

Once when I was passing the tents I saw one between two carts that was surrounded by women, all of them facing outwards. I went closer, to find out what was happening, and an old woman asked me what I wanted. "A woman's having a baby in there," she said. "Don't come any nearer—she mustn't be disturbed."

ANOTHER THRESHER: I can tell you another story about the gleaners from Modica. It happened at Belice, where I had the job of keeping an eye on the shocks. Well, I noticed two women gleaning in a patch of stubble, but when I looked that way again, they were both gone. I wondered where they went and what they were doing. I thought they might have crossed the river nearby, so I made my way to the bridge, and sure enough, there they were on the other side. One was lying on her back with her hair all wild and her legs spread wide; she was in labor, and the other woman, that'd just given birth to a baby herself, was doing all she could to help her.

a country woman

Those thirty-odd *pagliari* you see were put up by smallholders and *mezzadri*. The walls are made out of a mixture of clay and stones and straw and mule dung, and the men pat it into shape with their hands just the way children make mud pies. The walls are generally about three feet high, though some may be a little bit higher. Long poles are fastened onto the walls to make the steep, pointed roof that's thatched with straw, and hay and grass. If it's done right, the rain won't come through. The roofs are thatched new every year.

In the winter the hands that are hired to break up the clods to get ready for the sowing live in the *pagliari*—share them with their animals. During the cold weather it's only the poorest of the poor that bring their families with them to the *pagliari*, and here, at Turrumè, none of the men are quite as needy as that. At Tudia, though, women and children live in the *pagliari* all year round.

When we go out to the fields to glean, we ask the *mezzadri* to let us stay in their *pagliari*, and they give us the keys. One year twelve *pagliari* caught on fire here; another year, twenty-four. Four summers back twelve more were burned down. We were asleep in our *pagliaro*, and were waked up by what we thought was a roaring wind. Then we heard a crackling sound, and I jumped up, ran to the door and saw flames. There were six of us: my husband, myself, our four-year-old daughter, my niece and two other girls, and we all rushed out just as we were. Later on, people gave us different things to cover ourselves with—dresses and shoes and things. We couldn't save anything. Our donkey and our four hens died in the fire, and we lost four blankets and every scrap of food we had: two hundred pounds of wheat, three boxes of pasta and over a hundred pounds of beans. Another two hundred pounds of wheat and sixty pounds of beans that belonged to my brother, who usually slept in the *pagliaro* with us, were burned too. Men, women and children ran around crazy, screaming for help. The *mezzadri* kept their scythes and plows and so on in the *pagliari*, and they came rushing to get their tools out.

Three times the *pagliari* have caught fire here and burned down, but how it happened nobody knows. Maybe one of the gleaners set them on fire just to spite the *mezzadri* after they made us give them sixty percent of all we gleaned.

Sometimes there've been such crowds of us living in the *pagliari* that people have come out from the villages to sell us potatoes and tomatoes, and the ice-cream man has made the trip from Vallelunga twice a day. The children all wanted ices, of course. "Buy me an ice! Buy me an ice!" they'd shout, and the way they enjoyed it when we did made us very happy.

When we're living in the *pagliari*, the smoke from the fires where we do our cooking keeps the black adders away. But if there's a baby in one of the *pagliari*, then they smell the milk, and back they come: they say that an adder'll wind itself around a baby's throat and choke it to death.

We country women can turn our hands to just about everything—we're not like women in the city that can go out and buy what they need. We knit and sew; we make blankets for the beds and all our dresses and underclothes. Sometimes we make a few lire by weeding in the wheat fields, or picking cotton or almonds or olives.

In the summer, when there's not a breath of wind, we leave the door wide open when we're cooking; the sun gets so fierce that even the stones are burning hot. There aren't any fleas or lice in the *pagliari*; there are in the villages, though, but they don't bite everybody, they don't like some people's blood.

It's against the law nowadays to sell American clothes. We could buy a dress from the man that used to come around with them for fifty lire, but people said if we wore what he sold, we might catch all kinds of diseases, so they chased him out of the village. At Marianopoli, though, they say he was chased out because everybody went to him for clothes and stopped going to the stores. Whenever we buy second-hand things, we soak them first in the alcohol that we use to disinfect our bodies.

When you don't have any money, life's a terrible trial. You have daughters and you can't buy them any linen for their dowry; it drives you to despair. When our *pagliaro* was burned down, I lost my donkey, my hens, my wheat—we barely escaped with our lives. I was in such a state that I tried to drag out the sack of wheat. I forgot all about my little girl inside. I pulled her out just in time; the fire had really caught on, and a second later the *pagliaro* was a mass of flames.

Santo S.

The estate of Tudia, a thousand *salme* of land, is just inside the boundaries of the province of Palermo. It belonged by tradition to a certain Cavaliere G., but it was finally split in two, and half was leased to D., the lawyer, and the other half to Cavaliere P. At first neither one of them owned a single animal—they had donkeys' reins, but no donkeys!

A *salma* of land on the estate cost the *mezzadri* seven measures of wheat or beans: four measures for the owner, one for the overseer, one for the upkeep of the footpaths, and one for the oil of the sanctuary lamp. On top of this, they had to give a present to the owner's hired man who carried the produce to his master, and another to the *carabinieri*.

Those *pagliari* you see there were put up by the *mezzadri* when I was still a boy, but even though they built them and used their own materials, they had to pay the owner for the right to live in them; they were taxed at the rate of a dozen hens a year. What's more, when the owner came to spend a few days at his house in Tudia, some of the wives of the *mezzadri* had to work as his servants without pay. Many *pagliari* have been destroyed by fire; in one fire five were burned down. From time to time another *pagliaro* or so goes up in flames.

In the early days, there were about two hundred *mezzadri* on the estate. Probably when they went out at four in the morning to the threshing floor to shovel up the wheat, they'd see a window in the master's house being opened, and they'd move away fast; the owner had a nice little habit of making water over the balcony regardless of who was below. If you don't believe me, ask Giuseppe B., Antonio T., Francesco M., Mario P. and a dozen more—they saw him with their own eyes. What a scandal there would have been if a peasant ever did such a thing.

The owner kept a number of gorgeous peacocks in his poultry yard. So did the Duke of S.—not only because they were beautiful creatures but because they gave more beauty to an estate.

At certain times the *mezzadro* had to go to the owner's house—he still has to today—and give a full account of what he had laid out on seed, tools, water and so on. The master settled the bills, and the *mezzadro* paid him back in installments. Oftentimes, though, the owner would make the total much more than it really was, and when the *mezzadro* opened his mouth to complain, he'd suddenly get up. "That'll be all —good day to you," he'd say with a wave of his hand.

D.'s heir raised the money to buy an estate by making the *mezzadri* pay far more than they should have. I came to Tudia in 1941. I brought six head of oxen with me, and the owner, Don Cesare D., suggested that they should be valued and that we should go shares in them, and I agreed. A few months later, he brought me the contract, but the valuation price of the animals was far less than they were worth and I refused to sign it. He began to threaten me, said he'd evict me if I didn't agree, and since there was nowhere for me to go, I was forced to accept his terms.

The following spring he asked me for more than his fair percentage of the hay. This time, though, I stood firm, and from then on he had it in for me. One fine day the eviction notice came. I was out at the time, and when I got home my wife was in a terrible state. "Look what the master's sent you!" she burst out. This was before I'd heard of the peasants' unions, and I just didn't know where to turn. It was through asking different people for advice that I learned there was a political party in Petralia that would help me and do everything possible to see that I got my rights. So I saddled my horse, rode over to Petralia—it took me six and a half hours to get there—and went to the Party headquarters. There I told my story to a young man—he was a student, the miller's son—and when I finished he said: "Go and see Dr. B., he'll tell you what to do." Dr. B. was out visiting patients, and I had two hours' wait before he came back. He gave me a friendly smile and said: "I haven't seen you before, have I? Sit down and tell me what I can do for you." As soon as I gave him the facts, he said: "You stay on your land—don't budge even if the owner sends the *carabinieri* to evict you.

I'll write to Palermo immediately and I'll let you know exactly what to do." After I gave him my address and said good-by to him, I rode back to Tudia.

On June twenty-eighth, when I was in the village of Petralia Soprana for St. Peter's Fair, I noticed some posters stuck up on the walls which I read. (I got as far as the fifth grade in school.) They explained the details of the new laws that had been put into force on the distribution of produce and were signed by the Minister of Agriculture, Signor Gullo. I took some of these posters, and when I got back to Tudia I pasted them up, and I spoke to all the *mezzadri* and told them that, under the new laws which were now in force, the owner's share of our total produce was fixed at forty percent.

Well, just before we finished reaping the owner arrived in Tudia, and though he never bothered before about the time it took us to thresh, he ordered us to start threshing at once. Only a few of the *mezzadri* were ready to begin, and the minute they threshed their wheat, he demanded his usual percentage, taking no notice whatsoever of the new laws.

When they refused to give it to him, he threatened to send for the *carabinieri* and have them all arrested. They came to me and so did the *mezzadri* from the L. estate, and this gave me courage. I rode over with them to Petralia to make quite sure from the party that we were acting in the right, and that evening Comrade Giovanni and Comrade X., the student, started back with us for Tudia. We spent the night on the mountaintop in a shelter that was used for the animals in winter. We slept on the ground, and to see Comrade X. lying there uncomfortable with us peasants made a deep impression on me. What made him, a student, throw in his lot with us? I couldn't get over the fact that he was ready to share our hardships—I'll never forget him.

Early next morning, one of the *mezzadri* who lived on the land nearby brought us some milk, and then we made our way to Tudia. Some three hundred peasants and *mezzadri* were assembled there to hold a meeting of protest. I was the last to arrive in the village, and by the time I got there the meeting was over, and I was told that the comrades had gone to see the owner. "Nothing'll come of it, though," everyone was saying. "It'll be the same old story—they'll sell us out to him as usual." So I spoke to them and told them they were wrong. "Our leaders are here to defend our rights," I said. "They won't let themselves be bribed. They're on our side, and we've got to trust them." I was trying to make my way through the crowd, when I heard someone call my name. It was my brother—we hadn't spoken to each other for two years on account of a quarrel we had. "Look out for yourself, Santo," he said. There was a detachment of *carabinieri* there and he was afraid I'd be arrested. I stopped, but after a minute or two I told myself I hadn't done anything wrong; there was no reason why I should be arrested, so I continued on my way.

I went to the owner's house, and I had just climbed the steps when he came out to meet me. "Oh, it's you, Santo," he said in a friendly way. He shook hands with me, slapped me good-naturedly on the back and whispered in my ear, "Come on, Santo, let's behave sensibly like the men we are, not like children."

He led me into the room, where I found our leaders, two or three of the police and a *carabinieri* corporal. As soon as we came in, the comrades said:

"Don Cesare has agreed to split the produce fifty-fifty with the *mezzadri*. He's also agreed that when the talks between Aldisio[1] and Gullo are finished, he'll give you back whatever may be due to you. We suggest you accept."

"Comrades," I said, looking at the owner, "this noble gentleman's got millions in the bank—the distribution of the produce isn't a matter of life and death to him as it is to us with our families to keep."

"I've said I'd return whatever's due to you," said the owner. "Don't you trust me?"

"No," I said outright. How could I trust him, I went on, seeing that every time the crops were distributed he'd always taken more than his fair share, and though he'd promised to give me back what was mine, he'd never done it—he'd put me off with this or that excuse: he'd lost the key to his granary, or he was too busy to take care of me. "God knows how often I've walked those four miles and back," I wound up, "and every time, I felt as humiliated as if I'd asked you for charity."

[1] Then High Commissioner for Sicily. *Translator's note.*

"You've received your notice to leave, haven't you?" asked Don Cesare.

"Yes," I replied. "And I'd be glad if you'd explain right here and now why you're turning me off the land."

"You're a good fellow, but we just don't hit it off together," he said.

"I'm sorry about that," I said, "but just the same I, Santo S., mean to stay in Tudia as long as the law allows. After all, we don't have to sleep in the same room!"

With that, I got up to go. Don Cesare stepped out onto the balcony and spoke to the *mezzadri*. He told them they must give him fifty percent of the wheat they threshed, but promised that he would adjust things later. "Excuse me," I said to him, "but since the talks between Aldisio and Gullo are still going on, I suggest you take forty percent instead of fifty. In any case, we've still got to thresh most of our wheat." He wouldn't hear of this, though, so I said, "All right, there'll be no distribution today, and we won't thresh the rest until a contract's been signed between us that'll insure our getting our rightful percentage."

Don Cesare got furious, and he began to threaten all of us with eviction. I'm ashamed to tell you what happened. We behaved like cowards—we were so terrified that we all gave in.

In 1947, during the general strike, the peasants who were angered by the tax that made them give so much wheat yearly to the state, often leaving them without enough for their own needs, took advantage of the situation to besiege the tax office; they broke in and set fire to all the records. As I was trying to calm them, the *carabinieri* arrested me and twenty other men, and took us to prison. We were held there for eighteen months; for eighteen months we were completely cut off from our families. After we were tried and had appealed, we were sentenced to four months. While I was in prison, Don Cesare did all he could to frighten my wife; he kept threatening her with eviction, then, finally, he told her that if she'd leave of her own accord, he'd give her a hundred thousand lire. But my wife refused to budge.

A year later, exactly the same story was repeated over the distribution of the hay with the new owner, Don Vittorio.

He made it clear that he had no intention of sticking to the laws, and the fight began all over again. When I finished threshing my beans, I said I'd give him the percentage that was due to him and no more, but he wouldn't listen to me. I went straight over to Caltanisetta to ask the union leaders for advice, and while I was talking to Don Totò, my son telephoned to tell me that Don Vittorio had hired men from Modica to thresh the bean crop and that they had already started to thresh the wheat. I hurried back to Tudia, and found out that a truckload of *carabinieri* had arrived. Next day, Comrade Totò came over to hold a meeting, but it had hardly started before a squad of *carabinieri* marched into the piazza, led by a corporal. "You know very well such a meeting's strictly against the law," he said to Comrade A., and ordered him to break it up at once. "My dear corporal, kindly don't interrupt," said Comrade A. "If what I'm doing is unlawful, go get a warrant."

Half an hour later, when the meeting was over, the commissioner and a truckload of police appeared on the scene. You should have seen the ugly look on their faces. I invited the commissioner to come with me to my house, and Comrade A. said immediately: "We don't want to break the laws —just the opposite, we want to enforce them, at any rate, some of them . . ."

On July thirteenth, at four P.M., we leaders went to the prefecture, but the noble gentlemen didn't deign to show themselves, so we couldn't do a thing. The peasants were anxiously waiting for news, but just as we got back, a Fiat— the latest model—pulled up. In it were Don Vittorio and the corporal of the *carabinieri*. Don Vittorio called me over and said, "Take your percentage, Santo. Don't worry about the others, let them deal with me themselves." "They come first," I said. "I come last—you and I can arrange things later." He drew himself up. "You think of yourself as a very important fellow because the police, instead of enforcing the law, appear to be taking an interest in your affairs," he said coldly, and told his chauffeur to drive on.

I went back to the *mezzadri*, but a few minutes later I saw the Fiat coming back. It stopped, and the chauffeur told me to get in. "The corporal wants to talk to you," he said.

"I don't have to go, but since my conscience is quite clear, I have no objection," I said.

The minute we arrived at the house, the corporal asked me, "What made you say what you did to Don Vittorio?"

"What made me? The fact that you ask proves I was right to say it," I answered.

Don Vittorio then asked us to come into his office, and the same old discussion started about the distribution. The servant came in shortly and said that supper was ready. I got up to go, but Don Vittorio said, "Please, you must give me the pleasure of sharing a meal with me." So I stayed, and he kept pushing things at me like a waiter: "Have another helping, Santo—fill up your glass, Santo—we're friends, eh?" and he patted me on the back. All the time it was: "We're the best of friends, aren't we, Santo? Try some of this—pour yourself some more beer." I laughed till my sides ached, I couldn't stop myself—I wasn't used to this sort of treatment. When Don Vittorio got some of us *mezzadri* to carry sacks of chickpeas or wheat from one storehouse to the other, he never as much as offered us a glass of water!

"Eat, Santo, drink, Santo—you're a good fellow, and I'll look after you." Don Vittorio winked at me. "Be smart, now, and don't let your family down. I'll do the right thing by you, and if you think you ought to have a bigger share of the produce, well then, you'll have it!" I was suspicious, though; I drank very little—I had no intention of getting fuzzy. Meanwhile the agent had typed out the contract, and when we finished supper we went into the office. Don Vittorio sat down, signed the contract and handed it to me, but I refused to put my name to it. "Read it, man, read it!" the corporal ordered. So I read it all and threw it back on the table in front of Don Vittorio. "Why won't you sign it?" demanded the corporal. "Because I won't, and you can't force me to, either!" I said.

The corporal got up and turned to Don Vittorio. "Take four witnesses with you," he said. "You have my authority to take all the crops and put them into your storehouse."

I went to the door.

"Wait!" called the owner. "The chauffeur will drive you home."

"Thanks, I'd rather go on my own two feet," I said.

The peasants were all assembled outside the house. I told them what had happened, and we made our way to the road. The corporal came out and as soon as he saw me, he said:

"What right have you got to hold a meeting?"

"The law of the Italian Republic gives me the right," I said without hesitation.

All of us then went to the threshing floor where one of the owner's hired men was filling the sacks he'd brought with him with our beans. I called to my son Giuseppe and said, "Come on, let's take our sacks before he empties them, and the measures, too—we'll give Don Vittorio what he's entitled to by law." The corporal hurried to Don Vittorio's house to tell him what we were doing, and he immediately drove off to inform the police commissioner that we had started, in front of witnesses, to distribute the beans—sixty percent for ourselves, forty percent for him.

At about eight o'clock that evening, when I was at home playing the harmonica, the commissioner drove up with a squad of police. I stayed just where I was, and went on playing. The police surrounded my house, arrested me and fourteen other men, and took us out to the police wagon. They also confiscated our beans. They drove us to the Resuttana barracks, where we spent the night; in the morning we were taken to the Polizzi Generosa prison. We were questioned that same evening. Two days later we were transferred to the Termini Imerese prison. At the end of eight days we were released provisionally, and when we appeared in court we were all acquitted.

A week later, the same old thing happened over the distribution of the wheat, and I stuck up for my rights. I was arrested and held in prison for twenty-eight days. When I was tried, I was acquitted again since I hadn't been guilty of breaking any law. During my absence, though, Don Vittorio adjusted the distribution in his favor, and had twenty-eight hundred pounds of my wheat carried into his granary.

At last came a year when the produce was distributed according to the law: sixty percent for us, forty percent for the owner. But that was the one and only year. Because I'm all alone in the fight, you see, I'm too weak—I'm so completely alone, so completely powerless. We used to hold meetings, and I'd be in a fury: "Be on your guard, beware, be careful or they'll come and arrest us—me first, and then the rest of you." Then they'd swear that as long as they were free the fight would go on. But time and time again the sight of the police or the *carabinieri* threw them in such a panic that they went to the owner and said, "It's Santo that's to blame—he eggs us on in spite of ourselves. He ought to have his head cut off!" And as a sign of remorse and to get into his good graces, they would take baskets of eggs to his house.

It's not that they're unaware of what's being done to help them. If you talk to one of them, he'll tell you: "The trouble is there's no unity."

"But if you believe in what we're doing," I'd say, "why not stand by me and then there'd be two of us? Unity isn't any gift from heaven."

"You can talk about unity," another one would say, "but when I take the lead at a demonstration, and turn around to see who's following me, there's nobody, or almost nobody. What's more, the police keep on calling us agitators . . ."

One day or another . . . Listen—only six miles from here, Epifanio Li Puma was murdered by the Mafia of the estate. In the end, though, the estate was expropriated. And life goes on . . . We only get work for some ninety days in the year, and when we're unemployed we pick oregano, capers, fennel, wild cabbages and chicory, and hunt for snails—it's all according to what season it is and what we can find. There's nothing we can do to make things better; it's hard and bitter, the life we lead . . .

pagliari at Túdia, Turrumè and Arcia

There are thirty-nine *pagliari* at Tudia in which families live the year round. The actual buildings are the house where the owner of the estate lives, a tiny church where Mass is said only on those occasions when the owner's wife visits it, and a tumble-down school with no toilet, to which the children bring their own chairs.

In winter the peasants share the *pagliari* with their animals; part of the interior is set aside for their use. The door of the *pagliaro* is roughly two and a half feet by five, and always faces south. In the center of the one room is a tiny stove which has been set in the earth floor, but the thatched roof has no outlet for smoke. A few families sleep in the straw, but most of them have cots which sit on stakes driven into the ground. These "beds" are covered with charming and unusual patch-work spreads.

Sacks of wheat and a few American clothes dangle from cords that have been strung across the interior. Outside some of the *pagliari* there are pots of flowers. One family owns a radio—an antique crystal set. All the *pagliari* are outstandingly neat and spotlessly clean.

The *pagliari* are only a yard or two apart. They nestle against the mountain slope which protects them from the mistral.

At Arcia, the twenty-five *pagliari* are inhabited for most of the year, but in winter some members of the families who live in them go back to their homes in the village. At Turrumè, the *pagliari* are only lived in for a few months.

There are fifty families under consideration; twenty-five at Tudia; eight at Turrumè and seventeen at Arcia. These families, numbering two hundred and eighteen persons, live in forty-four *pagliari* which also house fifty-three mules, three horses, three donkeys, eight goats, one pig, and many dogs and hens.

The families have very few pots and pans. Some have none, and do their cooking in battered old cans. The furniture consists of very light wooden stools; in many cases, though, blocks of stone do duty for chairs.

Twenty-eight of the *pagliari* have floors of packed dirt; nine have floors of stone; five have floors half of packed dirt for the family and half of stone or brick for the animals; two have entire floors of broken brick.

About ninety percent of the children go to school. About half of the men and about three-fifths of the women have had a little schooling. On the average, the people over six years old have not quite finished the second grade.

As for the occupations of the heads-of-family,

thirty-nine are *mezzadri* who own from seven to fifteen acres of land, eight are farm hands, and two are cowherds and shepherds.

Among the more frequent illnesses are fifteen cases of acute rheumatism, eleven of malaria and nine of undulant fever.

Luciano

My brother Luciano's twenty-four. He got married when he was very young. He already had two kids by the time he was eighteen, so he wasn't taken into the service.

One day I had to go to Palermo, so I left home at four in the morning. I only got a step or two when I saw a man go into Luciano's house. I was surprised, then I thought: "It must have been Luciano himself—maybe he has to go to Palermo, too." So I went over to the house, but when I was standing outside the door, I could hear a deep voice talking love talk—the words got hotter and hotter. I knew that whoever the man was, he wasn't any stranger to my sister-in-law.

I knocked at the door. "Is Luciano in?" I shouted. Nobody answered. I knocked again. After a minute or two, my sister-in-law called:

"Who is it?"

"It's me, Beppo."

"Oh, it's you. What do you want?"

"Is Luciano home?"

"No."

So it wasn't Luciano!

"Open the door!" I yelled.

"What for? What do you want?" my sister-in-law called back, but she didn't open the door.

I started to hammer on it.

"If you don't let me in, I'll break the door down!" I yelled, and that brought her to the door. I followed her in, and found the room was dark.

"Put on the light," I said.

I knew there was a man in the house, so as soon as she put it on I looked under the bed, and sure enough, there he was! He was lying flat on his back in his shorts, holding onto his pants with his hands. I lifted up the covers, and there was enough light from the lamp for me to see his face. It was Don Luigi.

The Sunday before that, Luciano and I borrowed eighteen thousand lire from Don Luigi so we could buy a mule. After talking a little, he told Luciano that he had always liked him and trusted him, and that he would do whatever he could to help him. So, finally, he hired Luciano to look after his wine shop. I didn't know it till later, but on this particular morning, Don Luigi had said to Luciano: "You take the keys and open up—I'll be in later."

"Come out from under that bed, Don Luigi," I said. "So this is your way of helping my brother, you bastard—by making him wear the horns!" He crawled out, and started to pull on his pants. "I've mixed my blood with your brother's," he said. "You keep your mouth shut or there'll be trouble, real trouble!" I had no knife, and I knew he had. "I better keep quiet or he'll kill me," I thought, and I ran out and went across the road to the house where my sister lived. I banged on the door, and my brother-in-law came running to see what was up. When he opened the door, he was just in time. He saw Don Luigi come out of Luciano's house and finish buttoning himself up in the street. "I found him half-naked under the bed," I said, and was just going after him when my brother-in-law stopped me. "We haven't got any knives—let him go, or he'll kill us," he said.

I ran home and told my youngest brother to get on his bike and go get Luciano from the store. I told him what had happened, and he went. As soon as Luciano locked up the store, he got on the bike with him, and they were nearly at his house when they met Don Luigi. "What's your brother been telling you, eh?" asked Don Luigi. "He hasn't told me anything," said Luciano, though it wasn't true and he knew the whole story. "There's been a little trouble over at your place," said Don Luigi. "If your family starts talking about it, just say it was you that asked me to go there. You'll always find a friend in me, remember that." Then he told Luciano to come back to the store as soon as he could.

As soon as Luciano got home, he told his wife to get out. She started to scream and shout—she made such a racket that all of the neighbors came running to see what was happening. Luciano kicked her out in the street, but she ran in again. "Don't listen to lies!" she yelled, "I haven't done a thing, I swear I haven't. They want to ruin me out of spite! They want to take my husband away from me! Oh, Oh, Oh!" "Get out!" Luciano shouted, but as fast as he threw her out, she came back. "Kill me!" she screamed. "Throw my dead body out, but as long as I'm alive, I won't go, do you hear? I won't go!" Then Luciano, seeing that she was determined not to budge, gave her a clout, went to the police, and came back with two *carabinieri*. And still she wouldn't go. "You'll have to leave—your husband won't have you in his house," the *carabinieri* said. "Where am I supposed to go?" she yelled. "I was forced into this—I'm not to blame!" Was she saying that Luciano and I agreed to let Don Luigi have her for the money we borrowed from him? Or was she saying that we trusted Don Luigi too much to think he would do such a thing? I can tell you this—we valued our honor too much to have it stained. She went on and on for an hour and a half, and then the *carabinieri* took her and Luciano to the barracks; they kept her, but they let him go. When he went back that afternoon to have his case put down in the books, she had gone to her mother's.

Zu Procopio lives close by and he's got a name for being a *mafioso*. He came to see us—he wanted to make sure we wouldn't do anything. "After a brawl or a murder, you can call somebody in to fix things up with both sides," he said. "But this is a question of honor, and nobody's got the right to interfere." Zu Procopio was followed by another man. The other man said: "Listen to me. Accept whatever Don Luigi offers you. There's a fixed rate for losing your honor, and if Don Luigi won't open up his purse, we'll send a certain person to see him that'll make sure he pays."

What are we doing about it? People like that won't stop

at anything. Tomorrow he could turn on me because I didn't keep my mouth shut about seeing him under Luciano's bed— who knows? We go through hell. We have to face him all the time, we can't get away. Luciano refuses to support his wife. "Be careful," people say to us. Must we be horned and hang-dog, too, like the saying goes? "Be careful," they all say. What are we going to do?

Nonna Nedda

Well, of course, a husband's got the right to beat his wife. If she gives him cause to beat her, of course he has the right. Say she starts arguing with him, answering him back—he won't put up with it, and no wonder, so he beats her. But has a wife got the right to raise a hand against her husband? She has not! If we hear of a woman doing such a thing, we're disgusted—"Trash, that's what she was," we say. But if a hus-band's got a reason to beat his wife, we take his side, not hers. "Don't tell us he beat you for nothing," we say to her, "we know a few things about you!" and then she's ashamed. The sort of woman who's no better than she should be, she's always raising a hand to her husband. "Fine business!" we say to her. "Shows how you've been brought up." We've got a name for a woman like that, who doesn't take care of her home and runs around with other men—a mare, we call her, a mare that's always got somebody on her back. When her husband's giving her a beating, she'll scream: "I only please you when you're on top of me!" That's why we call her a mare.

Every wife gets beaten once in a while, but it's only the mares that go to the police station and complain. I ask you: Is it right for a woman to speak bad about her husband just because he gives her a thrashing? A decent woman would never think of doing a thing like that, she'd never say a word against her husband. Take my granddaughter, Sariddu, for instance; her husband thrashed her so hard she couldn't get up off the floor and her face was all bruised. "What have you done? How did you get that black eye?" I asked her. "I fell down the stairs, Nonna," she said. "Oh dear God, and you expecting!" I said. "It's all right, Grandma," she said. "The baby wasn't hurt—I can feel it moving." A well-brought-up girl like Sariddu wouldn't tell her own mother her husband hit her. Once my husband gave me such a beating that he broke one of my ribs—it hurt so much I had to get down on my knees to make the bed. When people asked me what was wrong with me, I said, "Nothing, my head aches, that's all." I never told a soul what my husband did to me.

When a woman spends all her time gossiping, we don't have any use for her, I'll tell you that much.

"Look at her!" one of us'll say. "Wasting the whole day talking instead of doing her housework. Slut—no wonder her place is always filthy!"

"Look at that dress she's wearing—she doesn't even know how to wash and iron!"

"Why don't she clean her place up instead of gabbing from morning till night?"

"She hasn't got a good word for anybody—she's always saying things behind people's backs. It's a good thing her husband beats her—shame he doesn't do it oftener, though!"

"Leaves her children crying at home while she's out in the street—a scandal, I call it!"

No, we've got no use for a woman like that!

We women do enjoy a good talk, though. When the sun comes out, we bring our chairs outside and settle down for a nice chat. You can breathe better when you're sitting in the sun—there's nothing more pleasant. We talk about this and that, we get to know what everybody's thinking and doing. "Hi! Come on out and look at the sun," we say—what we mean is, "Let's bring the chairs out and chat!"

A wife who wants to keep her husband happy and contented has to stay home, keep everything neat and clean, cook his meals, wash and mend his clothes, never say no to him, and never even look at another man. He's the master of the house, and her master, too. Everything belongs to him except the dowry linen. And a husband has to be firm with his wife, he has to keep her in line; if he didn't, she might end up bad. We women know what kind of treatment to expect when we get married. How do husbands treat their wives in other countries? How do they treat their wives in America? How do they treat them in Russia?

My mother died when I was still a baby at her breast. My sisters told me how she died. One day, her head was very bad—she'd been baking, and the heat had made it bad—so she put a cushion on a bench and lay down. My father came in a little high. "Get yourself up, Rosalia," he said, "I want my bed made." "My head's so bad I can't move—ask one of the girls to make it up for you," my mother said. So my father told my sister Rosaria to go get the mattress. "I won't!" she said. "You've drunk up all our money!" She was cross because she was hungry and he hadn't brought us back anything to eat. (It didn't happen often, though; he was a good father to us.) Well, my father turned to my mother. "You'll have to make up my bed, Rosaria won't," he said. "I can't," my mother said, "I can't raise my head." Then my father lost his temper; he didn't mean to hit her so hard, but he was a blacksmith and he didn't know his own strength—he gave her such a wallop on her poor head that her teeth became wedged together. He rushed and brought my godfather, who was a barber and who doctored people, and he tried to force her mouth open with a spoon, but it was too late—she was dead.

If a man gets sick, his wife prays to Our Lady and begs her to cure him. She makes many promises to the Madonna. Sometimes a wife will say: "Santa Maria, leave me my husband—take one of my sons in his place." Then she makes a solemn promise: "Blessed Lady," she says, "if you'll make my husband well, I'll go down on my knees and lick all the stones right from the church door to your altar."

If Our Lady cures her husband, she carries out her promise the following Sunday. She walks to church barefoot, and when she kneels down and starts to lick the stones, the people say: "Make room for her—she's come to church to thank the

Madonna," and they cry as they watch her. My daughter-in-law licked the stones when Our Lady cured my son.

This is what you do. You kneel down outside the church, and you start licking the stones, which are covered with dust and mud and filth. When you're inside the church, you crawl forward on your knees, licking each stone as you go. The church is always crowded—people move from one place to another and spit, and the little ones do pi-pi. When your mouth is so sore that you have to stop for a minute, you raise your head and you say: "Blessed Mother, I thank you," and then you crawl some more, licking and licking. Then, when you're almost to the altar, you get up, you hold out your hands to Our Lady and you thank her with all your heart. You raise your voice so everybody will hear you, and you praise her for the grace that she's shown to you. While you're praising her, the tears stream down your face, and all the people cry, too. After you've finished thanking the Madonna, you wet your handkerchief and wipe your tongue, which is cracked and sore and bleeding, and you dry your eyes. It's not only here that women lick the stones—they do it at Romitello and Tagliavia, too. We used to make other vows to the Madonna when I was young—this one didn't become a custom till five years ago.

I've had many sorrows in my life—five little ones the Lord took from me. One of them was three when he died; I was still giving him my breast. My married son who lives here, I nursed him till he was past four—as long as I had milk, I thought it was right to feed him, and I didn't want to wean him. "Mama," he used to say when I was sewing, "titty, Mama," and I'd unbutton my dress and let him suck away. But I was telling you about my three-year-old. One day he was playing horses with another little boy who had the whooping cough; he put the reins in his mouth, and he caught the whooping cough, too. He was such a pretty little fellow, so delicate he was, with a head of gold curls—he took after my husband's side of the family, his sister was fair—my grandson Fifiddu has his looks. Everybody who saw him said how beautiful he was—his name was Carmeluzzu.

Well, he coughed-coughed-coughed, poor little fellow—he wasn't strong and I was frightened he might die. So I went to the druggist, and I said: "My little boy of three's got whooping cough—I want some syrup for him to bring up the phlegm." He made up a mixture and told me to give him a spoonful three times a day. I took Carmeluzzu into my arms. "Here's something to take away that nasty cough, darling," I said, but he wouldn't touch it. Then I pretended to drink it. "See, Mama's drinking it—baby have it," I said, and at last I coaxed him into swallowing a spoonful. But not long after that, he began to scream and cry and rub his little tummy. "What is it, darling?" I said—I couldn't think what was the matter with him. "Go 'way, go 'way, bad old pain!" he sobbed. "Great big fire burning me up inside—go 'way, go 'way!" he screamed. I thought maybe he was making a fuss the way children do if they have to take medicine, but all day long he never stopped twisting around and crying.

My little girl of five drank some of the syrup—it tasted sweet and children love anything sweet. She began to cry, too, and she said her tummy was hurting her. By evening Carmeluzzu was worn out. Every time he cried in the night, I gave him my breast to try and soothe him. The next day he was worse—he turned his little head away and wouldn't suck any more. When it was night, and I took him into bed with me, he closed his eyes, and I was so tired I fell fast asleep. Early in the morning, the young signorina who paid me to walk to the convent with her where she took lessons in sewing and cooking, knocked at the door. "Are you ready, Donna Nedda?" she said. "I can't leave my little boy, Signorina," I said. "He's very sick, I'm afraid he's dying." She came in, went to the bed, looked at him and burst out crying. I went a little way with her, then I went back and took Carmeluzzu in my arms. I couldn't make him take the nipple, so I put a drop of the syrup into a glass of water, poured out a spoonful, tilted back his head, and tried to get him to swallow it so it would freshen his poor little mouth. But he couldn't swallow it—he was dead. His little body was still warm, but he was dead.

My husband and my oldest son were out. I sat there sobbing, holding Carmeluzzu in my arms. "Look, Ciccina," I said to my daughter, "baby's dead," and I couldn't stop crying. We dressed him in his best clothes and Ciccina went out to buy him a little pair of white shoes, and my godmother sent me in a beautiful blue ribbon for him.

And then . . . in less than one hour . . . when I think of it, something comes over me and I . . . the death certificate was signed, and they took his little body away. As soon as the druggist who made up the syrup heard that Carmeluzzu was dead, he asked the owner of the *carrozze*, who was a friend of his, to send one of them to take this baby away, quick, quick . . .

My little girl of five said, "I couldn't cry when baby died, Mama—I had such a pain I thought I was going to die, too," she said. "It hurts me—my tummy started to hurt me after I drank some of his medicine—" As soon as she said that, my oldest son smashed the glass where I'd poured a drop of the syrup into little pieces, and I grabbed my little girl and ran to another druggist, who had a store near the fish market. "Please—she took some cough syrup and it's made her ill— do something for her quick," I said, and he looked at her and took me into the room in the back. I was sure she was dying. He examined her and felt her tummy and gave her some medicine, "Are you the mother of the little boy who was poisoned?" he asked. "Poisoned?" I said. I didn't understand. It seemed that the man who made up the syrup for Carmeluzzu was a beginner who didn't know his job—he'd mixed some stuff in it that came out of a bottle with a skull and crossbones on it.

The druggist gave me something for my little girl to clear everything out of her tummy. "I'll take it, Mama," she said to me. "Then I'll get better, won't I?" "Yes, darling," I said. I wouldn't let her have anything to eat for the next few days, I kept her on milk.

At the end of the week, a man came to see my husband. "Friend Peppino," he said, "I won't waste any words—I'll only say that this is a nasty business. But keep quiet about it. If you start making speeches—well, you're poor and they're rich, so what can you do? What could you gain, friend, by making a lot of noise? If you have your little boy's body dug up, you'll have to pay for it, all the expense'll be on you. Don't think you can show them up—they're rich, I tell you, they'll get the best of it. Take my advice, leave things alone . . ."

E.A.

The first time I was arrested—in August, 1944—I was taken to the P. barracks and put on the *cassetta* to make me "confess." The *cassetta* has two wooden boxes about a yard long; I was stripped, and I had to sit with my legs stretched out on the top box, and the rope that passed through two rings in the bottom box was tied around my ankles. My hands were tied behind my back with the rope that was hooked onto a ring in the floor, and the leather straps fixed on both sides of the *cassetta* were hooked tight around my waist to stop me from getting loose. A gas mask without the cover on the mouthpiece was pushed down over my head, and the *sbirro* that was standing behind me jerked me backwards with the rope my hands were tied with. Then the torture started. A cop came over to me with a can of salt water (there was a bucket of salt water nearby so he could fill it as soon as it was empty) and began to pour it through the mouthpiece. While he was doing that, Sergeant M. beat the soles of my feet with a rawhide whip as thick as two fingers, and another cop grabbed me by my testicles and kept twisting them every minute. The pain was something terrible, but pretty soon I became barely conscious of it: I was suffocating, I was choking to death in the gas mask—and death would have been a relief.

But the cops didn't let me die. They knew exactly how much a man could stand, and as soon as they saw I'd reached my limit, they stopped, took off the gas mask, and forced me to sit up. "Are you ready to talk now, you bastard?" the sergeant shouted, but I wouldn't talk. "Maybe you'll change your mind after another taste!" he said. They jerked me backwards again, the gas mask was clamped over my head, and it was the whole lousy business all over again. I couldn't breathe, I kept swallowing salt water, and when they figured they'd filled me up with it, they untied me, and one of them pressed my stomach with his hands till I threw it all up.

There's no danger of anybody getting to know that somebody's being tortured inside the barracks—you can't scream with a gas mask on. After I'd heaved up the water, they strapped me down again, and they tortured me the same way another two or three times. Then, when it was clear to them that I couldn't stand any more of that treatment, they took me off the *cassetta*. I couldn't use my arms or legs, they were numb, and two *sbirri* took me by the arms and marched me up and down till my blood began to circulate again. A cover was thrown over the *cassetta* so no prying eyes could see the signs of the fight I'd put up to free myself; from instinct, in spite of all the torture and agony, I fought to save my life.

As soon as I could stand up without help, they made me get dressed and I was taken from the barracks to my cell in the prison.

Sixteen days in a row, I was put on the *cassetta*. Towards the last few days my feet were so swollen from the steady lashes of the whip that I couldn't put on my shoes—I had to be carried from the *carrozza* they drove me in to the barracks, into the torture chamber. I still refused to "confess," so Sergeant M. tried even worse kinds of torture: he put lighted matches on the soles of my feet and burned them all over.

I was arrested again in 1947. It was eleven at night when they brought me to the barracks in Corso C. They didn't even go through the formality of the investigation, they put me on the *cassetta* right away. It was the same dirty stuff like before, except they didn't lash my feet. They had made up their minds I was guilty of certain crimes, and they were determined to make me confess: the fact that I might be innocent—and I was—was something they didn't even bother to think about. The pain I felt was so great, I'm telling you, that if I would've had the strength to talk, I would've gladly confessed that I killed Jesus, set Rome on fire, or anything they wanted, just so they'd stop torturing me. Many men have confessed to crimes they never committed when they couldn't stand any more, and have rotted in prison for three or four years before going to trial, and then have been found innocent.

But to go back to where I was, the torture chamber. After an hour or an hour and a half, I was taken off the *cassetta* and marched up and down by two *sbirri*. But instead of taking me back to my cell, they hooked my hands and feet and tied me onto a camp bed. They were afraid I might follow some of their other victims' example and commit suicide in the cell by banging out my brains against the wall or cutting my throat with a nail or a piece of glass. Except for a few minutes when they untied me to take me to the toilet, I stayed on that bed till ten o'clock the next night, when I was tortured again. I went through this treatment twenty-two days on end —no, I'm wrong, there was a break of two days when they were busy with some other business.

E.A. speaks of another incident in his life.

In Partinico, as soon as the good weather starts, the ice-cream men come out hoping to make a few lire. The second the kids catch sight of their bright wagons, they all yell: "I want an ice!" Some mothers are too poor to buy them, and the scene that goes on is really heartbreaking. "Why can't I have one?" some kid'll say to its mother, its lips quivering, and the mother makes up a story in a hurry. "Because it's garbage," she says. "It's mixed with donkey's piss, it's not fit to eat." But the kid sees the other kids licking away at their ices, and doesn't believe her. It starts to cry, and she pets and fondles it, with tears streaming quiet down her own cheeks. How can she buy ices when she can't even afford to buy bread? Cheap greens are the main food of poor families like them.

There's one case of poverty that I'll never forget, it was so terrible. I got engaged to a girl in 1944, but we couldn't get our hands on any money for a decent wedding, so in 1945, like a lot of other working-class couples, we ran away together, and got married a little later with as little noise and dough as we could. We came to Partinico, where a friend of mine had lent us his house for a while. It was in the Via Madonna section, and almost right across from us there was this family, the father, the mother and four kids; the baby was only four months old, the rest were about nine, seven and six. The day after we came, the nine-year-old girl came over to our place to give my wife a hand, hoping maybe to get a piece of bread.

Frankly, we had no idea what trouble this family was in, because even though the kids were ragged and barefoot and all, still, ragged, barefoot kids are such a common sight in Partinico we didn't think much of it.

On the third day, my wife was cooking some pasta for our supper when the little girl came in. "Donna Titidda," she said, "Mama says when you've finished cooking the pasta, can she have the water you boiled it in, please?" My wife nodded like she didn't even hear her, but the thing struck me as being so strange that, just out of curiosity, I asked the kid why her mother wanted it. She told me that except for a crust of bread and a spoonful of pasta, they hadn't had anything to eat for three days. "Mama hasn't got any milk to feed the baby with," she wound up. "She thought may be if she drank the pasta water, the milk would come back."

When I heard that kid's story, I cursed the God that made me, I cursed the government that allowed such misery to go on, I cursed the kid's father for being some kind of a goddamn freak who just stood there watching his family starve to death. I know if I'd been in his shoes, I'd have stolen, I'd have done anything to get food for my kids. I wanted to go and say to one of the decent ministers in the government: "Change places with this man for a week, and see what you'd do—you'd become a thief or a bandit or worse rather than just sit there doing nothing, knowing that your own children hated you because you were letting them starve to death."

We gave the kid a couple of pounds of pasta that we'd found in the house, a little oil, and our one loaf of bread. "Tell your Mama it's for her," we said. "Instead of water, she has to eat this bread and pasta."

We both had tears in our eyes. As soon as the kid had gone, we set the table and sat down to our supper of pasta and no bread. But my wife kept looking at her plate and saying she didn't want it, she had no appetite, and when she thought I was convinced that she really didn't want it, she said, "Franco, I'm not hungry, would you mind if I gave my share to the kids?" "That's funny—I'm not hungry either," I said. "We'll take them over the whole works." That night, it was the third night of our honeymoon, we went to bed starving, but knowing that for just one night we were able to give those kids a meal, more than made up for the loss of our supper.

A few days later they were evicted; they couldn't pay the rent and the landlord wouldn't wait any longer. The police came along, tossed out everything they had in the world, a few broken chairs and a broken-down bed, and threw them into the street.

Giuseppe Z.

For twenty years and more, houses around here have been falling down because of the river that runs underneath them. The people here wrote and asked the government to do something about it, and in the meantime they began digging a tunnel to find what was happening down below. They went so deep down they couldn't see each other, though they could hear each other's voices. But they didn't find anything except earth and water. Oh, how I wish the government would hire some men and give them the right kind of tools and tell them to keep on digging till they got to the bottom of the world. I walk around the countryside and I think about it and I'm positive I'm right: there *is* something that holds the world steady. But where does it end? Where *does* the world end?

In lonely parts of the country like this, where there's hardly any roads and no railroads and it's not very easy to get around, the Mafia's very strong. The people that live here are so scared they might say something that would bring the *mafiosi* down on them they're afraid to open their mouths. They're not so quick-thinking like city folk; if you're in a city you're more alive, you learn how to use your head, but when all you see is mountains and sky day in and day out, why, you're just like sheep, and when there's wolves around . . .

You ought to see the big shots that come down here and

talk to us right before the elections. "Work on the state projects will begin in June, and you'll all get regular jobs," they tell us. Believe me, if God Himself came down out of heaven and said the very same thing, we wouldn't believe it! Maybe by the time I'm old, there *will* be regular jobs for everybody, but then it'll be too late—I won't even care . . .

When we have to take a coffin to the cemetery, we strap two baskets onto a mule's back, one on either side, and fasten the coffin in between them. Sometimes we take the corpse just the way it is—some houses are so far away from a village there's no way of getting a coffin to them. We wrap the body in a blanket or a sheet so as not to scare the people passing— or the mule either, for that matter—and then we tie it onto the mule's back. If somebody gets seriously sick in one of these lonely houses, we take him down to the village in the same way; if we were to wait till the doctor got here, he'd be dead—a thing that's happened more than once. A few roads have been built, but some of them are in such condition that they're not even fit for walking. The ones we use aren't much better, and many times the mule with the corpse on its back suddenly sinks knee-deep in mud. Then we take a stick, a slab of wood and a rope, and we push and pull till we get him out. We have to ford the river at one point, but when it's running in full force, we can't get across. We have to stay where we are, corpse and all, and wait for the tide to drop. In spring, when the snow's melting, we've had to wait sometimes for as long as a week, even two weeks. There's a cemetery at Petralia Soprana, and another one at the Trinità. The villages are very small in these parts: Raffa has a hundred houses, Lucia only six, then there's Salice, Scarpette, Acquamara, Saline—there are thirty-two villages altogether, and from some of them it's three hours by mule to the cemetery.

There's hardly any of these villages you can get to by road. I make my way to them up the mountainside to buy eggs, and hens and roosters. There's no running water, no electric light. There are kids of twelve that've never seen a wheel— they've never been past the walls of their villages. When a couple gets married, the peasants, riding mules or horses, form up into a procession, and those that've got harmonicas bring them along. The bride in her white veil rides up in front—sometimes, though, she don't put her veil on till she gets to the church for fear it might get torn. Just behind her comes the bridegroom. After the wedding, there's a feast and everybody gets presents: candy, trinkets, roasted melon seeds and *confetti*.[1] In the evening everybody dances to the harmonicas—there aren't any radios around here. Couples always get married in the summertime so they can be sure the weather'll be good for the procession—and then, too, people've got their harvest money.

If a woman's in labor, we go by mule to the village to bring the midwife. If we see it's going to be a difficult birth, then we make a litter and carry the mother all the way to Palermo. It's rough going. Once a woman got so shaken up that her baby was born before we got there. If we go to a dance in a big village, we put on our heavy shoes, carry our light ones in a bag, and change into them when we get there. All the men in these small lonely villages have rifles. They're good folk, plain folk that the world knows nothing about, and if anybody does them any harm . . . well, they take the law in their own hands, and nobody says anything about it.

I make a living for myself by buying and selling. I buy eggs, for instance, for twenty-seven lire, and sell them for thirty lire. Many of the old people don't know the value of money, but the younger ones do—the war opened their eyes. They're picking up a bit here and a bit there—it's not very much, but still it's a beginning . . .

The estate's divided up now, but when it belonged to the Marquis the peasants used to starve to death because he wouldn't let them kill the rabbits. The rabbits used to eat up all their lentils, wheat, beans—whatever they sowed—but the Marquis wouldn't let them set their traps; the rabbits had to be kept alive for his pleasure, just so he could go rabbit shooting every week . . .

Not long before I was born, a young man that lived here—

[1] White sugared almonds, which are arranged in tiny china or filigree dishes and distributed as keepsakes to guests at a wedding. This is the custom throughout Italy. *Translator's note.*

Giovanni, his name was—ran away and joined the bandits up in the mountains. I've heard many a story about how he robbed the rich to help the poor; he forced the great lords to give him wheat and money, and he shared it out among them that were needy and starving. They caught him and put him in prison, but as soon as they let him out, he joined up with the bandits again and lived with them for another ten years. Three years ago he was murdered in the woods where he had his hideout, but who did it, nobody knows . . .

When I've got eggs to sell, I pack as many as I can in a basket—a hundred, a hundred and fifty, two hundred—and I take them from village to village. I always break three or four eggs; if they're cracked I eat them, but if they're completely smashed they're a dead loss. In winter, when eggs are scarce, I ask forty-five lire apiece; it's hard to get around in the slush or in the thick snow, with an icy wind blowing, and when it's dark it's worse still—long after the villagers have gone to bed, I'm still stumbling and groping my way home. There's about ten of us egg sellers in Petralia. In Gangi there's five or six, but they go by mule, and they sell other things besides eggs— for instance, the rubber shoes made out of old car tires that all the peasants and shepherds hereabouts wear, and that cost two hundred lire a pair.

In the old days the folks around here were honest and didn't try to cheat you—you could earn a little money by going around. But times have changed. They're a pretty sharp bunch now, and they know the prices of things better than us sellers that walk from village to village. They've taken a leaf out of the book of the strangers that come here sometimes, they're beginning to learn city ways . . .

Down there in the valley, Li Puma was murdered by the Mafia. He was one of our leaders, he was a good man: "The estate ought to belong to the peasants," he said. So they killed him, but in the end some of the land—it was the poorest land, though; it was full of rocks—was given to thirty families, and a village was built on the lowest slope of the mountain. But times have changed. People are too afraid of the laws to stand up for their rights; nobody makes a move, the party just stands still, though maybe one or two are working for it secretly. But when Li Puma was alive, the movement was really strong. The students used to march side by side with the peasants. (Some of the *contadini* send their boys to the training schools for elementary teachers.) They used to march in a column three hundred strong, carrying banners that they'd plant in the soil of the estate. The leaders always managed to trick the *carabinieri* who had machine guns trained on them when they assembled in the piazza. "We're only going to hold a peaceful demonstration," they'd say, and the *carabinieri* would believe them and calm down.

Li Puma was shot through the heart at two o'clock in the afternoon. All that morning he'd been shelling almonds. The two men that meant to murder him had arrived about midday, and while they stood talking to the agent of the estate, they kept their eyes on him to make sure that the second they were ready, they could get him. As soon as the agent got on his horse and rode away, they walked over to Li Puma, said a few words to him, drew their revolvers, fired, and walked away. Li Puma's eleven-year-old son was working right close by. He saw the whole thing. He knew the agent by sight, of course, but the two men were strangers to him. No investigation was ever made—there was no trial, nothing. They took the little boy away from his mother and put him in an orphanage in Rome. Soon after that he was found drowned.

Not so long ago Li Puma's family put in for some land, but their application form just disappeared. They didn't get any land, but other people did, and it was for the others, not for himself, that Li Puma died . . .

In Petralia there's a sodality that arranges all the processions, and any man that belongs to it gets a free funeral procession when he dies. The members get paid fifteen hundred lire for walking in a procession, but if they don't walk, they get fined five hundred lire—that's to make sure they'll turn up. The sodality also provides free funeral processions to follow the coffins of the members' wives or children. There's three sodalities in Petralia; one wears white robes, one blue and one black. The men wear these robes for the Easter procession. It starts out from two different places: the Madonna's half of the procession starts out from the Town Hall, and the other half, the procession of Jesus, from the main street. When they both get near the barracks the trumpets blow, three men fire rifles, and a whole string of firecrackers is let off. The two processions meet, the Madonna is unveiled, she and Jesus come face to face and they look just as if they were kissing each other. After they've kissed, they're carried along side by side and we all follow behind: the band, the sodalities, the mayor, the *carabinieri*, the police. The two statues are taken back to the church, and the priest and a monk praise Jesus for His Divine Sacrifice. After Mass we all go home and feast. If it's been a long spell of dry weather, then the peasants and the Communists, too, walk in the Easter procession to pray for rain; they all wear crowns of thorns on their heads.

When I've got no eggs to sell and no work, I pick mushrooms and collect kindling—for a bundle that weighs sixty-five pounds, I get two hundred lire. Sometimes I get a little charcoal, but not very often because there's snow up here in the mountains for six months of the year. Like nearly all the rest of the people hereabouts, I manage in winter by selling greens, fennel, orach, loosestrife—but loosestrife tastes bitter and people don't buy it much—cockles and chicory. Chicory's more plentiful than the rest. And I hunt for *babbaluce*, too; I find plenty in wet weather, but in a dry year none at all—if there's no rain, they die. In summer I go down to the valley where the estates are, and I glean. I also go out picking wild asparagus—there are two kinds, one's taller than the other—and hazelnuts. We have to do what we can— all the people here in Petralia are poor. But though they're poor, they're proud—they always put on clean things before they sit down to their supper.

When there wasn't a store up here the women had to trudge all the way to the big village to buy what things they needed. The schoolmistress used to take the kids for a walk down to the road—she still does—to watch the cars and the carts go by. It's a real treat for the children. "You be good, and we'll take you down to the road to see the wheels go round!" we promise them.

a goatherd and three young shepherds

THE GOATHERD: There's the Mafia, but I've got my own picked men to look after me—every one of us thinks he's more *mafioso* than the rest—it gives us a feeling of safety. If the *mafiosi* have a falling out with each other over the money they've made by selling stolen cattle, the ones that complain about their share are put out of the way fast; they're ambushed and killed. If a landowner won't hand over the money that's demanded from him, the *mafiosi* kill him, too. They cut one woman to pieces. They slashed a bearded bandit to death. They buried another man alive. If they find out that somebody's a spy, they kill him, tear out his tongue and leave it lying on his nose so everybody'll know what happens to people that squeal and that poke their noses into other people's business. Sometimes, instead of tearing out his tongue, they chop off his hands—to show they'll do the same thing to anybody that interferes with them. They killed another man because he molested a little girl—they cut off his balls and hung them around his neck. They kill out of jealousy, too. There was this egg seller that used to go from village to village. He had an affair with a farm hand's wife, and one day the husband found out what was going on. "Get out, and don't show your face around here again!" he shouted. But the egg seller came back just the same. The farm hand went to the police and the egg seller got a warning, and still he wouldn't keep away. So one evening the farm hand said to his wife, "I'm going out to play my pipe," and she didn't suspect anything because he often used to go out to play his pipe—sometimes he played just to please his friends. Well, out he went, and hid in the barn. He saw the egg seller go into the house, saw him sit down to supper with his wife. After they ate they went to bed, and the husband waited till they were both asleep. Then he ran in and stabbed them both with his knife—the wife, she was screaming, she tried to save herself by hiding behind her little girl . . . maybe the husband cut off the egg seller's balls, maybe he didn't. I don't know . . .

We've had some famous bandits in these parts. F.'s dead—the first person he ever killed was a woman, he strangled her. A.'s still alive. C., that was tied up with the Mafia, he was shot by the police; they pumped so many bullets into him he was chock-full of lead. He was so strong all he had to do was grip a man's arm to snap the bone. The *mafiosi* cut the breasts off of one woman, and burned her to ashes in a bread oven. At Gangi they slashed another woman in her private parts. Sometimes they're content just to spit in their enemy's face. In the old days they'd've gone further than that and sliced off his nose or his ears. See those oak trees over there? Since 1922, not a year's gone by but a man's been found lying murdered under them.

I've been a goatherd for forty years—I became a goatherd when I was ten years old. In the morning I take the goats out into the fields and at night I bring them back to the farm. Once or twice a month I go to Gangi for a bath; after I've cleaned up I go over to the licensed house and have a woman. There are some young fellows here, some of them boys of twenty, that've never once been away from the estate. A funny thing happened to Antonio. He was born here but his birth never got recorded, so when he went down to Palermo for his military service he found out his class had been called up two years before. I went to Palermo when I broke my arm. I once spent a day at Catania and that was enough for me. What would I do in Catania? Swallow flies?

I count my goats in my own way. I can count up to fifty and that's all, so when I get to fifty I begin again: "One, two three . . ." Goatherds have to be able to tell one goat from another, to make sure that each nanny has her own kids. You have to be able to tell, too, which way the wind's blowing. You don't like being out in a high wind, do you? Neither do the goats. We look around for a place to shelter them from it, and we take them there. They can't stand a cold wind, it freezes their blood and they get sick. These two hundred and thirty goats I'm tending now belong to the Cavaliere. I've been chilled to the bone and soaked to the skin so often that

I've got pains in the back that make me feel like a dog is gnawing at me.

I use up all the marrow in my bones scraping a living together. You think I'd throw away my hard-earned soldi on a movie? You think I'd pay to see a puppet show and give my money to the puppeteer? He don't work a quarter as hard as I do . . .

They talk about land reform, but what have they done? Get hold of some land, give it to men that've never even handled a hoe, men with friends up at the top. There's less and less grazing ground—they take everything away from us poor people. All us goatherds and shepherds are worried—pretty soon, if they go on parceling out the fields the way they are now, there won't be a blade of grass left for our animals. We don't vote for the Socialists, though; fact is, we don't hit it off too bad with the *mafiosi*. The barons haven't robbed us of our pasture land. They still own the estates in these parts— so far, nothing's been done about dividing them up . . .

LEONARDO, A SHEPHERD OF SEVENTEEN: What did I do when I was little? I played leapfrog. When I was thirteen, I hired myself out as a shepherd. My father's a shepherd, and I used to help him with his sheep—after you've been tending them for a year, you know all about them.

I've tended goats, too. When I was at San Giorgio they didn't want me to milk the goats, but I milked them just the same because I loved doing it. If you squeeze their teats too tight when you're milking them the first time, they never forget, and they won't ever let you milk them any more. You've got to take care, too, never to scratch their udders with your nails. Some of them stand still while you milk them and others'll kick out. When they've got very short teats or crooked teats, they're hard to milk. Some people goats can't stand, but they always let me handle them.

I can't count, but even when I was a long way away, I could see if one of my goats was missing. I knew every goat in my herd—it was a big herd, but I could tell every one of them apart. I could tell what kid belonged to what mother. I've tended big flocks of sheep, too, flocks of a hundred or two hundred. The master used to count them to see if they were all there, but I knew they were all there without counting them.

I love sheep and my sheep love me. I watch them, follow them, pet them, coax them, pick tiny beans for them to eat, and they come right up to me—they're not timid with me. When a ewe stops cropping the grass and her udders are all hard and swollen, I know she's ready to drop a lamb. She lies down, begins to bleat and the water breaks. If everything's going well, she stops bleating, but when I see she can't manage by herself, I make the opening bigger with my hands. The lamb's feet and its tiny muzzle stick out, and then when it's born, the mother starts to lick it clean and dry it. As soon as she's finished, she gets up, and a quarter of an hour later the lamb gets up, too, and begins to suckle. I was with my father the first time I saw a lamb born, and I helped him, so I learned what to do at lambing time.

We call the maiden ewes *renische*; when they've lambed, we call them *pecore*. We call young nanny goats *ciaravedde*: The ones that only have one kid we call *primarole*. We don't have any special name for the ones that've had two or more kids, we just call them goats.

Very young kids don't follow their mothers when they go too far away for them, but when the ones we've kept for rearing are a month old, they follow them all right; a few won't, so we slaughter them. But boy, how tired them little kids get skipping after their mothers! We let them out twice a day, in the morning and in the evening, to suckle—the rest of the time we keep them shut up. They'd much rather be out of doors, but if we let them caper around for hours, they'd get far too thin. A kid's navel cord shrivels up and drops off by itself.

I love goats. I always take them where the grass is juiciest. If they can't find anything to eat, you ought to hear the noise they make. When the sun comes blazing down in the middle of the day, they all huddle together and stand in each other's shade.

The only places I've ever been to are Castellana and Alimena. I don't understand anything about soldi.

If sheep nibble on the berries of jack-in-the-pulpit they die right away. But the berries don't poison goats, so when we see them growing in a field we drive the goats on ahead; as soon as they eat them up, we can graze our sheep safely.

To pass the time, I make a doll out of clay, and then I set it up and throw stones at it and try to knock it down. Some shepherds have reed pipes and they play tunes on them. I haven't got a reed pipe, I don't know how to make one. I can make clay dolls, though, and knock them down, too. It's a game that all shepherds play.

What are stars? I've seen them many many times but I don't know what they are. In the pictures of Jesus, there are stars. The stars are some queer sort of eyes, maybe—how can I tell what they are? The moon is the Madonna. I've heard people say the moon's the Madonna, and that's what I say, too. The sun is Our Savior. I pray to the moon and the sun. When it's cold I pray to the sun to come out, and when the sun comes out and it's too hot, I pray to the sun to go in. "Make me warm," I say to the sun when I'm freezing. "Give me some light," I say to the moon when it's dark. When the sun comes out and warms me, I'm happy, and when the moon gives me light, I'm happy too. I love to watch the moon moving along in the sky. I pray to the stars, too. "Please shine for me," I say. I love to watch the stars—they're so pretty.

What I like best is going back home to my village for a day, and seeing my mother and my father and my sisters and brothers and all my uncles. Boy, what a time I have! But I like being with my animals, too. I like working. I wish I were a farmer, though, so I could sow and reap and eat as much as I liked.

Sometimes I pray for good weather, or I pray it won't rain all through the winter, or there won't be any thunderstorms. I pray to Our Father. "Oh, dear little Father, please don't send us bad weather," I say to him out loud.

When the wind blows, it turns cold. The wind brings the cold. What is the wind? I see the grass swaying this way, that way, and that's the wind. If it's very cold, I pray to the sun. "Please come out and warm my animals or they'll all get sick," I say. My mother and father taught me to pray to the sun and the moon. All us shepherds pray to them.

What's the sea? The world is a sea. I live here summer and

winter and I don't know what the sea is—I've only heard people talk about it. I've heard them say the world is a sea, so I say the world is a sea.[1]

I've seen clouds, but I don't know what they are. The wind blows them out of the sky.

We're in the world because we have a house in it and we work in it. We eat in it too. Why do we come into the world? To work. To eat. To work. I don't know anything else. Men grow old, everything in the world grows old, the animals grow old and so do Christians. But the sun never grows old.

GANDOLFO, A SHEPHERD OF THIRTEEN:
If I could choose, I'd live with men, not animals.

LEONARDO: I wouldn't. I'd rather stay with my flocks. I love my sheep.

VINCENZO, A SHEPHERD OF FIFTEEN: I'd rather be with men. Men are company.

ALL THREE TOGETHER: Italy? Never heard of it!

GANDOLFO: I've never heard of America—

LEONARDO AND VINCENZO: We have, but we don't know what it is.

GANDOLFO: I've heard tell of the Pope, too, but what sort of thing is it?

LEONARDO AND VINCENZO: The Pope? Never heard of it . . .

---

[1] Our own saying, "The world is a sea of troubles," is common in this part of Sicily. *Translator's note.*

the Santa Rosalia quarter, Alia

On January 19, 1947, the Council of Alia (the population of Alia was eighty-one hundred and thirteen when the census was taken in 1951) asked the appropriate authorities to include the Santa Rosalia section (where approximately eleven hundred persons live in some two hundred houses controlled by the Council) among the landslip zones. No reply was received. On August 25, 1955, the Council made a second application, couched in even stronger terms, pointing out that every year, owing to the hazard, five, six or seven houses were found to be in such a dangerous condition that notices to evacuate had to be served. This second request also remained unanswered.

The streets of the quarter are in a very bad state; they are no longer level, and in places there are deep depressions at the bottom of which are pools of water. One house presents an extraordinary appearance: the upright of one wall is still in position, but the wall itself and the roof are in ruins. The water is sucking at the foundations of the entire area, which is gradually crumbling to bits. But water is rationed in Alia; it is only turned on for four hours a day.

The water has channeled its way below almost all of them at a depth of about three feet. The walls bulge and crack, the joists work loose. The thin floorboards of the rooms on ground level are reeking with damp rot—from time to time the entire floor of a room caves in.

In the course of the last ten years, apart from innumerable minor repairs, a hundred and sixty-four major repairs have had to be carried out. The hazard during this period has caused four million, four hundred thousand lire worth of damage to these houses.

The fifty families under consideration, numbering two hundred and three persons, live in eighty-two rooms. Seventeen houses have no water taps, forty-three have no toilets, eleven have no electricity and all forty-eight are sparsely furnished.

All the families share their living space with their livestock. In sixteen homes there were hens; in fourteen there was a mule; in four there was a donkey; in two, a goat; in one, a pig; and in one, a cow and her calf.

As for the occupations of the heads-of-family, twelve are farm hands, five are *mezzadri,* five are laborers, one is an agent, one is a quarryman, one is a stone mason and one is a stone breaker. The farm hands work about eighty-five days out of the year and the rest about a hundred. Ten heads-of-family are either pensioners or disabled men and now do no work.

There are fifteen cases of malaria, three of typhus, three of glandular disease and two of mental disease; there is one case of undulant fever and one of t.b.

Crocifissa M.

Please sit down. Don't be afraid—we won't be killed today. But tonight—only God knows . . .

Three times we've had to leave this house because of landslides. The first time was 1935—we got orders from the mayor to leave. There were cracks in the earth floor, then in the walls. They bent inwards so much that we couldn't close the door. A week before my daughter Pina was born, the floor split wide open, the walls started to crumble and the roof started to press down lower and lower. It was winter; I had to leave everything, and take my three children to my father's house.

It wasn't only my house that was falling to pieces, all the other houses in our section of Alia were tumbling to pieces, too. We wrote to the Council and they sent an engineer; after he looked around, he ordered everybody out. "I'm responsible for your safety," he said, "and you can't stay here. All the ground under your houses is slipping away."

We stayed with my father till June, then we started to repair our house, and in September, when we couldn't find any place else to live, we went back.

But in 1940 the same thing happened again. The floor split open and part of a wall crashed down. I had four children then—I was glad, because three didn't seem enough to me. In February we got another order to leave, and the engineers came and said they wouldn't answer for what happened if we stayed. So in March we moved to another house we managed to rent. We weren't there long when my husband died, and I was left to take care of myself and my four children. I got the insurance money, and with the little I'd saved I repaired the house, and by September we were living in it once more.

Year after year, when the heavy rains come, the houses sink down a little more—sometimes as little as a fraction of an inch, sometimes as much as six or eight feet. If the weather's fairly dry it's not so bad. We leave when we're told to leave, but we always come back. As the houses sink deeper in their foundations the ones on the higher ground begin to slide, and they press down against the ones below and everything begins to tumble down about our ears. The electric cables break and we have no lights. Big holes open up in the street, and the drains burst. Down come stones and plaster—sometimes a whole house falls down.

We sow the fields in springtime, but nothing ever comes up—the earth cracks and crumbles and slides away down into the ravine below.

Even the water pipes burst. They burst in Uncle Vincenzo's house, and in many other houses, too. The walls don't crash down all at once; we can tell when they're going to cave in, and as soon as pieces of them start to fall we rush out. What do we do at night? Last year, when my son was here, he woke up to find pieces of plaster falling on his bed, and he shouted to warn us and we all ran out just as we were.

Our animals always know when there's something going to happen. They sniff around, they can scent danger under the earth. Once, in 1940 it was, I heard the mules stamping around in the middle of the night. Plaster and stones had started to come down and they were wild with fear, they were trying to escape. A violent death is a horrible thing—even the thought of getting killed is terrifying.

We all have telephones without wires in this section of Alia. Not real telephones, of course; I mean we can hear every word our neighbors are saying through the big cracks in the walls; a thief wouldn't stand a chance! If we want to talk privately, we have to whisper. We can see each other, too, through the cracks. If the light's on in the house next door, there's no need for me to put on mine. It's as bright as daylight in here. When you undress you do it in the dark unless you want people to see you with nothing on. Sometimes just when you sit down to eat, crash! down comes a lump of the ceiling, and then you have plaster with your soup!

Whenever the wind blows the house shakes all over—it's just like somebody staggering around. If there's a gale we go outside, bury our faces in our hands and pray to God to protect us. At night, when there's a high wind I stay indoors sometimes. I crouch close to the shaking walls and pray to St. Rosalia to make the wind drop down.

The smoke from our fires creeps through the cracks in the chimneys from one house to another. No sooner do we fill them up than they crack open again.

Once upon a time my floor was level—now look at it! It's all lumps and bumps like a mountain chain—you can't set a chair straight. Two years ago I fixed my kitchen up good, I had the walls and ceilings repaired—everything. But pretty soon there was one crack, and then another one, and then down came a big lump of plaster, and another and another; since March, I've been under notice to get out—so have seven other families. Every year some of us have to go. You see that stony mountain right opposite—the Ilice, we call it—well, that's where the landslide is, right underneath it.

The river used to drain into Totò Battaglia's land and flood it when it overflowed, so he made a dam. Now the river runs underneath the houses and we're all ruined. The water's been turned away from the river, it's got no outlet, so it just spreads and spreads. It's already under this section. It ought to be channeled away before it gets to other parts of Alia.

About two hundred and forty houses in the St. Rosalia area are caving in. The foundations are being eaten away bit by bit, and they're all shaky. The whole section's slipping and slipping; so is the mountain.

People complain plenty, you can be sure of that; they protest to the Council, but the Council's only interested in its own affairs. So the landslide gets worse and worse, and the men go on filling up the cracks, and as fast as they fill them up, there are new ones.

When we ask the Council to do something about the landslide and then repair our houses for us, they tell us: "We're going to start work at once—today, tomorrow." But nothing ever happens.

Do they ever give us a thought? Sure—just before the elections. Then they come around with a key and they say to us: "Here, take this, we've found you a new place." But any other time of the year, it's: "Your house is not safe, you'll have to leave."

"But where are we going to go?" we say to them.

"You'll have to manage the best you can—stay at the inn of the moon!"—camp out, that's what they mean.

Then the engineers and the other authorities come around again.

"You poor things!" they say, and they look at us with pity.

When our houses are ready to fall down about our ears, they tell us to leave, but they never offer us new ones. It's always: "We'll start repairing them on Monday . . . we'll start repairing them next month . . ." And as for the landslide, "We're hard up—we're heavily in debt," says the Council, and that's how it goes—each one thinking of himself and not us.

My son only works two or three months out of the year. Poor people like us don't know much about what's going on in the world, we don't understand that kind of thing. Only the rich can afford to buy papers every day. If there's important news, like a big disaster, or the store owner says there's something special in the paper, then one of the women goes and buys a copy, and we all go over to see her and somebody reads it out loud while the rest of us listen. I've got a relative in Palermo, and every now and then she pays me a visit and brings me the news. "You remember that couple I told you about the last time I was here?" she may say. "Well, he's had another fight with his wife," or, "He's thrown himself under a train . . ."

There are more than twenty-seven people around here that've gone crazy from hunger or fear. Last week—Saturday it was—a woman was in her house when half the wall fell in and pinned her against the window. She got out all right, but her mind was gone; she rushed up the Ilice and threw herself into the ravine. She's alive, but she'll never be right in the head again. There's a man living in the alley that's raving mad. He screams and shrieks, stops for an hour or so, and then starts all over again. Such awful things he screams: "He must die, he must die! You've eaten human flesh!"—that's the way he goes on. He used to be a good worker once, poor man. The neighbors all complain about him, they want to get him put away in an asylum.

None of the men in these parts get more than two or three months' work in the year. When they're out of work they run up bills at the store, and when the store owner won't give them any more credit, they go picking greens in the mountains—fennel, chicory, whatever they can find—and sell them for a few lire a bunch. Many times they get arrested for trespassing. The greens grow wild in the fields, but the fields belong to the master, and us poor people, you know . . . We hunt for snails, too—they're sold by the measure here, we don't bother about scales and weights. The women shell almonds, and sometimes they do a man's work: they transplant lentils, or they reap wheat, or pick beans and chickpeas. But they're always paid short—their papers are never in order, never . . .

Oftentimes, in the middle of the night, the sound of somebody screaming wakes us up, and shaking with fear, our faces white as plaster, we run out into the open.

The beams get loose from the walls and come crashing down. We don't know what it is to be free of fear—any minute we may be crushed.

On St. Joseph's Eve, the old house that used to stand three doors away from here came down just like that. Tano's little granddaughter saw the stones starting to fall. "Look out!" people shouted to her. "The whole place is going!" The cat ran away meowing. The child stood there shrieking and shrieking and the house caved in.

Our doorways keep shrinking. When we can't close the doors we call in the carpenter, but the doorways get narrower and narrower all the time. Once I dreamed that mine got so small that the only way I could get out was through the window. If only it was a dream—but all you have to hear is that quiet rumble of the walls when they come loose from the beams to know that it's no dream. At night, we're wakened by the thud of falling bricks, and we put on the light, and take a look around, and then put it out again. An hour later, maybe: thud; this happens two or three times every night.

In the winter we hardly ever sleep a wink. The water

spreads and spreads, and when it's on the move, so are we: the houses slide, everything slides. People scream in fear, but the people that could put a stop to it don't do anything about it—their own interests come first. We gave six hundred lire each to a man that knew how to write and he made out the complaints for us, and we signed our names to them. We sent the complaints to the police inspector, the Regional Assembly and the government, but we never heard a word.

A few months ago, the Honorable F. came to Alia. "A landslide?" he said. "Nonsense! There is no landslide here!"

Then Antonino and some of the other men got a letter. Wait a minute, I'll go get it so you can read it . . .

CROCIFISSA GOES OUT AND RETURNS WITH THE LETTER:

Republic of Italy, Region of Sicily

The President, Division III, N.
Ref. 22/589   Palermo, 26 October, 1955

To: Sig. Todaro Antonino fu Francesco
Via Savoia
Alia

With reference to your request for help, we wish to state that we have been in communication with the technical experts regarding the displacement of soil in Via Gorizia, and have now been informed by them that these do not constitute a true hazard. The Council of Alia, therefore, is the responsible authority, and no claims for state assistance for damage caused by the said displacement can be entertained.

(Signed) Chief Surveyor

statistical-sociological survey

When you are unemployed, how do you manage to live?

One hundred and six answered that they managed as best they could, but added nothing specific; seventy said that when they were out of work, they borrowed and ran up debts. The rest replied as follows:

1 I go gleaning.
2 I gather greens and go round selling them; that's what I do.
3 I go gleaning, and collect firewood.
4 I hang about the piazza in the hope that someone'll come along and offer me work.
5 I do any job that comes my way; when there aren't any jobs, we go hungry—we can't afford to buy anything but some bread. I pick greens and collect firewood for our own use.
6 I go into the country and collect firewood and pick fennel.
7 I sell greens and brooms in Palermo. We use *disa* that grows on the mountains, summer and winter, for the bristles. We also make a kind of vegetable horsehair with *disa*.
8 I go into the woods and pick up a few sticks.
9 I pick fennel when it's in season, and we eat it at home. When there's no fennel and nothing to do, I go to bed.
10 I've two brothers in regular work; they help me when I'm unemployed.
11 I ask my father and uncles for help, but how can they possibly go on keeping me for weeks on end? During this last spell of unemployment, I nearly went crazy. I didn't know what to do. My children were crying with hunger, my wife and I had grown so weak for lack of food that she kept crying too. One day, I couldn't stand it any longer, and I suddenly made up my mind that I'd go out and steal. I kissed my wife and children, and began to sob, and when they saw

me sobbing, they sobbed too. My poor babies—they were too young to understand why I was kissing them—they didn't know that I was saying good-by to them. The police don't arrest big-time thieves, you know, but poor devils like me—they arrest us right away before we've so much as moved. I went out weeping in my despair, and I met a man who, seeing the state I was in, stopped me and asked me what was wrong. At first I couldn't bring myself to speak, I was too ashamed, but I wound up by telling him what I had in mind. He managed to persuade me to go home by promising that he'd help me. He kept his word, and I've been working for the last four days. I'll probably get two weeks' work altogether; it isn't much, but it's better than nothing. If I hadn't met this man, I'd have stolen for sure—I wouldn't be here talking to you. I'd be in prison. This is my baby daughter, my youngest—what a sin it would be to leave such a sweet little thing without a father, wouldn't it?

12   I sell chicory and fennel; I sell brooms as well at 30 lire each. I manage to make 200 lire a day.

13   Some days, I just wander here and there. I just manage to make enough to keep us alive. When I've no money and no work, I run up debts.

14   I do any kind of work I can find. I make a few trips into the country to buy coal which I sell to different people. The weather's been very bad this winter, we have one heavy snowstorm after another. We were starving so I went to see a man who let me have a sack of charcoal on credit and I loaded it on to my mule, and went from village to village, through drifts a foot deep, to sell it. I trudged for fourteen or fifteen hours in bitter cold and snow—I was fed up with life, full of despair.

15   I do a bit of business. I'm an agent for one or two lines of goods.

16   I just walk about aimlessly.

17   I walk round and round the piazza, counting the cobblestones.

18   I collect firewood and pick greens.

19   When I'm out of work, I grow desperate. I curse Italy. I curse everything and everyone. I'm a C.D. member of the

village council, but I think all politicians are money-grubbers who are simply out to feather their own nests. I'd like to be independent of all of them. I'm not a C.D., but I'm not a Communist either, so I vote for the Christian Democrats.

20 I just go on from day to day in the hope that something will turn up.

21 I don't do anything. If there's work, I work. If there's none, I just stand around in the piazza. In the winter, I'm always in despair.

22 I go into the country to look for fennel and greens so that my family can have something to eat.

23 When there's no work, there's no work—that's all there is to it.

24 I climb up into the mountains, and if I find any greens, I pick and sell them. When it isn't the season for greens, I stand around in the piazza; when it is, I go gathering, and so it goes on.

25 I don't do anything.

26 I manage to get along by running up bills at the shop and borrowing from friends—what my debts come to, I couldn't tell you. When one man gives me a nasty look, I move on—I just go to someone else and ask him if he'll lend me a little money.

27 I just stay in the village.

28 I do whatever I can. I sell greens and brooms which I make myself, and I get a few odd days hoeing in the fields.

29 I just despair—I walk about feeling that I'm going to die of despair. I get a day's work now and then, but I'm only paid half the regular rate. In this bitter winter weather, if it wasn't for my bit of unemployment money and the family allowance, we'd all be out in the street in the snow—we wouldn't even have a roof over our heads.

30 I get a few days' work. When I've nothing to do, I just walk about.

31 I pick greens in the fields and woods.

32 I go gleaning, and I pick and sell greens.

33 I do any odd job that comes my way.

34 I walk to the piazza and I walk back again—back and forth, day after day.

35 A man loses heart and doesn't know what to do.

36 I go and look for greens, and collect sticks for firewood.

37 I gather greens which we eat ourselves.

38 My father has a pension of 6,000 lire; I get money from him.

39 If there's a man in this place who doesn't run up debts, then all I can say is he isn't made of flesh and blood.

40 I stand about in the piazza.

41 When I'm out of work, I can't bring myself to steal; instead of having three meals a day, I only have one.

42 There's nothing to be done. I pick a bit of greens and bring them home; if I didn't, we'd starve to death. We lead a miserable life.

43 I pick greens and hunt for snails.

44 I pick greens and collect sticks for firewood.

45 I run up debts and get my mother-in-law to give me some of her pension money.

46 Sometimes I just stand about in the piazza, sometimes I go into the country and collect a little firewood. I grow a few tomatoes on a bit of land close to where I live, and I sell a small quantity of greens.

47 I pick a bit of greens.

48 I collect firewood and pick greens.

49 When I've no work, I either stay at home or stand around in the piazza. The woods are a long way off, and if I was caught picking up a few dead branches, I'd be clapped into jail.

50 I pick up a few sticks and gather greens.

51 I walk all over the place looking for a job.

52 I do whatever odd jobs I can find. I load and unload trucks, go into the country after greens—I don't care what I do as long as there's something to put in the pot.

53 I make charcoal.

54 I go into the woods, cut down brambles, arrange the twigs in neat heaps, and set them on fire. When they've nearly burnt away to ash, I put the fire out with water, and as soon as the charcoal I've made has cooled down, I load it onto my mule. I sell it for about 30 lire a *tumulo*.

55 My in-laws in America send me a few parcels.

56 What can a poor devil like me find to do? I run up

debts, borrow a little here and there. It's bad, but it's better than stealing—I couldn't steal.

57 I'll tell you what I do. I go to the mayor, the police sergeant, and say: "If you don't give me some work, I'll turn thief—make no mistake about that!" But there isn't any work. I don't steal, but I despair. I walk round and round in circles, stop, start off again; I walk from place to place keeping my ears open in case I should get to hear of a job that's going.

58 I go gleaning. With luck, I get a few days' hoeing.

59 I go gleaning. In the winter, I borrow money—I have to give I.O.U.'s.

60 I try and find some work to do.

61 I do anything I can.

62 I collect sticks and faggots in the woods. I go gleaning.

63 I make a bit selling *disa*. I collect firewood, and sometimes, if anyone offers me work, even if he refuses to pay me more than 400 a lire a day, I'm forced to accept it in sheer desperation.

64 I don't know how to manage. When I've no work, I just walk around; on the twenty-fourth of each month, I go and sign my unemployment card.

65 I manage as best I can. I've been all over the place—I was in Greece during the war, and spent two years in a p.o.w. camp in Germany.

66 I go gleaning, and I gather greens and collect firewood.

67 I manage in this way and that. I pick a bit of greens, collect firewood, and get a bit of help from friends. I hunt for *attuppatedde*. For days and days, I don't do a thing.

68 I tighten my belt and go with my belly half empty.

69 I go into the country looking for greens, whatever I can find.

70 I carry loads from place to place. I pick greens and collect firewood.

71 I gather a bit of greens in the fields and woods; I do a little work that hardly brings me in a thing.

72 I've got four hens.

73 When greens are in season, I pick and sell them. In the summer I go gleaning, and that way I just manage to get along.

74 I sell wheat. I borrow money from my uncle, go into the country and buy a quintal. I sell the wheat in Termini, but the profit I make is so small that it's hardly worth while.

75 "I've got a day's work for you," someone'll say. In September, I go to Marsala for the *vendemmia*. I started going to Marsala three years ago as there was no work to be found in these parts. A few days' work here and there—the *vendemmia* in September—and that's all, absolutely all.

76 I buy this and that, and make a little of profit by selling it. I pick greens, too, but don't sell them—we eat them at home.

77 The day before yesterday, a man paid me to take a cow to Termini. I go into the country to pick greens; I've no mule, and sometimes I trudge I don't know how far before I find any.

78 I get asked to play music once or twice a month. I'm paid 1,500 lire a time.

79 I climb into the mountains and pick fennel and chicory; I sell some of it and we eat the rest at home. I sell about twenty-five to thirty bunches a day at ten lire a bunch. I also sell a few bundles of firewood and *disa*, and, as I get a day's work from time to time, I make just enough for us to exist on.

80 I hunt for snails. I make a few lire doing odd jobs for different people.

81 I get to such a state that for two cents I'd steal; Giuliano was a good man—he robbed the rich to help the poor.

82 I sell newspapers. I do a little hoeing. I gather greens and collect firewood.

83 I can't manage. It's impossible for a man to manage—there's no work to be had in the winter. I help unload trucks—carry crates of greens and blocks of salt to the shops. For carrying about 120 pounds of stuff a distance of maybe 300 yards, I get paid 25 lire a time.

84 I earn a few lire whitewashing. I also do some electrical work.

85 I'm waiting till they find me a job with some firm.

86 I collect sticks for firewood. I also go into the fields and pick greens; if I didn't, what would we have to eat?

87 I get as much credit from the shops as I can.

88 I ask the priest and the mayor to give me free vouchers for food. I do a few odd jobs. My wife's mother's in America, and she sends us a few parcels. I go about in rags so that people will see I'm poor.

89 I go into the woods for sticks, and carry them home on my back. I pick greens and sell in the village. I hunt for snails and sell them too. Then there's always a chance that something'll turn up. . . .

90 I do whatever I can to get by; I pick greens, collect firewood, and so on—I do anything I can think of to make a few lire to buy food for my children. Five little ones I've got. . . .

91 How do I manage? I can't manage. There's no work to be found.

92 I manage as best I can. I buy on credit and run up debts, and the shopkeepers write down what I owe them and read me the list.

93 I go from shop to shop. "Can I have some pasta?" I say, "I'll pay you as soon as I get work." I've been from one shop to another today. I'm up to my neck in debt—how I'm ever to get clear, I don't know.

94 We kick up a fuss outside the council offices and in the piazza, but what's the good? They can't make work for us— they can't do anything, so what can we do? Stealing—that's all that's left to us—I buy on credit in the winter, and pay off what I owe in the summer. Whenever we protest, out come the *carabinieri*—I don't know how often we've come to blows with them and been forced to break up.

95 I either pick and sell greens, or I borrow money from those that have got it to lend, and pay back by working for them. They always stick on twenty percent, or thirty percent, though.

96 The shopkeeper won't let me have more than a certain amount on credit; after that, he's got me at his mercy, and he takes advantage of it to charge me more for everything.

97 I sell firewood at 100 or 120 lire a bundle, so I manage to buy a little food for my family. I pick greens for us to eat, and go up the mountain for *disa*.

98 I glean, pick up sticks, gather greens, and so on. What else can I do?

99   I rack my brains day after day wondering what to do. To get by, you've got to scrape up a little here, a little there. If you don't, you die.

100   As soon as there are any greens, I go into the fields and woods to pick them.

101   When I'm unemployed, there's nothing for me to do.

102   When there's any food in the house, I eat; when there's none, I go without.

103   I go gleaning, I collect a few bundles of sticks, but that's all.

104   I gather greens when they're in season. I may find some growing fairly near here, or I may have to trudge along for miles. I pick orach, chicory, and so on; it takes me a whole day to collect enough to make ten bunches. Some people sell the greens they pick, but I take mine home and we eat them ourselves. I can't get any sticks as the woods are too far away, and I haven't a mule.

105   Even though the sky falls, we've got to eat. I do whatever I can when my luck's out. I run up bills at the shop, I pick greens—if we were all poor, I wouldn't be able to sell them, would I? I've got a few hens, and a young pig. I'll sell it to someone when it's slaughtered, those with the money to spend'll have pork to eat, we won't.

106   I used to collect sticks in the woods, but you're not allowed to do it any longer—if you're caught you're fined. And if you're fined—well, you're cleaned out, and you're forced to go right and left, cap in hand.

107   I get a few days' work. I grow a few artichokes, glean, pick greens, and run up debts.

108   We can chop down brambles and make charcoal. I don't pick fennel. When times are really bad and people are starving, so many of them go gathering fennel that soon there's hardly any left. When I can't find any work at all, I get up to my ears in debt.

109   I manage in the worst possible way: I sign I.O.U.'s and borrow money.

110   I don't do anything; I walk about the piazza.

111   I try to manage by doing anything that comes along. Sometimes I get a day's work or a couple of days' work, then I wait for something else to turn up.

112 I earn a few lire emptying sacks.

113 My friends lend me a little money, and I run up bills in the shops, bills I can't possibly pay.

114 I walk around. I've no hope of getting any real work.

115 I keep an eye on a car for somebody. I load and unload stones and sacks.

116 To earn money to buy food for my family, I carry sacks. I lend a hand with the slaughtering, and carry the carcasses on my back. I collect a load of firewood and carry it on my shoulders—I carry it for four or five miles. I gather greens too, fennel, wild cabbages, and so on—I walk and walk and pick up whatever I can find. I run up bills at the shop which I settle yearly; if I haven't the money to settle them, then I pay them off in the summer of the following year.

117 Sometimes I'm called in to repair a Calor gas stove, sometimes people pay me to write letters for them and fill up forms.

118 I can't do anything. I stay at home with my wife and four children and run up bills.

119 I collect sticks for firewood, and pick up greens for us to eat.

120 Sometimes I get a load to carry; I collect sticks for firewood.

121 I run up debts, and wander around doing nothing.

122 I don't do anything. I run up debts and walk around aimlessly.

123 I manage as best I can. What should I do—steal?

124 I work for a few odd days. I'm loaded down with debts.

125 How can I manage? The shopkeeper gives me credit, and when I get a little work in the summer, I settle the bill— I don't always make enough to pay it all off, though. I collect and sell firewood; with the few odd lire it brings in, I buy food.

126 I lend a hand in the office of our local trade union—I fill in the claim forms, and so on.

127 I do what I can to get by.

128 I go into the woods.

129 I don't go out and steal. I borrow money and sign I.O.U.'s.

130 I do whatever job comes my way.

131 The only way I could manage would be by stealing, but stealing's not in my line, so I run up bills at the shops.

132 I get a few days' work loading trucks and carts.

133 I collect a few sticks for firewood, and in winter, I pick greens. Now, when there's nothing to do, I just stay in bed and sleep.

134 I'm forced to work for a blacklisted employer who pays me far less than the proper rate, and doesn't give me my family allowances.

135 I climb into the mountains for *disa*, which we use for making brooms.

136 When I get the chance, I do some gleaning. In the winter, I pick greens.

137 There's nothing I can do.

138 When I'm unemployed, I ask some landowner to give me 500 lire, maybe a bit more. When he's in need of a laborer, he sends for me, and I work for him for nothing till I've paid him back. When the wheat's been harvested, I go gleaning, and in this miserable way, I just manage to eke out a living.

139 I run up bills. I can't find anything to do. When you're out of work, you either stand around in the piazza or you stay at home.

140 My father-in-law has a tiny pension, and we manage as best we can. I go into the country and gather sticks and pick greens.

141 My father sometimes gives me something to eat. I roam about the countryside, so weak with hunger that I can hardly see out of my eyes. I do a few odd jobs, but they don't amount to anything.

142 There's nothing I can do except tighten my belt.

143 I go gleaning, run up debts at the shop. I'm a dead weight to my sons.

144 I just walk about.

145 I get into debt. My mother who's a war widow sometimes gives me a bit of help, and I get along somehow.

146 I have work for the moment—there's the threshing to be done. I used to make a bit by collecting sticks in the woods, but it's against the law now, so I don't risk it. Like many others, I will probably be forced to leave Sicily, and to

settle, if I can, in France or Germany or Belgium—it's impossible to make a living here.

147 I go into the country and gather greens. When it rains, I hunt for *babbaluce.*

148 I do a day or so's work here and there. I spend the rest of my time walking in the piazza, nine times out of ten with an empty stomach.

149 I'm single. My dad draws a pension—10,000 lire every two months—and he gives me a few crusts of bread.

150 I wait for some work to come along.

151 I ask friends to lend me some wheat. Some men make you pay back much more than you've borrowed—fifty percent more, very often—and others won't lend you any at all.

152 I collect sticks for firewood and pick greens.

153 When my belly's rattling with hunger, I fill it with greens.

154 I just walk around.

155 I sell a few bundles of firewood. Sometimes I work for a miserable 400 lire a day so that I can buy my family a bite to eat.

156 I manage by collecting firewood for our stove and picking greens for us to eat.

157 I make a little carting sacks.

158 I get a few odd jobs.

159 I go into the country to pick fennel, but as I don't know one herb from another, I gather whatever I can find; my wife sorts out the stuff I bring back and throws out anything that's no good. I'm not up in country matters, all the plants look alike to me. I manage by tightening my belt and running up bills at the shops.

160 I pick a bit of greens, but the only way I manage to get by is by running up debts—when I'm unemployed for weeks and weeks, I can't keep them below 40,000 lire.

161 My father gives me a bite to eat.

162 I manage by doing a bit of business.

163 I try to earn a few soldi by selling greens and firewood.

164 A friend pays me to do a day's work for him.

165 I collect sticks in the woods, I earn a few lire carting stones.

166 I tighten my belt—what else can I do?

167 I go around begging. I'm ill, and they won't give me a pension.

168 I collect sticks for firewood, and every now and then, I get a few days' work on the land. I run up debts.

169 I do my best to manage. I run up bills.

170 I don't do anything.

171 We're slaves. We manage by making ourselves do anything and everything.

172 I do some gleaning.

173 I sell the wheat I've gleaned.

174 What can we poor devils do? Sometimes I collect a bit of firewood to burn in our stove.

175 I run up debts and do some gleaning.

176 I get a loan from the money lender and sign I.O.U.'s. In the summer, I go gleaning. In the winter, I run up debts.

177 I live on credit. I'm in debt to at least ten shops. If I didn't get credit, I couldn't manage—we'd all be dead now. I collect firewood to burn in our stove.

178 I make and sell charcoal, so we manage to eat. I also sell bundles of firewood and greens.

179 I go into the country to collect firewood. I make a few lire carting sacks, and so on. When we've no food in the house, we eat chicory which I pick in the fields.

180 I don't know how to manage. I'm desperate.

181 I get by by collecting wood and picking greens.

182 I pick fennel and whatever greens I can find.

183 My wife gets a bit of sewing to do. Our hens lay eggs.

184 I pick wild asparagus and hunt for *babbaluce*.

185 I gather herbs.

186 I try to turn my hand to anything.

187 I collect firewood and gather greens.

188 I pick greens when they're in season, and collect a bundle or two of firewood.

189 I gather herbs which we eat.

190 I hunt for *babbaluce*, pick greens and run up debts.

191 I pick up sticks for firewood, and I glean a little.

192 In wintertime, I go into the woods to get a few sticks.

193 I do whatever I can.

194   I go gleaning.
195   I go into the country and pick greens. I run up debts.
196   I sell greens, and make cord with *disa*.
197   I watch the sun rise, I watch it set.
198   I gather greens, do a few days' work, go gleaning.
199   I go around selling vegetables and fruit.
200   I don't do anything.
201   If there's anything to do, I do it; when there's nothing to do, I stand about in the piazza.
202   I pick mushrooms and herbs and hunt for snails.
203   I manage as best I can by going into the country and picking greens, doing whatever comes my way.
204   I gather greens; when they're scarce, I hunt till I find some.
205   I don't do anything.
206   I collect and sell firewood; I gather greens which we eat.
207   I go gleaning—I don't do anything else.
208   I do a bit of business on commission.
209   When I've picked a bit of greens and brought it home, we've at least got that much to eat.
210   I gather greens when they're in season.
211   I won't steal—I haven't had my employment card long, and I won't blot it by stealing.
212   I pick greens in the fields; when the wheat's been harvested, I go gleaning for a few days.
213   When I'm out of work in the summer, I go gleaning. My brother's in a job, and when I'm unemployed, he gives me something to eat.
214   I go into the country and pick greens.
215   I glean a bit, pick greens and hunt for snails.
216   I get a few odd days' work—between times, I just stand and stare. Most of us would give anything to go to Brazil or France, but in those countries, there's no call for unskilled labor. In 1950, I was determined to cross the frontier into France, but the frontier guards spotted me and fired at me, so I had to run for my life. I never did get across, and so, after two months, I had to make my way home again.
217   When the first rains fall, and the herbs begin to sprout, I go into the fields and pick them for us to eat.

218   My brother makes a living as a hawker, and he and my mother between them keep me in food.

219   I gather greens, collect firewood and hunt for *babba-luce*.

220   I get a few days' hoeing; I gather greens, collect wood, do a bit of everything.

221   I collect a bit of firewood and gather greens, and so I just manage to get by.

222   I manage as best I can—I make and sell charcoal, collect firewood and so on.

223   I carry a few loads of wood.

224   I gather greens when they're in season.

225   I go a long way into the country with my mule; I collect firewood, pick greens and hunt for *attuppatedde*.

226   I've got a donkey, and I go into the country to collect firewood. I glean in the summer, and I also run up debts.

227   I pick greens and collect firewood.

228   I go gleaning and pick up whatever I can find.

229   I make a little carting loads.

230   I go gleaning.

231   I go gleaning, and collect and sell a few bundles of firewood so that I can buy bread.

232   I run up debts. I gather greens, collect firewood and so on.

233   I either stay at home or stand about in the piazza.

234   I never have enough to put in my belly. I gather a bit of greens, collect a bit of firewood.

235   I go gleaning and collect firewood.

236   I don't do anything. I stand around in the piazza or I stay at home.

237   I stand around in the piazza.

238   I carry loads and crush olives.

239   I make the food I'd otherwise eat in a day hold out for a whole week.

240   I used to make a few lire collecting and selling firewood, but there are three electric stoves in the village now, so that's no good anymore.

241   I load stuff onto trucks; I run up debts, go and walk about into the woods and fields to pick greens. I collect sticks

in the woods and bring them home, so at least we don't burn any money in our stove.

242 I manage to get along in one way or another.

243 I pick greens and collect firewood. I spend the rest of my time at home or in the piazza.

244 I sell a sack or two of charcoal, collect firewood, pick greens, hunt for snails and so on.

245 I gather greens and help to pick the grapes.

246 I make a bit as a porter—I carry a sack of corn for 50 lire, a suitcase for 60 lire, and in that way I get by.

247 I'm always free and ready to take anything.

248 Debts, debts, debts. I get a few days' hoeing. Never-ending rows with my wife.

249 When I'm out of work, I wait around day after day in the doorway. I stand in the doorway and kill mosquitoes.

250 I do anything that turns up, but it's more likely that nothing'll turn up.

251 Once, I was out of work for so long that I had to sell every stick we had in the house.

252 I fish without a license, and sell *frutti di mare*.

253 I draw my unemployment money, and my relations help me out.

254 I go wherever I'm likely to get a job, and I pick greens and collect firewood.

255 I go round peddling stuff.

256 I do anything that chances to come my way. Sometimes, I get a day's work, sometimes I load trucks. I also pick greens, collect firewood and so on.

257 I'm not in the least bit ashamed to tell you that I make out by carrying loads. I go into the country and bring back whatever I can find—greens, wood and the rest. If there's anything to be done, I'm always on the spot. I go gleaning, too.

258 I spend a day or two picking greens and collecting wood. I run up debts and hang about in the piazza.

259 I carry suitcases for the bus passengers, do other small jobs. I sell a bit of contraband stuff. I pick greens and so on, and collect firewood.

260 I wait in the piazza in the hope that I may get a job unloading a wagon or truck.

261 We walk about in the country.

262 I pick greens.

263 I collect firewood.

264 I do the first thing that comes along; I pick greens, collect firewood, carry sacks and loads, go into the mountains to bring back *disa* for brooms, make charcoal.

265 I collect a load of sticks, look for mushrooms, greens, *disa*, make charcoal, and so on and so on.

266 I've nothing to do. I collect firewood for our stove.

267 I do the best I can, but I'm not handy. I'm a dead weight on my father-in-law, I'm ashamed to say.

268 I'm in a bit of a mess with debts. If I don't get work soon, I'll be in a spot, and I'll be forced into planning to commit a crime.

269 I do a little casual labor. Five days off, then two or three days on, maybe, and then another sp ll with nothing to do. I just manage to get by.

270 I dredge up oysters and clams and sell them.

271 I'm always free and ready to take anything.

272 I get called in to move furniture, or carry loads from place to place. I'm forced to run up debts.

273 I manage as best I can, do some tiny bit of work, sell *frutti di mare*.

274 I gather greens and collect firewood.

275 I shell almonds, and pick greens when they're in season.

276 I draw my unemployment money, and my son who's got a job helps me.

277 When my employment card was stamped the right number of times, I drew my unemployment money, but as I haven't had enough working days, my card's no good, I don't qualify for the hand-out.

278 I sell *frutti di mare*.

279 I have to look to my brother for help. I've a tiny pension for my war service, and I buy on credit at the shops.

280 I pick greens, and now and then I trudge the woods to collect sticks. I run up debts.

281 I carry suitcases, and I get a few odd jobs as a waiter. Naturally I don't go out stealing.

282 I pick greens and collect firewood. I run up debts.

283 Last year, I drew my unemployment money. But when

my card hasn't been stamped often enough, I buy on credit here and there.

284 I walk around, hoe, do a bit of carrying, I get a couple weeks' work when the *vendemmia* comes round.

285 I collect firewood for our stove, and when it's the season, gather greens for the family.

286 Because we lack bread, because my family's starving, I go into the country to pick greens so that my wife can make a drop of *minestra*.

287 I decant wine, work when I can as a waiter, help in a bar, and so on.

288 I make baskets and hampers.

289 My father has a tiny pension, and we can buy a bit of food.

290 I struggle with all my might to earn a crust or two of bread. I collect firewood, hoe, and gather greens which is pretty nearly all I have to eat.

291 I hunt around for greens, anything I can put in the pot. When we've no food in the house, not even a scrap of bread, my children go hungry to bed.

292 When I was in work, we were all right; but now we're in want, but we don't let on about it, we don't beg.

293 I do a bit of wood-polishing. I make chicken coops and get a little casual work.

294 My wife earns a few lire embroidering and sewing. I pick a bit of greens, collect firewood and so on.

295 I can't possibly manage. I was offered a few days' work at a miserable 300 lire a day, and things were so desperate that I had to take it. I'd got credit at the shop, and I suffered for it, I can tell you. No sooner was I unemployed than the shopkeeper came down on me for his money and wouldn't listen to reason. I had to borrow the money to pay his bill, and the interest on the money I'd borrowed kept mounting up and up; as I wasn't earning a thing, I couldn't pay it off, and so all my household goods were seized. That's the second time my stuff's been taken on account of a debt I couldn't settle.

296 I sell clams. When the sea's calm, I get plenty of them, but when it's rough, it's hopeless, and I'm desperate—I can't make a soldo.

297 I'm a hawker. I sell my goods along the coast and travel
to all the fairs where I work the three-card trick. If they gave
me a license, I wouldn't take it—why should I bother to work
when I can make easy money inviting the mugs to spot the
lady.

Do you think it is God's will that you are unemployed?

One hundred and sixty-eight contented themselves with saying: "No." Twenty-five said: "God does not concern himself
with such affairs." Twenty-five said: "No. Men are to blame
for the unemployment." Seventeen said: "No. It's the government's fault." Ten gave vague and inconclusive answers.
Eight said: "I don't believe in God." Seven said: "I don't
know." Six said: "It's not God but the mayor who's to blame."
Three said: "Wicked people are to blame." Three said: "The
priests are to blame." Two said: "Yes, it's God's will." One
said: "No—the capitalists are to blame."

The more detailed replies are given below; the most varied
are those in section (d).

a

1 To tell you the truth, I'm a believer; I've got faith, but
only up to a certain point. The fact is that no one on earth has
any knowledge of heavenly matters; what's more, there are
so many different religions, and every single one of them
says: "I'm the only true religion." There's someone above
who has power over this world, that's certain, but who this
someone is, nobody knows. Neither I nor anyone else can
rightly say what God's will is, what His thoughts are.
2 We don't know anything about heavenly matters.
3 How do I know what God wills or doesn't will?

4   How do I know?

5   I believe and I don't believe. That's all I have to say.

6   God and the saints exist, so they say. But how can they say for certain whether they exist or not?

7   I don't think it *is* God's will that I'm unemployed, I've always trusted in Him. But who can tell for certain whether it's His will or not? I can only say I don't think it is—I was taught to believe in God, and I do believe in Him, but I've never seen Him.

8   I don't know whether it's God will or not—everything depends on the party.

9   Perhaps—I only say "perhaps," mind you—it *is* God's will. But it's men who are to blame. Maybe the Rights are the most to blame, eh?

10   That's a riddle none of us can read. Who can possibly say whether it's the will of God or not?

11   I don't think it's God's will, but . . .

12   I can't see God, and I can't possibly say that it's His fault.

13   We're not politicians. We don't know who God is or whether He's to blame.

14   I went to Catechism classes when I was small, but when I was ten, I stopped going. The other day, we went on strike; the police seized all our tools and took them to the police station—they're still there. People always say "It's God's will," but I don't know whether it's His will or not that I'm unemployed. God's up above where we can't see Him.

15   I don't know whether it's God's will or not. I only know that I've tried to find work, that I don't want to be unemployed; I'm ill, I've got a hernia, but that wouldn't stop me from taking a job if I could only find one.

16   I don't know if God exists, but if He does, it wouldn't be His will—we're taught that God is love and that He is good to His people. But God's laws have been buried.

17   I don't believe that it *is* God's will, but who can say?

18   I've never talked about such things; I don't know, but I believe there is *someone*. I can't possibly say, though, that it's through the will of Jesus that I'm unemployed. How can I say such a thing seeing that I've never spoken to Him?

19   I go to church when I've time, but I don't know God.

20 I believe in God, but I don't know Him.

21 It's beyond our powers to know whether or not God's to blame. He made the world, and gave us free will; we can take whichever path we choose. If God didn't exist, there'd be no world, no wheat, nothing at all.

22 God sees all and knows all. It's all a mystery. God made everything, and He knows everything.

23 Me? How do I know what God's got in His stomach?

24 I don't know whether it's God's will or not, I've never seen Him. I don't know whose God He is. I wish I could see Him just once so that I could ask Him whether He wants me to be unemployed.

b

25 How can God be to blame? What must be, must be.

26 It must be God's will. If God willed it, there'd be work for us all.

27 We follow God blindly wherever He chooses to lead us.

28 He tells us what to do and we do it. That being so, it stands to reason that everything He does is right.

29 Men are to blame; not all men, but those at the top.

30 We were born into the faith, and so I believe in it. God is an epoch, and when the epoch changes, so does He. There are too many of us, and they don't give us work. There was the Fascist epoch and there was the Middle Ages epoch. Now it's the epoch of unemployment, and there's no work.

31 Is it God's will that I'm unemployed? No, it's destiny. I was in the *carabinieri*, and I ran away because my girl insisted on my marrying her, and she was quite right. Who's to blame for my being unemployed? It's fate. It's everybody's fault.

32 I always go to church when I've got time. Whatever happens to us is the will of God.

33 Who can tell whether it's God's will or not? It seems to me that it *is* His will—He can't help everybody.

34 I've no way of knowing whether it's God's will. I don't know whether God exists or not—if it's written in your stars that you'll be unemployed, well, then, you'll be unemployed.

God said: "Heaven helps those that help themselves." I can't help myself, so He doesn't help me.

c

35 If there was truly a God, it wouldn't be His will.
36 I don't think it's God's will. There *is* a God, but He's not everybody's God—He's the God of the rich, the God of those on top, not the God of us poor folk. It's His fault that there are poor folk in the world, that's sure and certain.
37 We never talk about God.
38 Leave God to the priests.
39 God's will that we're unemployed? The privileged class say it's God's will because they want to maintain slavery.
40 They say that God exists; our parents and grandparents tell us so, but they never saw Him and neither have I.
41 I don't know whether it's His will or not. I pray to someone who'll give me a chance to live.
42 Don't talk to me about God! When my mind's at peace, I believe in Him and His saints. I believe there was one Supreme Being, and so on. But when a man can't find work, he's filled with a black rage. I feel as though there were a wheel in my brain which keeps on missing a turn—it drives me into screaming out: "F . . . the lot of you!" to God and all His saints.

d

43 How can it be God's will that I'm unemployed? He doesn't interest Himself in such things. He doesn't come into it—it's our affair. God made laws of the Catholic Church, but men are to blame for unemployment. How could I possibly think that it was His will? If it was, what sort of God would He be?
44 God said: "Heaven helps those that help themselves."
45 We're a wicked lot, we Christians, and God doesn't meddle with such affairs. God said, "Love one another, help one another," and we don't love one another, we don't help one another, so God does nothing.

46   I believe there's a God, but I do as much as I can for myself—God won't carry a sack of corn to my house.

47   In Marineo, the mayor, the parish priest and the police sergeant are God Almighty, and that's that.

48   God brought us into the world, God will never fail us—we must always have faith in Him.

49   I believe in God—all I ask for is work.

50   I believe in God, but I don't believe it's His will that we should die of hunger.

51   I had two excellent mules, but thirteen years ago—on August 13 it was—they were snatched away from me. Two soldiers took them, they beat up my son, and when he fought back, they got hold of him, tied him up so tightly with leather thongs that he couldn't move and threw him into a ditch.

52   If God is as powerful as they make out, He could make it clear to those who govern us that they oughtn't to let us starve to death.

53   We're left to die.

54   We're religious folk here, and we're sure it's not God's will. There's a doctor who's the ruin of this place—he works for the rich. He makes us vote for them by not charging us for his visits.

55   Men are to blame for unemployment. God's not to blame, He suffered for our sake, but we—we make each other suffer.

56   It's God's wish that we should make everything equal; we know that, but instead, we make everything unequal.

57   I blame the Government more than I do God. God gives us the light, and we ought to make the most of it. We ought to work as hard as we can while the sun shines, because in winter, when the ground's covered with snow and slush, we can't work.

58   I believe that there is Someone up there. We have to have faith because we can't see Him. Our Lord can't please everybody, can't make all of us contented.

59   What has God to do with our affairs? God can save us, He can think about us—I mean if I fall and break my leg, I can say it's the will of God. But it's the government, not God, that ought to think about finding work for us.

60   God made the world, and left it free to follow its own course. If a man knows how to get on in the world, he flour-

ishes; if he doesn't, so much the worse for him. God can't do anything for him and doesn't do anything for him. It's no use his lighting candles and saying prayers.

61 God doesn't bother His head about such things. And I don't bother my head about Him.

62 How do I know whether it's God's will or not? (*He laughs, much amused.*) If I were ill, He'd tell me to lay off work, but as I'm not ill—well, I ask you . . . !

63 I'm not sure about God, I believe in Him and I don't believe in Him; I wouldn't swear to it that He exists. There are the priests, of course, but that's another matter, and God's got nothing whatever to do with work. What's more, there are two who've got power over us: God and the Devil. Instead of fighting with one another, they ought to put their heads together and make a bit of order in the world. But God's got one way of thinking and the Devil another.

64 God sees us, but we can't see Him.

65 It's God's wish that all of us should have work and enough to eat. I've always been a good Catholic, and I know it isn't by God's will that we're unemployed—it couldn't be His will, even for those who don't go to church, and who don't believe in anything. God wishes nothing but good for us, and we share one another's sufferings.

66 I've never spoken to God. God sees that they're (the government) to blame; they're God and the Devil in one.

67 They say that God exists, but I've never seen Him. I see the rich, with their great big bellies, stuffing themselves like pigs, while we poor devils haven't even a crust to gnaw on.

68 God made men in order that they should work.

69 What God means to me is that we must have food to eat.

70 God might will a man to be out of work for a couple of weeks, but for a whole year—no, never.

e

71 I believe that if God were there, we could talk to Him, and He couldn't be against us, He'd be on our side; but He's not there, and we can't get together with Him.

72 God doesn't mix Himself with these affairs. He thinks of other things.

73 It's got nothing to do with God.

74 How does God come into it? God and the Church keep to their own affairs. Our Lord's in Heaven, and we're on earth.

75 I believe in God, but He doesn't come into it.

76 It can't possibly be God's will. God's busy with his own affairs.

77 God doesn't come into it. God is in heaven and earth, God is everywhere, and He attends to His own affairs. We men ought to clear things up and put them to rights between us.

78 As I see it, God's got nothing to do with it.

79 How does God come into it? If He does, it doesn't worry Him; He doesn't bother about us.

80 God sticks to his own affairs.

81 It isn't God's will. God's got nothing to do with it. He's in heaven, and we're on earth.

82 I don't believe it's God's will. Each of us studies his own interests, thinks of himself—God does the same thing.

83 God attends to His own affairs. Men are to blame. God made us and we must love Him because we're Catholics.

84 It's nothing to do with God. It's the boss—he's the one to blame.

85 God's in heaven—He doesn't exist here on earth.

86 How can God come into it? I trust in God, but in other men—no. They've got no decency, no sense of right and wrong.

87 What's God got to do with it? God made us and now He doesn't bother His head about us any more.

88 God pitched us into the world in the midst of the woods, and left us to tend to our own affairs, so He doesn't have anything to do with our being out of work.

89 God doesn't come into it. We who live on the surface of the earth—we're the ones that come into it.

90 *U Signure non ci trase.* (God doesn't enter into it.)

91 What! God come into it? God's in Paradise and tends to His own affairs.

92 God has nothing to do with it. God said: "Love one another like brothers—get busy, all you others!" and then He

went to Paradise. Now we're like lost sheep. I saw a film once about Him—men begged Him to forgive them after they'd crucified Him.

93 God's up above where He belongs—I've never seen Him. The unemployed are far away from where He is, and they don't come into God's affairs. There's a whole list of saints— St. George, St. Anthony—but how do the saints come into our business?

94 God has more important matters to attend to—He isn't concerned with unemployment.

95 Our Lord doesn't live among us working men.

96 Our Lord doesn't lift the burden from our shoulders, He says: "Fend for yourselves." I don't believe in God—if He'd show Himself to me, I'd believe in Him.

97 God isn't interested in such affairs, that's my opinion.

98 God doesn't come into it. He sticks to His own business, and leaves us to stick to ours.

99 There's no need for God to meddle in such matters.

100 God's in the Church and has His own affairs to attend to.

101 It's not God's will that I'm unemployed—men are to blame, they're not like God.

102 God has his own affairs to see to, He doesn't mix Himself up in ours.

103 Is it God's will that I'm unemployed? What am I supposed to say?

104 God thinks of Himself.

105 God doesn't come into it. Very old folk say that God exists, but I've never seen Him. All the same, there *is* Someone.

106 God doesn't come into it. We've never seen Him, but they tell us that He's there, and we believe them. We don't see God, but we see the rich.

107 It can't possibly be God's will that we're unemployed. God is a saint, how can the fault be His? He has no faults. It's men who are to blame, the men who give the orders. God doesn't dwell on the earth.

108 It's not God's will—God doesn't know that unemployment exists.

109 *Lu Signuruzzu* is too busy with His own affairs to bother His head with us.

110 If God exists, He isn't down here; He's up above.

111 No, no—God isn't to blame. Jesus Christ is in Heaven, isn't He? Well, then!

112 God tends to His own affairs and those of the Church.

113 Unemployment didn't come about by God's order. Where's this God you talk about? You go and find Him. He's not on earth—we are.

114 God comes into it. He made us, and when He'd created us, He said: "Hurry up now and manage your own affairs." So now we're God.

115 God has nothing to do with unemployment. God's only concerned with things that come within His own province.

116 It's not God's will that we're unemployed. He's not responsible at all. How can He be? He's in heaven, and we're on earth.

117 He doesn't really come into such things. I don't think you can blame Him.

118 God made the world, and put it into the hands of men. Can He always give His mind to what's going on there? There are times when He does, that's certain—He seizes the opportunity whenever He can, but He's nearly always taken up with His own affairs.

f

119 Yes, I believe in God. We are God, you might say, because there's only one God and He is the sun and the moon—there's only one God, that's all. The others give orders and do as they choose. The sun and the moon are the only ones that do good. Why did the others turn down my demand for land reform? It's the government's fault that I'm unemployed.

120 Could unemployment ever be God's will? No, it's impossible—work is men's concern, not God's. It's only in the weather that God counts—he sends the sun and the rain.

121 The One up there doesn't come into it. The One up there sends rain when it's needed. It's up to us to work.

122 How can unemployment possibly be God's will? It's we

ourselves who are to blame, we all prey on one another. Our Lord wishes us well, He sends us the sun and the rain, and because some people don't believe in Him, He punishes us.

g

123 God comes into these things, He ought to help us because the world's in His hands.

124 Perhaps it's not His will that we're unemployed, but He's to blame for the fact that we're starving.

125 God knows for sure that I'm unemployed. He's to blame—even in church we're told that His will must be done. So if I'm unemployed, it's plain that God's responsible for it.

126 It's God's will. Yes—He's responsible for not giving us work.

127 Most certainly God's to blame. Why should some have such an easy time of it while others get all the kicks and knocks. It's unjust.

128 If there *is* a God, He'd certainly be to blame, but I'm forty, and in all my life, I've never so much as caught a glimpse of Him, so how do I know if He does exist?

129 I think God is responsible. He doesn't live here on earth, He lives far away in Heaven, but He looks down on us and sees everything that's going on. He ought to do good to us all, but instead of that, the rich grow richer, the poor grow even poorer.

130 I don't think it's God's will, but that doesn't alter the fact that I'm unemployed. That's certainly His fault.

131 Whatever happens to us is God's will. The fault is ours, but the will is God's.

132 I think God is in league with those who govern us.

133 I believe in God up to a point, but when I'm out of work, I despair. I don't understand very much about God and such. It's all the fault of Adam and Eve who stole the apple. It's God's doing if there's no work to be had, so He's partly to blame.

134 God's responsible, because the poor are born into the world through His will; some are born with a golden spoon and some are born to have nothing at all.

135 Of course it's God's will. If it weren't His will, I wouldn't be unemployed—He'd make them give me work.

136 God wishes all men to have work, that's sure. God is all-powerful—He can do everything. Let's hope He'll make work for us.

137 God is responsible for our being unemployed. God is the father of all men, and He ought to provide for us all. He ought to shed light into the minds of the leaders of every country.

138 God's responsible for all of us, isn't He? Wasn't it God who made us and brought us into the world?

139 I tell you straight God's to blame—He reigns over the world and rules us all. If it's true that we're all equal, He ought to take a little food from those who've got too much and give it to those who are starving. The priests? I'd bury the lot of them in the cemetery. Those crows ought to be put out of the way so they couldn't do any more harm. They've reduced us to slavery. Things have reached a point where we're forced to work for them.

140 Even God Himself has forgotten us.

141 Yes—if we're unemployed, it *is* God's will.

142 God exists, but He doesn't give a thought to us.

143 God's guilty all right. He sees the filthy things men do and doesn't attempt to stop them. God's to blame for everything that happens—He's responsible for it all.

144 It can't be God's will that we're unemployed, but He's to blame because He allows men to be unhappy—when a man's happy, he doesn't curse God for having made him, does he?

145 I think God's to blame, for nothing can happen unless He wills it.

146 They say, don't they, that everything that happens to us is God's will. By God's will, then, there are the rich and the poor. Destiny counts, of course, but if a man's destiny shouldn't happen to be what God has ordained for him, then God would have to overcome destiny.

147 Yes, it's God's will that we're unemployed.

148 It's God's will, because if it wasn't, He'd see that I had work.

149 God doesn't want to give me work. o, as I'm unemployed, it must be His will.

150 It's God's will, because if it weren't, we wouldn't be unemployed. There'd be no misery in the world if God didn't will it. God sees everything, and misery is His way of punishing us.

151 It shouldn't be God's will, but it is.

h

152 No, I don't think it's God's will; He's not revengeful. I don't think He's to blame.

153 God doesn't want us to be unemployed, He wants us to work. God is responsible for the salvation of men.

154 It can't be God's will, I'm sure of that. But it's His fault that we're unemployed and desperate and starving.

155 It can't and never could be God's will to see us suffering like this. But He's responsible for it, because He's our heavenly Father, and He doesn't send us work.

156 Could it be God's will? I say, no. But He's to blame because He doesn't think about the welfare of men.

157 God's responsible up to a point, but it's men who are really to blame.

158 I don't think it's God's will that we're unemployed, He wouldn't take pleasure in seeing so many of us suffer. All the same, though, He's responsible for the troubles we're in, since He himself created us.

159 God wishes us to work. But he's responsible for our misery because He created the world and He ought to think about all of us, and treat us all alike.

i

160 God wishes all of us to have work. God was a Socialist.

161 It isn't God's will that we're unemployed. Jesus was a Socialist.

162 God could never have wished such a thing. In his day, He walked about the earth and helped the poor.

163 God has no hand in unemployment—religion tells us

that. God came down to earth to preach social equality, to teach men to respect one another and live together in brotherhood.

164　I think it's God's will, but as to its being His fault—when God was on earth, He loved men, so He can't wish them to be unemployed and starving. It's people on earth who are to blame, not God—we can't put the blame on God.

165　I'm a good Catholic myself, but I'd like the world to be a just place, I'd like it to be a place where everyone could work and eat and live in freedom. God has no hand in unemployment—He wanted a world in which all of us would be equal and all of us would live as the *signori* live today. They say God was a Socialist.

166　I don't think it's God's will that I'm unemployed. God is dead, but He made bread, He made work. Now others have stolen the bread and the work, so God can only act as Providence and give us our health—that's all He has left to give.

167　I've always heard tell that when God was here on earth, He lived among the poor people like us; then the rich, together with the priests, betrayed Him, and now He's dead.

168　If God willed it, He'd revenge Himself on us, just as men take revenge on each other. But God preached that we were all equal, and said that the poor should have the biggest share. It was because He said these things that they put Him to death. God doesn't mix Himself in such affairs as unemployment, but He ought to try and put into practice what He preached when He was alive—He ought to see to it that we're all equal.

169　It isn't God who wants me to be unemployed, it's the capitalists. The capitalists are much stronger than God, it was the capitalists who killed Him. The capitalists murdered him, and ever since then they've profited from it by living on us.

170　God sticks to His own affairs. This is what He said: "I shall make men and women and they'll couple amongst themselves. Then I shall have done my part, and it'll be their turn to manage as best they can." God once walked on the earth, but He doesn't walk here any more. Does God still walk on the earth in Switzerland?

171　If God were alive, it wouldn't be His will—He'd never

allow a whole population to die of hunger. But they crucified Him because He preached: "Give to the poor." The rich preach sermons about Him now, but first of all, they killed Him.

172 God's responsible for unemployment. I used to believe in a real God, but now—what is God? There are only the different parties.

173 Once, God walked on the earth and gave men work to do—He was a good man, He wanted us all to be equal. At least they tell us that God existed and walked on the earth, but I don't think He exists any more—He's dead.

174 Once, there was a God, He was the Father of us all, but that was a long time ago. He's no longer the father of all men as He used to be, but we can't lay the blame for things on Him; the only thing He's to blame for is for having created the world.

j

175 I don't think it's God's will that I'm unemployed. I believe that if God came down to earth again, He would never enter the Vatican, because God belonged to the people, and the Vatican is against the people.

176 God isn't responsible for unemployment. It's the fault of the priests who meddle in politics and drive us to starvation instead of following the divine laws and saying Mass. The crows are to blame for all the abuses, all the rottenness.

177 One thing's certain: it's not God's will that we should be out of work. When we're out of work, we curse and swear —our children cry with hunger, we've no bread to give them and we fall into despair. First and foremost, I blame the government and the Vatican, then the priests and authorities, but God—no.

178 God doesn't wish me to be unemployed. God said: "Love one another, respect one another."

179 Unemployment isn't God's will, because God wanted us all to be equal, and He said: "Love the poor." But the C.D.'s don't love the poor. They favor the rich. They take sides with the capitalists against the poor. I know what I'm talking

about, because I've studied the Bible and the Apocalypse—I was in a seminary for six years. I went to the seminary when I was eleven years old, but when I was seventeen I left because I realized that all they want to do is to dominate people instead of living as Christians.

180 God wants all of us to be equal, but there's no equality in this world—people make sure of that.

181 God wants us to work, but the landowners won't give us any work.

182 It's not God who's to blame for unemployment, it's the capitalists.

k

183 God doesn't bother Himself with such matters. It's the people of this world who ill-use each other. Man ill-uses man.

184 The bosses are to blame for unemployment because they only hire those who've got a "pull," who've been recommended to them.

185 I get so desperate that I let off steam by cursing God right and left, but it isn't His fault if we're unemployed; we've only got ourselves to blame, we can't stick up for ourselves, we don't know anything about our rights.

186 We ought to be ashamed to implore God to do for us what we can and ought to do for ourselves.

187 It's not God's fault but ours. We've sunk very low.

188 Who made the world? A Heavenly Being made it, but it isn't the fault of this Being that we're unemployed. Men are to blame.

189 No—God doesn't want us to be unemployed. He made the world so that all of us should have bread to eat—He meant us to be Christians, not beasts. He isn't to blame—men are.

190 God has nothing to do with unemployment—He's in heaven and He said to us: "Love one another." But instead of living like brothers, men are swine, specially those at the top.

191 God wanted to make the whole world equal, and He preached justice. It's not God's fault—it's the fault of wicked

men who break His laws and take the bread out of our mouths.

|

192   I don't believe my heavenly Father put me on the earth just to make me suffer and despair. If God truly exists, I think He will be sorry for His children.

193   God brought us into the world to work; the rest's up to us.

194   I know God doesn't want me to be unemployed. There are times when I curse Him, but I only do it to let off steam.

195   I don't think it's God's will. God wants us all to work and be happy.

196   I find it difficult to believe that unemployment should be the will of God.

197   Does God want me to be unemployed? It's a bit risky, that question! God wants us to have work, schooling, etc. Men are to blame for the state we're in, not God.

198   It's not God's will, for sure. God meant us to work. He put us on the earth to work.

199   No, it's not God's will that I'm unemployed, and I won't give way to despair. If I did, I'd be lost.

200   In my opinion, God's got nothing to do with unemployment.

201   Our Lord doesn't want us to be unemployed. When He blessed the earth, He blessed it for all mankind.

202   Let me think, now, what shall I say? Well, then, I'll say it's not God's will that I'm unemployed.

203   If I had work, I'd find it easier to believe in God.

204   I believe in God, but at such times as these when I'm starving and desperate, I can't believe in Him any more.

205   I need work to make me believe in God.

206   I used to believe in the Gospels. When I was twenty-one, I was baptized, but now I don't believe in anything. I can't go on believing that Jesus exists; if He did, He'd surely know where I live, and He'd come to my house and help me —He wouldn't just stay up above and tend to His own affairs, would He? I can hardly believe in Him at all.

207   God must be responsible for unemployment, that's plain, but if I've nothing to eat today, no one'll give it a thought except me. It's only when there's work that there's a true God.

208   I don't think God exists because I only believe in Him when the sun rises on the morning when I can go to work.

209   To me, God means that I've got work to do and can buy food for my family. When I can't bring them back a bite to eat, it's excommunication.

What do you think the various parties in Italy ought to do to get rid of unemployment?

One hundred and sixty-four replied: "Give us work," or: "Give everyone work." Forty-seven replied: "They ought to unite," or: "Come to some agreement with each other." Twenty-five replied: "Carry out land reforms" and "Give the land to the peasants." Thirty-one either had no ideas on the subject or evaded the questionw. Eighteen replied: "Start up new industries. Reform the banks." Fifteen said: "I don't know." Fifteen replied: "They ought to carry out social reforms" and "They ought to carry out land and industrial reforms and reform the economic system." Thirteen said: "Put the Communists into power." Eight said: "They ought either to find work for us or allow us to emigrate." Eight said: "Put the Lefts into power." Eight said: "Introduce free trade and lift the restrictions on emigration." Four said: "Smash up all the machinery." Three said: "Put the Socialists into power." Three said: "Give the reins into the hands of a single leader." Two said: "Go on strike." Two said: "Vote Left." The most significant of the answers are given below. The least classifiable are those which have been grouped together in section (d).

a

1 I don't know. As we hardly ever buy a newspaper, we don't know anything about such matters.
2 I don't know what to say. If we had a single leader, it would save spending all this money on political demonstrations. I don't understand politics.
3 I ask you! How do you expect me to know what the parties should or shouldn't do?
4 I don't know. I can't read or write. The government should know what it ought to do.
5 Now if you asked me about hoeing. . . . I don't know one party from another. Is there any difference between them?
6 I don't understand a thing about politics—politics are nothing but confusion!
7 The parties themselves know what they ought to do—they know perfectly well that they ought to give us the means to earn our bread.
8 I'm poor and ignorant—I couldn't understand politics if I tried.
9 I don't understand a thing about politics. I don't take any interest in them—I don't read the papers, so I can't take any interest in them.
10 What ought the parties to do? Being out of work's made me sick in the head, I can't think straight—I can't put my mind to politics.

b

11 They ought to open up work in a big way, but before they do anything else, they ought to scrap every bit of machinery, because one single machine takes away the jobs of a hundred men.
12 The party I have in mind will never be in power again, unfortunately.
13 All industries ought to be nationalized. There was no unemployment in Germany when I went there in 1941.
14 They ought to provide work for us. If there was enough work to go around, there wouldn't be any parties.
15 They ought to get rid of the head of the Labor Bureau

and put a man in his place who'll have his heart in his job, who'll do his best to see that we get work.

16 They ought to start a revolution and march on Rome—that's what they ought to do.

17 What we want is a change. What Mussolini did was good, not bad. The Socialists ought to follow his example and do something.

18 They ought to give us work. When people are working, they don't interest themselves in politics, they live quietly and peacefully. The State should open up new works.

19 They could do something or other, give us a bit of assistance money.

20 The parties can't do anything. It's only the contractors who can give us employment.

21 The parties are short of funds—what can they do?

C

22 They ought to unite and form a single party that would look after all of us. As things are, you don't know which party to turn to.

23 The parties are only interested in getting into power—none of them do what they ought to do. What we need is a single party with a single leader, like Mussolini or the King. As it is, one party promises you this, another party promises you that, and they all end up by doing absolutely nothing. The parties should be governed by a single law.

24 I've never mixed myself up in politics, and I don't intend to start now.

25 We ought to have just one party—the Facist party.

26 They're only interested in getting into power—Communists, Christian Democrats, the whole lot. All they think about is their pockets.

27 We ought to have a democracy, but a real democracy such as they've got in America—a democracy that's really Christian.

28 We'd be far better off without any parties—the parties we've got only think of their own interests.

29 We ought to be governed by a single party that'd have the interests of the poor at heart as well as those of the rich.

30   We ought to get rid of all the parties except one.
31   We ought to have just one party in power. What are all these parties anyway?

d

32   What they ought to do is create more work, see that more jobs are available, especially in the summer. Then we'd be able to put away something for the winter when work's scarce; things wouldn't be nearly as bad if we could afford to buy food while we're unemployed. If we had a little in hand, we wouldn't be forced to apply for relief. It's an awful business. When I applied for it, I was told I had to go to the Council and get a copy of my birth certificate or else my family record card (this costs 30 lire). Three weeks later, the welfare people came along to look into our case, and when they were satisfied that we really were destitute, they told us we'd be given help. At the end of a month, they came back and handed me 500 lire—I had to make do for two whole months on 500 lire. I'm a married man with two children and a widowed mother to support—that makes five of us altogether, and 500 lire doesn't go very far in a family of five. I had to keep asking for assistance; it'll be the same winter after winter till they find us work to do.
33   In the first place, we shouldn't bother about whether we're red, pink or blue; in the second, we ought to get rid of all the *mafiosi*.
34   All the parties ought to unite, and if they don't, start a revolution to get rid of the government. A revolution's the only way out.
35   They ought to work out a scheme for full employment.
36   The parties ought to unite and ask themselves: "How do the unemployed manage to live?" They ought to unite and think of us.
37   They ought to find work for us, and take measures about machinery—instead of being a help to us, it does more and more harm.
38   We ought to have one single party to govern us, a party that would remove the restrictions on emigration; we could then go to any country where labor's needed.

39   They ought to carry out their promises and act in an up-right way.

40   The parties ought to be different from what they are. I've no use for all the agents they employ—there's too much favoritism for my liking.

41   They ought to have a real sense of duty to the people, and stop taking them for a ride.

42   If you look at the Communist party, it seems to be going ahead, but then, if you look at the Christian Democrats, they seem to be doing well, too.

43   They ought to unite and discuss ways and means of helping people to live.

44   We're like a stone that is thrown into a well.

45   We ought to be friendly with all other countries, Western and Eastern, we ought to trade freely with them and not allow ourselves to be dictated to by any foreign power. We want to collaborate with all nations, but we won't submit to military domination. We want to be united and independent. Economic reforms ought to be introduced to raise the value of the lire.

46   Instead of always siding with the rich—the higher-ups—the parties ought to help the people because they aren't smart enough to get along by themselves. The Left ought to give them every chance to go ahead; the people may not be intelligent, but they're shrewd and honest.

47   They ought to think about the poor.

48   They ought to make work for us. They should stop spending money on armaments, and start new enterprises that would benefit our country.

49   Each party has its own supporters.

50   I'm a liberal. If a government's no good, the best thing to do is to chop off the heads of the leaders. I want work, I want my rights.

e

51   It's a good thing to have several parties, because opposition's a good thing.

52   I'm satisfied with the parties.

f

53   None of the parties are any good.

54   The parties ought to be united and sincere; we'd be better off if they talked less and made good their promises.

55   The trouble about the parties is that they only act in their own interests, not in those of the nation.

56   As far as I'm concerned, there's nothing to choose between any of the parties. They are all schemers, one's as bad as the other.

57   I'm not satisfied with any of the parties—how can I be? To my mind, they could all do with improvements.

58   The parties ought to change their ways—they ought to consider the poor.

59   What should the parties do? Let me ask *you* a question —do any of them do anything for the working man? No—not one of them bothers about him. They could help him all right if they wanted to, but they don't do a single thing for him.

60   The way things are going, we'll end up with a civil war.

61   They ought to do their utmost to make work for us. My feelings are that at the present moment, none of the parties, neither the Left nor the Right, take any interest in us.

62   If the parties wanted to give us work, they could give us work, but they don't want to, and that's that.

63   All the parties are good in their own way, but not one of them's any use at present. How can they allow the people to go on living in such fearful misery?

64   As I see it, the parties ought to make the party that we've always hoped for and never had. That's my view, for what its worth—I'm ignorant, and I don't know much about such things, I can't put it right.

g

65   Wipe out communism.

h

66   As long as there are rich men in the Chamber, we'll go on being poor.

67 Get rid of all the crooks.

68 We ought to put in power the party that's got a social conscience.

69 We need a real workers' party which would create jobs for us. I think the Socialists and Communists are on the right track, but they ought to fight a little harder.

70 The parties ought to be different, they ought all to be Communist.

71 There ought to be only two parties: the rich man's party and the poor man's party.

72 They ought to organize strikes and demonstrations.

i

73 They ought to carry out land reforms, improve the mines and get irrigation schemes going.

74 Enrich the soil.

75 Take the land away from the landowners.

76 They ought to create new industries.

77 They ought to carry out land reforms and irrigation schemes, build council houses for the people, put up new school buildings, construct roads, and raise the poor above the level where they're forced to live on charity.

78 They ought to carry out reforms: they should nationalize industry, change the banking system, improve industrial conditions and go ahead with land reforms.

79 They ought to carry out land reforms and provide sufficient work for the people. The C.D.'s don't break our backs with work, that's for sure.

80 Land reform would go a long way. In these parts, the only mention we hear of land reforms is when a meeting's held—they talk about it but that's as far as it goes, nothing's been done.

81 They want to keep the working classes under for good.

j

82 The parties ought to join forces—they ought to work as one to solve the problem of unemployment.

83 They ought to do what's right and just, split up the es-

tates among the peasants. They ought to work together for the good of the people of the whole world; that's the law they ought to go by.

84 They ought to unite. They ought to start a revolution.

85 What should the parties do? I think they ought to unite and say: "Let's have no more difference of opinion—let's work together for the common good."

86 They ought to form a socialized government and organize the whole country; they ought to stop quarreling among themselves and think first and foremost of the people.

87 They ought to come to an agreement with one another, and provide work for all. But the trouble is that, instead of agreeing, they come to blows, and we're caught in the middle.

88 When it comes to work, we all ought to be equal.

89 The majority and the minority ought to reach an agreement and put party differences to one side when it comes to tackling the problem of how to provide work for all.

k

90 To my mind, they ought to make the Constitution effective.

91 They ought to put the Constitution into effect, with its rights and duties.

92 The parties ought to make just laws. The parties of the Left haven't succeeded in fulfilling their program.

93 They ought to put into effect Italy's present Constitution.

94 They could improve the present state of things. First and foremost, they should observe the Constitution because it's based on ideals and laws that are the finest in the world.

95 They ought to respect the Constitution.

96 They ought to honor the Constitution, not just pay lip-service to it.

l

97 They ought to put an end to exploitation, form co-operatives, carry out social and land reforms, take away the estates from the wealthy landowners and split them up among the peasants.

98   They ought to put the Constitution into effect and over-throw the capitalists.

99   They ought to do away with all class distinction.

100   They ought to make all things equal for everybody.

101   They ought to socialize Italy, narrow the gap between the classes, and give everyone a chance to earn his bread. What we want is a society of workers—a society in which there aren't any dreams.

102   They all ought to be Socialists.

103   They ought to tax all those who have any property.

104   They ought to tackle the housing situation, and give all of us decent houses.

m

105   They ought to try and provide work for everyone. They know very well what they ought to do.

106   They ought to see that all men with families to support have jobs. If only we could get work, everything would go better.

107   They ought to get rid of unemployment which causes so much misery.

108   They ought to agree among themselves, and provide work for us all.

109   They ought to provide work for us all.

110   They ought to open up new fields of work and give everyone a chance to live.

111   All that matters to me is work and I'm in favor of any party that'll provide it. At present, as the Communists are on the side of the working classes, I'm with them, but if they swung the other way, I'd have nothing more to do with them.

112   When we've got work, we don't bother about parties.

113   They ought to give us work—work means everything to us who've got no income. All we ask for is work.

114   We're not looking for this party or that—what we're looking for is work.

115   They ought to be able to think out new work projects and put them into effect to provide employment for all of us.

116 They ought to make sure that there's enough work for us always.

117 They ought to give us work, that's all—just give us work.

118 They ought to provide us with work, and if they can't— well, shoot all of them, that's what I say.

Is the ballot secret?

saying: "Yes, the ballot's secret." Sixty couldn't be sure whether it was secret or not. Forty-four said: "It's not secret." Twelve said: "Sometimes it's secret." Six said: "The ballot's secret, but they bribe us to vote." Five said: "I don't know." Three gave evasive answers.

The most significant answers are given below. Those in section (d) provide the key to all the affirmative answers. Section (b) contains the least classifiable answers.

a

1 It may or may not be secret—who can tell? I should think it's secret in the big cities, but in a village where you know everyone and everyone knows you, it's a different matter. The archpriests (the Christian Democrats) give us presents of pasta, so . . .

2 According to some people, the doctor who lives in these parts unfolds the voting slips and looks at them. Other people, though, say the ballot's secret. I really don't know . . .

3 The ballot's secret—at least, they say it is.

4 Let's hope it's secret.

5 When you go to vote, you're huddled into a box, a coop, you might say, but when you come out, who knows what happens to your slip.

b

6   There's not one of us that they don't know by sight.

7   Our eyes are open now—we know what tricks go on.

8   We go and vote and that's that. We vote with our eyes shut.

9   I've never voted. I've been in prison, so I don't get a vote.

c

10   It's secret—no doubt about that. If it weren't secret, would the Sisters have come to every house in Petralia, including mine, with presents of food and thousand-lira notes? I don't vote C.D., but they visited me just the same—that's how I know it's secret.

11   They bribe people to vote for them by giving them presents and promising them this and that.

12   Yes, the vote's bought all right . . . with packets of pasta.

13   The ballot's secret, but here's the catch. Ignorant people sell their votes to the *signoroni* who come along before the elections and distribute thousand-lira notes.

14   The ballot's secret, but some of the voters are bribed with promises of work which never come to anything.

15   The landowners force the people to vote for their candidates: "Vote for our party, and you can keep your land; if you don't, you'll be kicked off!"

16   Just before the elections, the owner of the land sends for the *mezzadro* and says: "Vote for me, otherwise out you go!"

17   This year everyone took bribes, and so no one voted against them.

18   The ballot's secret, but there are always a few people who haven't the courage to vote independently. "Put your mark against No. 1 and No. 8," the master says to them, and they don't dare do otherwise for fear they'd lose their jobs. The scrutineers check the slips as they come in, so they know whether you've voted for their party or not.

19   "I'll give you a pound of pasta if you vote for my party," They say to us.

20   It's impossible to say whether it's secret or not. The vote's bought, though. People are bribed with a thousand-lira note

or a pound of pasta. What's more, if you want to keep your job, you've got to behave like a rat and kow-tow to the master.
21 The ballot's secret, but you vote under pressure.
22 They try to make you vote for certain numbers by giving you presents of pasta.

d

23 The ballot's secret, but they know in advance for which party you're going to vote. If you vote against theirs, they make you pay heavily for it.
24 The ballot's secret, but they know in advance for which party you're going to vote. The landowners summon the *mezzadri* and say: "You must vote for our party . . . you must put your mark against these numbers . . . you must vote for so-and so." And if one of them doesn't do as he's been told, that's the end of him—he's kicked off the land.
25 The ballot's above board, it's secret all right, but many of the votes are bought. Ignorant people are blackmailed into voting for certain numbers. Wily owners come along and say to them: "You're to vote for these numbers. We'll know if you don't—don't forget that!" And so . . .
26 The ballot's secret. Quite likely, though, they know how you've voted.
27 They assure you the ballot's secret, but it seems they know in advance for which party you're going to vote.
28 The ballot's secret. They can monkey around with the votes, though.
29 It's secret, that's certain, and it's just as certain that there's lots of tricks.
30 The ballot's secret, but all the same, they have their suspicions about me, they know in advance how I intend to vote. I'm a free man and can't be bought.
31 I'm certain the ballot's secret, and I'm equally certain that a lot of crooked business goes on. They fix things among themselves to get their candidate elected.
32 The ballot's apparently secret, but you're blackmailed into voting for certain numbers. They either promise you this or that, or else they threaten you. I know for myself how they play around with the numbers system. The Communist

party makes use of it in this village to get people who are non-sympathizers to put their mark against the numbers of their candidates. All they have to do is glance at the slips to know whether they've done so or not. All the parties trick people in the same way.

e

33   They look at the slips for certain.

34   Tricks are as old as the hills.

35   There's always some crooked business.

36   The ballot's secret, but the Mafia and the agents of the Mafia violate the secret all right.

37   By means of the numbers system, they buy and control all the votes.

38   They play about with the numbers marked on the slips and combine them in the way that suits them.

39   It's all trickery. It's the same with everything today—the whole world's a trick.

40   They know how we've voted. They give us a combination of numbers and make their calculations. It's always been like this.

What do you think you and each of us should do to get rid of unemployment?

Ninety-five said: "Unite, struggle, go out on strike." Sixty-three said: "Organize ourselves, get all the poor to unite," and: "Union is how to reply—unity is strength." Forty-six gave evasive answers. Twenty-six said: "Strengthen the parties of the Left." Twenty: "I don't know." Eighteen: "There's nothing to be done." Fourteen: "Rise—start the revolution." Ten: "Demonstrate against unemployment." Nine: "Vote for the right party. Don't sell your vote." Six: "Join the trade

unions." Five: "Swell the ranks of the Christian Democrats."
Five: "Start co-operatives." Three: "Emigrate." Two: "Set
ourselves to work." Of the answers that follow, the least
classifiable are those in group (i).

a

1   I don't know.
2   They know, and we do what they order us to do—we
never disobey their commands.

b

3   As we can't read or write, we can't do much, we can only
talk to the people we meet. It's impossible for us to unite.
4   Blow out my brains—that'd make one less.
5   The working-man has nothing—what can he do? Add his
own hunger to the hunger of the rest?
6   We can't do anything. We can only wait. We're like children who stand around and cry till their mothers give them
some pap.
7   What can I do? Can I give anyone a job?
8   There's nothing we can do—nothing at all.
9   What can we do? Absolutely nothing.
10   There's nothing to be done.
11   I've never thought about it or talked about it. You've
taken me by surprise—I really can't answer.
12   Me, I'm poor and ignorant, what can I do? I don't know
how unemployment comes about, or how to get rid of it.
When we farm laborers strike, what good does it do? The
bosses know us, and if we strike, they see to it that we don't
get any more work. It's different when the railwaymen strike
—the whole lot of them come out, and everything's at a standstill. But if we strike, they call out the *carabinieri* if they can
—why's that? (Are you a C.D.?) We've struck all right, but
it's worse than useless.
13   It doesn't depend on us. We'll never be able to unite.
14   Wait for work.
15   What should we do? When there's no work, there's nothing we can do except starve to death.

16   There's no work to be had. We can't do anything.

17   We all do what we can, but there's no work—this is a poor village.

18   The Democracy would create new industries. What can we do?

19   What can I do?

20   I keep on counting the cobblestones in the piazza.

21   When a man's unemployed, everything looks black. Sometimes, I'm so ashamed that I can't bring myself to go into the street.

22   Wait till something turns up, and while we're waiting, try to keep ourselves alive.

23   What can poor working-class people like us do? We can protest against unemployment, yes, but it doesn't do any good.

24   What's the use of asking me? You ought to know better than me what people should do. You can't get people to agree —they've all got their own ideas.

25   In this part of the country, we don't know anything—we do what the Democracy does.

26   What can a poor beggar like me do? Walk around—that's all.

27   You know the answer to that better than me. All I know is that something ought to be done.

28   Wait for manna to fall from heaven.

c

29   Do what's right and just, and trust in God. Honor your father and mother. Love your neighbor as yourself, and help the poor.

30   We ought to pull ourselves together and use our brains. We ought to open our eyes a bit more to the vile things that are going on.

d

31   There are too many of us, there is always unemployment —emigration is the only answer.

32   Emigrate, with or without a permit.

e

33 Everything depends on the government.

34 It's a matter for the heads of the government. What can we possibly do?

35 We ought to unite, but we need someone who can really lead us. Otherwise, someone will come along and confuse us with his talk.

36 It's up to the heads of the government to get rid of unemployment.

37 The heads of the government may be able to do something about it.

38 I'm only a poor laborer, what can I do? It's those that live in the cities who ought to rouse themselves. We ought to have a leader who'd think out ways and means of getting rid of unemployment.

39 What can I do? Those that give the orders ought to do something about it.

40 Try your hardest to get work—that's all you can do.

41 What can I possibly say? There's only one way we can get work, you know, and that's by going and asking for it.

42 Hold protest meetings in every part of Italy. Make speeches and say: "We're fed up with all these promises. Get down to it and give us work!"

43 Make the government realize that it's got to provide work for us, that it's got to look after the welfare of every class.

f

44 I don't know what to think. It isn't right that nothing's being done about unemployment and that's a fact. They don't give us a thought—we don't count.

45 Manage as best we can.

46 Form a strong government. When we had the King, for instance, and there weren't any of these others, we had work to do and we did it—there wasn't all this talk.

47 When I've got work, I don't bother about anything else —I don't worry about the parties.

48   The C.D.'s wouldn't give me a chance to move—before I could do a thing, they'd have me in handcuffs. (*The speaker comes from Caccamo.*) If anyone puts a foot wrong there . . . (*he says meaningly, and presses his finger on an imaginary trigger*).

49   If I went to the Parliament in Rome, I'd be able to make myself understood. I've been to dinner with "Honorables," I have, and they always understood what I said to them.

50   Cut the throats of all those who won't give us work.

51   By fighting another war—there are too many of us, we need colonies, we need to expand. The only other solution is emigration.

52   We keep on insisting to the Council that the machinery ought to be scrapped, but nothing's been done about it.

53   Each of us ought to make out by selling greens and so on.

54   Anyone who has the money for the fare ought to go to North Italy.

55   Stage a strike every day, and smash everything up; when there are only ruins left, they'll have to start rebuilding and then there'll be plenty of work for all of us. It'll be the same as it was right after the war—I'm thinking, for instance, of the rebuilding of Monte Cassino.

56   There's never been a time when there weren't unemployed.

57   There are masses of us unemployed; I think of the speech Mussolini made about the rods and the sheaves—the speech that put him in power. When the masses are united, no one can stop them from imposing their will.

58   Striking doesn't lead anywhere. The people can't do anything—they need patriots to help them. Each party has its own patriot—we must make up our minds which of these patriots is the best.

59   (*The speaker takes up the story of what happened when he went to see the police sergeant to ask for work.*) "Go home and wait," said the sergeant. So I went home and waited but nothing happened. (*The suggestion is made to him that all the workless should go in a body to see the sergeant.*) It wouldn't do you any good. He'd only say: "What do you mean

by coming here like this and creating a disturbance?" (*He then goes on to say that if anything has been reported missing, if there's been a theft, the sergeant summons him.*) The sergeant: "Are you working? Me: "Oh, I'm doing a bit here, a bit there, you know." The sergeant: "H'm. Let's look at your hands!"

60 When a man's unemployed, he either has to steal or die of starvation. But if you steal, you end up in prison if you're caught. What should I do? What *can* I do?

61 We ought to go out and look for work, we ought to go on looking for it until we find it. Steal, and you wind up in the jug.

62 We ought to go and demonstrate in the piazza. All the people of Italy ought to rise up. If the masses won't unite, I'll become a bandit. That's what those at the top will drive you to, and I'll either win out or be killed.

63 The only thing to do is to get someone to recommend you. I'm acquainted with a Christian Democrat lawyer, and when I'm out of work, I ask him to give me a letter of recommendation to such and such a firm. If you haven't a letter to say: "I would consider it a personal favor if you'd give X. the vacancy," you'll never get taken on—you'll never get a job. I think it's perfectly right and proper myself because if you have a reference, the firm knows it's getting a reliable man. Once you've got a good job, you ought to turn a deaf ear and a blind eye to a lot that goes on; above all you should steer clear of the troublemakers, the agitators who go to the boss with complaint after complaint.

g

64 If every man stuck to his own trade, we factory workers would stand a chance of getting taken on, but as it is, any amount of agricultural laborers go into industry. If they went back to the fields, things would change for the better as far as we're concerned.

65 The agricultural workers should stick to the land. But more and more of them keep turning to industry, and the factory managements take them on in preference to us.

h

66   If we weren't afraid, we might be able to do something.

67   We ought to make the government realize the state of things. We ought to raise our voices and say: "There are thousands of us unemployed. What are you going to do for us?"

68   Keep putting pressure on the government.

69   Check the activities of the priests. They're getting so powerful that if we don't do something about it, the country'll be governed by crows!

70   All the parties ought to get together and start new industries to provide us with work.

71   We're badly in need of factories. Here, in Sicily, they ought to set up large-scale plants and workshops in the crowded working-class districts. At present, there's nothing here.

72   We ought to get together, set up a co-operative and make work for ourselves.

73   Only the State can put things right.

74   When I'm out of work, I try and force myself to think of ways out. But it's no good—I have to resign myself to begging and imploring this person or that for help. Sometimes a benefactor gives me a bit of work.

75   The people ought to unite, but it seems they can't. It's a desperate state of affairs.

i

76   We must never lose sight of the fact that they're making slaves of us.

77   If the people were less ignorant and more prepared, it might be possible to do something.

78   We ought to throw off our chains, teach ourselves to think by reading political matter, and take an active interest in what's going on around us.

79   Those who've got the ability ought to explain to the people what social progress means.

j

80   We ought to unite and do something for ourselves, over and above what the parties are doing.

81   We ought to make a community of the people.

82   We ought to do what we never do: unite. As it is, we just stray aimlessly like sheep.

83   We ought to unite and demand that work should be given to the poor.

84   We ought to keep on asking for work, but first and foremost, we ought to unite.

85   We ought to unite, raise our standard, and demand work.

86   We ought to force the government to give us work. We ought to unite.

87   It's no use for one or two to protest—we must unite.

88   The people must unite, make sure that there are no traitors in their ranks, and take up the struggle for work.

89   We must unite.

90   Instead of quarreling with one another, the parties ought to work together for the good of the people. If the government's rotten, we ought to unite and strike—keep on striking. We shouldn't steal jobs from one another—we ought to stand together.

91   We ought to unite, but we don't. "If I do this or that, such and such a party will have it in for me," each of us says to himself. The working man's afraid of what may happen to him if he stands out—he has to look out for himself.

92   We ought to organize ourselves and convince people that it's no use insisting on our rights until we're united. Suppose, for instance, I tried to do something alone. Suppose some guy had plenty to eat and I had nothing to eat and I fired at him and killed him. I'd be put in prison and the lawyer would gobble up every soldo I had. That's all that would happen—it wouldn't be fair!

k

93   Trade union organizations.

94   The people ought to struggle until the government cre-

ates enough work for them all—every category of work. They ought to back up the trade unions. But they don't do anything of the kind—they never do a thing.

l

95 We ought to unite and vote the C.D.'s into power here, in Piana—we'd be better off if we did.
96 We ought to support the present government and help it to find work for us.
97 We ought to collaborate with the bosses.

m

98 We ought to strengthen the Communist and Socialist parties if we want to throw off these shackles. The Chamber's filled with wolves and jackals. It's the Mafia, the powerful financiers who make the laws.
99 We ought to unite and put the Communist party into power; it's not the rich man's party, but it would carry out land reforms.
100 Unite—pass the word around to one and all, strengthen the Communist party, demand land reforms.
101 Each comrade ought to convert a Right.

n

102 Strike, strike, STRIKE.
103 What should I do to get rid of unemployment? How do I know? All I can think of is to keep kicking up rows at the Council, strike—things like that.
104 First and foremost, make proper use of one's vote and see that this government doesn't get in again. You've been in power for ten years, you C.D.'s, and you haven't been able to do a thing about unemployment. Then we ought to keep on striking—I'd like to see the strikers with guns in their hands if possible. When men are starving, they'll stop at nothing.
105 Keep on striking till we've smashed the lousy government. We've staged plenty of strikes but nothing's come of

them. If only there were more men like me. If I don't succeed the first time, I try again and I'll pull it off for sure. Don't think I'm telling you this just to build myself up. I was often the first to go out, but that's all over. The dirty sheep! At the start, they used to take part in the demonstrations, then they got afraid and hid themselves behind the doors.

106 If we kept going on strike, the village councils would have to act and find work for us.

107 Keep on striking, to make the government realize the horror of unemployment and starvation.

108 Strike day after day until they open up new works and industries.

109 A general strike that'll bring everything to a standstill, a strike that'll really make itself felt.

0

110 We've staged a good many strikes, some successful, some not. At times, they've agreed to our demands, at others, they've called out the police.

111 We demand our rights, we strike, but nothing gets changed. They promised us millions, a thousand million, but they don't do a damn thing.

112 We take action, we go on strike, but they don't take any notice.

113 I don't know what we ought to do—striking's no use. You don't get work through striking. Last year, we held several demonstrations, but none of our demands were met. When we struck, the sergeant came along and said to us: "Go home, all of you—I'll see that something's done for you." Well, we went home but nothing ever was done.

114 Go on strike? No. It wouldn't be any use if we're not united. Families can't agree among themselves, neither can we, so what can we do?

115 Strikes are no good. The best thing to do is to get into the good graces of the head of the Labor Bureau.

116 I'm all against strikes. If we get ourselves arrested, what's to become of our families?

117 Strike? Strikes only set us back further. It's no good striking—they are much too strong for us.

118   Strikes have never brought anyone good. The people can't succeed in uniting. There's nothing to be done. I march ahead of all the comrades, but as soon as the *sbirri* [police] arrive on the scene, they all bolt for cover. I'm the one that gets arrested—the only one!

119   We sometimes go in a body to the Council to protest, and, every so often, the police arrest us.

120   We demonstrate, but the *carabinieri* come along and shoot us down.

121   We can't strike because the people won't stick to it.

p

122   Instead of burying the book of the Constitution, they ought to put our laws into effect.

123   They ought to pass a law against unemployment.

124   We ought to unite and demand that the laws should be put into effect.

125   We ought to put pressure on the government and insist that the laws should be put into effect.

126   The Baron has a thousand to two thousand *salme* of fallow land. He won't cultivate it as he grazes his sheep on it. It ought to be taken away from him and given to us poor peasants.

q

127   Elect a government that'd see that we all got work.

128   At the next general election, vote for a new government.

129   Overthrow the government so that the people can find the sort of work they want—on the land, in the factories, and so on.

130   Get rid of this capitalist government. If you use your vote properly, you can win the fight.

131   We've got one weapon, the vote. We don't want revenge, we're not bloodthirsty, but with the vote we can get rid of the reactionaries, the exploiters of the people.

r

132 Revolution. The people of Italy ought to rise up and overthrow the government. We don't want riches—all we want is enough to eat and to stop living in this misery.

133 I think that strikes have left us exactly where we were before. I think the time is ripe for us to revolt, not to massacre the oppressors but to overthrow the government. We don't want to shed the blood of the masters, we don't want to commit crimes. We've had enough of prison.

134 We ought to unite and make our capitalist adversaries tremble. I say adversaries, because we mustn't look on them as enemies or hate them. We must stop being afraid, because we're in the right.

135 We ought to get rid of this everlasting C.D. government by staging a general strike that would bring the whole country to a standstill.

136 We ought to unite and fight the revolution till we force them to agree to our terms.

137 Revolution. Get hold of all the leaders and kick them out. Kick them out, not kill them. Replace them with men who've worked for the good of the people, honest, upright men.

138 Stand firm. Refuse to give in, even if it means dying of hunger.

139 We can fight and struggle and hold out for a whole year, even though we're dying of hunger. At all costs, we must reach our goal.

140 Revolt against the government, that's the only thing to do. Kill the leaders, but only the leaders—once they're dead and done with, the rest will change their ways.

141 One day, a decent party may emerge.

142 Revolution, but a bloodless revolution. It's wrong to kill—we must only do what's right and just.

143 Keep on striking. Struggle, strike, shoot down our enemies. Revolution, you understand, revolution. I'm in deadly earnest, you know—I'm not just spouting hot air. I'm an out-and-out revolutionary.

144 The best thing that could happen would be a war, then

we'd go into the army and fight and be killed, and there'd be so few of us left that there'd be work enough to go around.

145 Revolution or a war. Italy's poor, and she must go to war to get more living room for us all.

146 Revolution—get rid of the exploiters of the people.

147 One of these days, the revolution'll break out.

148 Resist, strike, or perhaps start the revolution seriously.

149 Revolution—revolutions soon level things. We've had strike after strike in Sicily, and much good they've done us, but a revolution. . . .

150 Keep demanding work and revolt. Sooner or later, the revolution's bound to break out—we can't go on forever like this.

151 Revolution—the real revolution.

152 Keep on striking. When we reach breaking point, on with the revolution! We wouldn't kill our enemies, but I don't say we wouldn't kick their backsides; I'd gladly give the capitalists a taste of the stick, but kill them—no.

153 Revolution's the only solution, but it's out of the question at the moment, because the people haven't succeeded in uniting. It would be far better to die than live as we're living, but if we're to die, let's cut off a few heads first and die side by side.

154 If we all had work and enough to eat, we would stop hating the rich.

155 Revolution—a bloodless revolution. No disorderly mob.

156 Keep on striking or start the revolution. This is the right moment to rise. The people are starving, working days are few and far between, and they can't earn enough to make a decent life for themselves. Do you think they ought to steal in order to exist? No, no, no.